PRENTICE HALL
LITERATURE

PENGUIN EDITION

English Learner's
Reader's Notebook

Grade Eleven

PEARSON

Prentice Hall

Upper Saddle River, New Jersey
Boston, Massachusetts

ISBN 0-13-165294-X

2 3 4 5 6 7 8 9 10   09 08 07 06

ACKNOWLEDGMENTS

Grateful acknowledgment is made to the following for copyrighted material:

Sandra Dijkstra Literary Agency
"Mother Tongue" by Amy Tan. Copyright © 1990 by Amy Tan. First appeared in *The Threepenny Review*. Reprinted by Permission.

The Echo Foundation
"The Echo Foundation Brings Henry Gates, Jr. to Charlotte" from *The Echo Foundation*.

Farrar, Straus & Giroux, LLC
"The First Seven Years" by Bernard Malamud from *The Magic Barrel*. Copyright © 1950, 1958 and copyright renewed © 1977, 1986 by Bernard Malamud.

Harcourt, Inc.
"A Worn Path" from A CURTAIN OF GREEN AND OTHER STORIES, copyright 1941 and renewed 1969 by Eudora Welty. "Everyday Use" from *In Love & Trouble: Stories of Black Women*, copyright © 1973 by Alice Walker. This material may not be reproduced in any form or by any means without the prior written permission of publisher.

Museum of Afro American History
"Museum of Afro-American History Mission Statement" from *www.afroammuseum.org/about.htm.*

The New York Times
"Review of the Crucible" by Brooks Atkinson from *New York Times*, Published: January 23, 1953.

Plimoth Plantation, Inc.
"Plimoth Plantation" from *www.plimoth.org/index.html.* Reprinted by permission of Plimoth Plantation, Inc.

Princeton University Press
From *Walden* by Henry David Thoreau. Copyright © 1971 by Princeton University Press. All rights reserved.

Scribner, a Division of Simon & Schuster, Inc.
"The Far and the Near" from *Death to Morning* by Thomas Wolfe. Copyright 1935 by Charles Scribner's Sons; copyright renewed © 1963 by Paul Gitlin. "In Another Country" from *Men Without Woman* by Ernest Hemingway. Copyright 1927 by Charles Scribner's Sons. Copyright renewed 1955 by Ernest Hemingway.

Sterling Lord Literistic, Inc.
"The Crisis, Number 1" by Thomas Paine from *Citizen Tom Paine*. Copyright by Howard Fast.

Syracuse University Press
"The Iroquois Constitution" from *Parker on the Iroquois: Iroquois Uses of Maize and Other Food Plants; The Code of Handsome Lake; The Seneca Prophet; The Constitution of the Five Nations* by Arthur C. Parker, edited by William N. Fenton (Syracuse University Press, Syracuse, NY, 1981).

Viking Penguin, Inc.
From *The Grapes of Wrath* by John Steinbeck, copyright 1939, renewed © 1967 by John Steinbeck.

Yale University Press
Excerpt from "Sinners in the Hands of an Angry God" from *The Sermons of Jonathan Edwards: A Reader* published by Yale University Press. Copyright © 1999 by Yale University Press.

Note: Every effort has been made to locate the copyright owner of material reproduced on this component. Omissions brought to our attention will be corrected in subsequent editions.

Contents

PART 1

UNIT 1 A Gathering of Voices: Literature of Early America (Beginnings to 1750)

Build Skills: The Earth on Turtle's Back • When Grizzlies Walked Upright • *from* The Navajo Origin Legend • *from* The Iroquois Constitution 2

The Earth on Turtle's Back from the Onondaga
  Preview 3
When Grizzlies Walked Upright from the Modoc
  Preview 4
from The Navajo Origin Legend from the Navajo
  Preview 5
from The Iroquois Constitution from the Iroquois
  Preview 6
  Selection 7
  Apply the Skills 10

Build Skills: A Journey Through Texas • Boulders Taller Than the Great Tower of Seville

A Journey Through Texas by Alvar Núñez Cabeza de Vaca 11
  Preview 12
Boulders Taller Than the Great Tower of Seville by García López de Cárdenas
  Preview 13
  Apply the Skills 14

Build Skills: *from* Journal of the First Voyage to America
by Christopher Columbus 15
  Preview 16
  Apply the Skills 17

Build Skills: *from* The General History of Virginia • *from* Of Plymouth Plantation

from The General History of Virginia by John Smith 18
  Preview 19
  Selection 20
from Of Plymouth Plantation by William Bradford
  Preview 24
  Apply the Skills 25

READING INFORMATIONAL MATERIALS

Web Sites 26

Build Skills: Huswifery by Edward Taylor • To My Dear and Loving Husband by Anne Bradstreet 30
- Preview 31
- Apply the Skills 32

Build Skills: *from* Sinners in the Hands of an Angry God by Jonathan Edwards 33
- Preview 34
- Selection 35
- Apply the Skills 39

UNIT 2 A Nation Is Born: Early National Literature (1750–1800)

Build Skills: *from* The Autobiography • *from* Poor Richard's Almanack
from The Autobiography by Benjamin Franklin 41
- Preview 42
- Selection 43
from Poor Richard's Almanack by Benjamin Franklin
- Preview 48
- Apply the Skills 49

Build Skills: *from* The Interesting Narrative of the Life of Olaudah Equiano by Olaudah Equiano 50
- Preview 51
- Selection 52
- Apply the Skills 55

Build Skills: The Declaration of Independence • *from* The Crisis, Number 1 56
The Declaration of Independence by Thomas Jefferson
- Preview 57
from The Crisis, Number 1 by Thomas Paine
- Preview 58
- Selection 59
- Apply the Skills 62

Build Skills: An Hymn to the Evening • To His Excellency,
General Washington by Phillis Wheatley..................................... 63
    Preview 64
    Apply the Skills... 65

READING INFORMATIONAL MATERIALS
Press Releases 66

Build Skills: Speech in the Virginia Convention • Speech
in the Convention 72
Speech in the Virginia Convention by Patrick Henry
    Preview 73
    Selection 74
Speech in the Convention by Benjamin Franklin
    Preview 77
    Apply the Skills... 78

Build Skills: Letter to Her Daughter From the New White House
• *from* Letters from an American Farmer 79
Letter to Her Daughter From the New White House by Abigail Adams
    Preview 80
    Selection 81
from **Letters from an American Farmer**
by Michel-Guillaume Jean de Crèvecoeur
    Preview 84
    Selection 85
    Apply the Skills... 88

UNIT 3 A Growing Nation: Nineteenth-Century Literature
(1800–1870)

Build Skills: The Devil and Tom Walker by Washington Irving 89
    Preview 90
    Selection 91
    Apply the Skills... 97

Build Skills: The Tide Rises, The Tide Falls by Henry Wadsworth Longfellow • **Thanatopsis** by William Cullen Bryant • **Old Ironsides** by Oliver Wendell Holmes • *from* **Snowbound** by John Greenleaf Whittier 98

    Preview 99

    Apply the Skills. 100

READING INFORMATIONAL MATERIALS

Memorandums 101

Build Skills: Crossing the Great Divide • The Most Sublime Spectacle on Earth 107

Crossing the Great Divide by Meriwether Lewis

    Preview 108

The Most Sublime Spectacle on Earth by John Wesley Powell

    Preview 109

    Apply the Skills. 110

Build Skills: The Fall of the House of Usher • The Raven 111

The Fall of the House of Usher by Edgar Allan Poe

    Preview 112

The Raven by Edgar Allan Poe

    Preview 113

    Selection 114

    Apply the Skills. 119

Build Skills: The Minister's Black Veil by Nathaniel Hawthorne 120

    Preview 121

    Apply the Skills. 122

Build Skills: *from* Moby-Dick by Herman Melville. 123

    Preview 124

    Apply the Skills. 125

Build Skills: *from* Nature • *from* Self-Reliance • Concord Hymn • The Snowstorm. 126

from **Nature** by Ralph Waldo Emerson

    Preview 127

from **Self-Reliance** by Ralph Waldo Emerson

    Preview 128

Concord Hymn • The Snowstorm by Ralph Waldo Emerson

Preview 129

Apply the Skills 130

Build Skills: *from* Walden • *from* Civil Disobedience 131

from **Walden** by Henry David Thoreau

Preview 132

Selection 133

from **Civil Disobedience** by Henry David Thoreau

Preview 139

Apply the Skills 140

**Build Skills: Because I could not stop for Death • I heard a Fly buzz—
when I died • There's a certain Slant of light • My life closed twice
before its close • The Soul selects her own Society • The Brain—is wider
than the Sky • There is a solitude of space • Water, is taught by thirst**
by Emily Dickinson 141

Preview 142

Apply the Skills 143

Build Skills: *from* **Preface to the 1855 Edition of** *Leaves of Grass*
• *from* **Song of Myself • When I Heard the Learn'd Astronomer
• By the Bivouac's Fitful Flame • I Hear America Singing
• A Noiseless Patient Spider** by Walt Whitman 144

Preview 145

Apply the Skills 146

UNIT 4 Division, Reconciliation, and Expansion: The Age of Realism (1850–1914)

Build Skills: An Episode of War • Willie Has Gone to the War 147

An Episode of War by Stephen Crane

Preview 148

Selection 149

Willie Has Gone to the War by Stephen Foster and George Cooper

Preview 153

Apply the Skills 154

Build Skills: Swing Low, Sweet Chariot • Go Down, Moses 155
Preview 156
Apply the Skills 157

Build Skills: *from* **My Bondage and My Freedom** by Frederick Douglass . . . 158
Preview 159
Selection 160
Apply the Skills 165

Build Skills: An Occurrence at Owl Creek Bridge by Ambrose Bierce 166
Preview 167
Apply the Skills 168

Build Skills: The Gettysburg Address • Second Inaugural Address
by Abraham Lincoln • Letter to His Son by Robert E. Lee 169
Preview 170
Apply the Skills 171

READING INFORMATIONAL MATERIALS
Public Documents 172

Build Skills: from Mary Chesnut's Civil War by Mary Chesnut
• Recollections of a Private by Warren Lee Goss • A Confederate
Account of the Battle of Gettysburg by Randolph McKim • An Account
of the Battle of Bull Run by Stonewall Jackson • Reaction to the
Emancipation Proclamation by Rev. Henry M. Turner • An Account of
an Experience With Discrimination by Sojourner Truth 177
Preview 178
Apply the Skills 179

Build Skills: *from* **Life on the Mississippi** • The Notorious Jumping
Frog of Calaveras County by Mark Twain 180
Preview 181
Selection 182
Apply the Skills 186

Build Skills: The Outcasts of Poker Flat by Bret Harte 187
Preview 188
Apply the Skill 189

Build Skills: Heading West • I Will Fight No More Forever 190
Heading West by Miriam Davis Colt
Preview 191

I Will Fight No More Forever by Chief Joseph

Preview 192
Apply the Skills 193

Build Skills: To Build a Fire by Jack London 194
Preview 195
Apply the Skills 196

Build Skills: The Story of an Hour by Kate Chopin 197
Preview 198
Selection 199
Apply the Skills 202

Build Skills: Douglass • We Wear the Mask by Paul Laurence Dunbar 203
Preview 204
Apply the Skills 205

Build Skills: Luke Havergal • Richard Cory by Edwin Arlington Robinson
• Lucinda Matlock • Richard Bone by Edgar Lee Masters 206
Preview 207
Apply the Skills 208

Build Skills: A Wagner Matinée by Willa Cather 209
Preview 210
Apply the Skills 211

UNIT 5 Disillusion, Defiance, and Discontent: The Modern Age (1914–1946)

Build Skills: The Love Song of J. Alfred Prufrock by T. S. Eliot 213
Preview 214
Apply the Skills 215

Build Skills: A Few Don'ts • The River-Merchant's Wife: A Letter
• In a Station of the Metro by Ezra Pound **• The Red Wheelbarrow**
• The Great Figure • This Is Just to Say by William Carlos Williams
• Pear Tree • Heat by H. D 216
Preview 217
Apply the Skills 218

Build Skills: Winter Dreams by F. Scott Fitzgerald 219

    Preview 220

    Apply the Skills 221

Build Skills: The Turtle *from* The Grapes of Wrath by John Steinbeck 222

    Preview 223

    Selection 224

    Apply the Skills 227

Build Skills: old age sticks • anyone lived in a pretty how town
by E. E. Cummings • **The Unknown Citizen** by W. H. Auden 228

    Preview 229

    Apply the Skills 230

Build Skills: The Far and the Near by Thomas Wolfe 231

    Preview 232

    Selection 233

    Apply the Skills 236

Build Skills: Of Modern Poetry • Anecdote of the Jar by Wallace Stevens
• Ars Poetica by Archibald MacLeish • **Poetry** by Marianne Moore 237

    Preview 238

    Apply the Skills 239

Build Skills: In Another Country • The Corn Planting • A Worn Path 240

In Another Country by Ernest Hemingway

    Preview 241

    Selection 242

The Corn Planting by Sherwood Anderson

    Preview 247

A Worn Path by Eudora Welty

    Preview 248

    Selection 249

    Apply the Skills 256

Build Skills: Chicago • Grass by Carl Sandburg 257

    Preview 258

    Apply the Skills 259

Build Skills: The Jilting of Granny Weatherall by Katherine Anne Porter . . . 260

    Preview 261

    Apply the Skills 262

Build Skills: A Rose for Emily • Nobel Prize Acceptance Speech 263

A Rose for Emily by William Faulkner

    Preview 264

Nobel Prize Acceptance Speech by William Faulkner

    Preview 265

    Apply the Skills 266

Build Skills: Birches • **Stopping by Woods on a Snowy Evening**
• **Mending Wall** • **"Out, Out—"** • **The Gift Outright** • **Acquainted**
With the Night by Robert Frost 267

    Preview 268

    Apply the Skills 269

Build Skills: The Night the Ghost Got In • *from* Here Is New York 270

The Night the Ghost Got In by James Thurber

    Preview 271

from Here Is New York by E. B. White

    Preview 272

    Apply the Skills 273

Build Skills: *from* Dust Tracks on a Road by Zora Neale Hurston 274

    Preview 275

    Apply the Skills 276

Build Skills: The Negro Speaks of Rivers • **I, Too** • **Dream Variations**
• **Refugee in America** by Langston Hughes • **The Tropics in New York**
by Claude McKay 277

    Preview 278

    Apply the Skills 279

Build Skills: From the Dark Tower by Countee Cullen • **A Black Man**
Talks of Reaping by Arna Bontemps • **Storm Ending** by Jean Toomer 280

    Preview 281

    Apply the Skills 282

READING INFORMATIONAL MATERIALS
Public Relations Documents 283

UNIT 6 Prosperity and Protest: The Contemporary Period (1946–Present)

Build Skills: The Life You Save May Be Your Own by Flannery O'Connor . . 289
    Preview 290
    Apply the Skills 291

Build Skills: The First Seven Years by Bernard Malamud 292
    Preview 293
    Selection 294
    Apply the Skills 302

Build Skills: Aliceville by Tony Earley 303
    Preview 304
    Apply the Skills 305

Build Skills: Gold Glade by Robert Penn Warren • **The Light Comes Brighter** by Theodore Roethke • **Traveling Through the Dark** by William Stafford 306
    Preview 307
    Apply the Skills 308

Build Skills: Average Waves in Unprotected Waters by Anne Tyler 309
    Preview 310
    Apply the Skills 311

Build Skills: *from* The Names by N. Scott Momaday • **Mint Snowball** by Naomi Shihab Nye • **Suspended** by Joy Harjo 312
    Preview 313
    Apply the Skills 314

Build Skills: Everyday Use by Alice Walker 315
    Preview 316
    Selection 317
    Apply the Skills 324

Build Skills: *from* The Woman Warrior by Maxine Hong Kingston 325
    Preview 326
    Apply the Skills 327

Build Skills: Antojos by Julia Alvarez 328

  Preview 329

  Apply the Skills 330

Build Skills: Who Burns for the Perfection of Paper by Martín Espada
• **Most Satisfied** by Snow by Diana Chang • **Hunger in New York
City** by Simon Ortiz • **What For** by Garret Hongo 331

  Preview 332

  Apply the Skills 333

Build Skills: Onomatopoeia • Coyote v. Acme
• Loneliness . . . An American Malady • One Day, Now Broken In Two 334

Onomatopoeia by William Safire

  Preview 335

Coyote v. Acme by Ian Frazier

  Preview 336

Loneliness . . . An American Malady by Carson McCullers

  Preview 337

One Day, Now Broken In Two by Anna Quindlen

  Preview 338

  Apply the Skills 339

Build Skills: Straw Into Gold: The Metamorphosis of the Everyday
• For the Love of Books • Mother Tongue 340

Straw Into Gold: The Metamorphosis of the Everyday by Sandra Cisneros

  Preview 341

For the Love of Books by Rita Dove

  Preview 342

Mother Tongue by Amy Tan

  Preview 343

  Selection 344

  Apply the Skills 350

Build Skills: The Rockpile by James Baldwin 351

  Preview 352

  Apply the Skills 353

Build Skills: from Hiroshima • Losses • The Death of the Ball
Turret Gunner 354

from Hiroshima by John Hersey

  Preview 355

Losses • The Death of the Ball Turret Gunner by Randall Jarrell

    Preview..356

    Apply the Skills...357

Build Skills: Mirror by Sylvia Plath **• In a Classroom** by Adrienne Rich **• The Explorer** by Gwendolyn Brooks **• Frederick Douglass • Runagate Runagate** by Robert Hayden...358

    Preview..359

    Apply the Skills...360

Build Skills: Inaugural Address • *from* **Letter From Birmingham City Jail** . 361

Inaugural Address by John F. Kennedy

    Preview..362

from **Letter From Birmingham City Jail** by Martin Luther King, Jr.

    Preview..363

    Apply the Skills...364

Build Skills: For My Children by Colleen McElroy **• Bidwell Ghost** by Louise Erdrich **• Camouflaging the Chimera** by Yusef Komunyakaa......365

    Preview..366

    Apply the Skills...367

Build Skills: *The Crucible* by Arthur Miller, **Act I**.........................368

    Preview..369

    Apply the Skills...370

Build Skills: *The Crucible* by Arthur Miller, **Act II**........................371

    Preview..372

    Apply the Skills...373

Build Skills: *The Crucible* by Arthur Miller, **Act III**.......................374

    Preview..375

    Apply the Skills...376

Build Skills: *The Crucible* by Arthur Miller, **Act IV**.......................377

    Preview..378

    Apply the Skills...379

READING INFORMATIONAL MATERIALS
Critical Reviews 380

PART 2 Turbo Vocabulary

Prefixes V2

Word Roots V4

Suffixes V6

Learning About Etymologies V8

How to Use a Dictionary V12

Academic Words V14

Word Attack Skills V16

Vocabulary and the SAT® V18

Communication Guide: Diction and Etiquette V22

Words in Other Subjects V26

Vocabulary Flash Cards V27

Vocabulary Fold-a-List V33

Commonly Misspelled Words V39

INTERACTING WITH THE TEXT

As you read your hardcover student edition of *Prentice Hall Literature* use the ***Reader's Notebook,*** English Learner's Version, to guide you in learning and practicing the skills presented. In addition, many selections in your student edition are presented here in an interactive format. The notes and instruction will guide you in applying reading and literary skills and in thinking about the selection. The examples on these pages show you how to use the notes as a companion when you read.

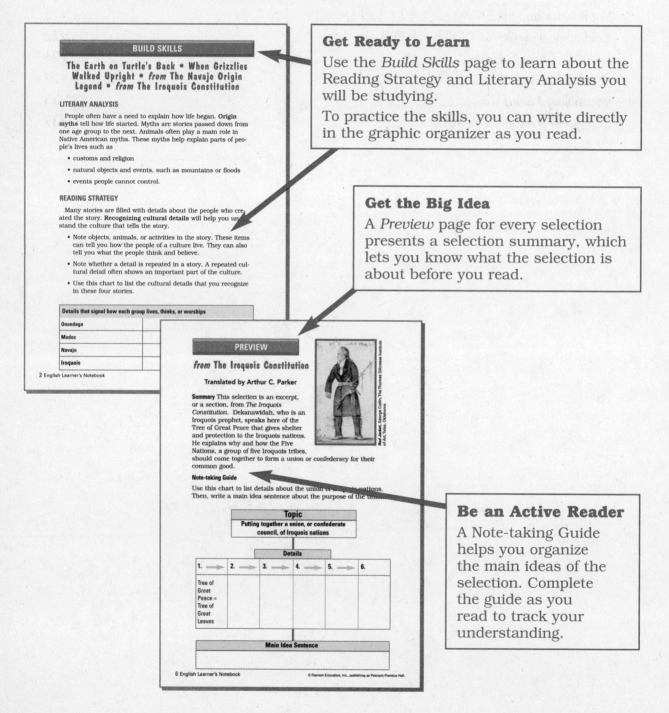

BUILD SKILLS

The Earth on Turtle's Back • When Grizzlies Walked Upright • *from* The Navajo Origin Legend • *from* The Iroquois Constitution

LITERARY ANALYSIS

People often have a need to explain how life began. **Origin myths** tell how life started. Myths are stories passed down from one age group to the next. Animals often play a main role in Native American myths. These myths help explain parts of people's lives such as

• customs and religion

• natural objects and events, such as mountains or floods

• events people cannot control.

READING STRATEGY

Many stories are filled with details about the people who created the story. **Recognizing cultural details** will help you understand the culture that tells the story.

• Note objects, animals, or activities in the story. These items can tell you how the people of a culture live. They can also tell you what the people think and believe.

• Note whether a detail is repeated in a story. A repeated cultural detail often shows an important part of the culture.

• Use this chart to list the cultural details that you recognize in these four stories.

Details that signal how each group lives, thinks, or worships	
Onondaga	
Modoc	
Navajo	
Iroquois	

2 English Learner's Notebook

Get Ready to Learn

Use the *Build Skills* page to learn about the Reading Strategy and Literary Analysis you will be studying.

To practice the skills, you can write directly in the graphic organizer as you read.

Get the Big Idea

A *Preview* page for every selection presents a selection summary, which lets you know what the selection is about before you read.

PREVIEW

***from* The Iroquois Constitution**

Translated by Arthur C. Parker

Summary This selection is an excerpt, or a section, from *The Iroquois Constitution.* Dekanawidah, who is an Iroquois prophet, speaks here of the Tree of Great Peace that gives shelter and protection to the Iroquois nations. He explains why and how the Five Nations, a group of five Iroquois tribes, should come together to form a union or confederacy for their common good.

Red Jacket, George Catlin, The Thomas Gilcrease Institute of Art, Tulsa, Oklahoma

Note-taking Guide

Use this chart to list details about the union of the six nations. Then, write a main idea sentence about the purpose of the union.

Topic					
Putting together a union, or confederate council, of Iroquois nations					

Details					
1. →	2. →	3. →	4. →	5. →	6.
Tree of Great Peace = Tree of Great Leaves					

Main Idea Sentence

6 English Learner's Notebook

© Pearson Education, Inc., publishing as Pearson Prentice Hall.

Be an Active Reader

A Note-taking Guide helps you organize the main ideas of the selection. Complete the guide as you read to track your understanding.

from The Iroquois Constitution
Translated by Arthur C. Parker

I am Dekanawidah and with the Five Nations[1] confederate lords I plant the Tree of the Great Peace. I name the tree the Tree of the Great Long Leaves. Under the shade of this Tree of the Great Peace we spread the soft white feathery down of the globe thistle as seats for you, Adodarhoh, and your cousin lords.

We place you upon those seats, spread soft with the feathery down of the globe thistle, there beneath the shade of the spreading branches of the Tree of Peace. There shall you sit and watch the council fire of the confederacy of the Five Nations, and all the affairs of the Five Nations shall be transacted[2] at this place before you.

Roots have spread out from the Tree of the Great Peace, one to the north, one to the east, one to the south and one to the west. The name of these roots is the Great White Roots and their nature is peace and strength.

♦ ♦ ♦

Other nations wishing to speak with the Five Nations will trace the roots to the tree. Peaceful and obedient people will be welcomed.

♦ ♦ ♦

We place at the top of the Tree of the Long Leaves an eagle who is able to see afar. If he sees in the distance any evil approaching or danger threatening he will at once warn the people of the confederacy.

Vocabulary Development

confederate (kon FED er it) *adj.* united with others for a common purpose
---

1. **Five Nations** the Mohawk, Oneida, Onondaga, Cayuga, and Seneca tribes. Together, these tribes formed the Iroquois Confederation.
2. **transacted** (trans ACT id) *v.* done.

© Pearson Education, Inc., publishing as Pearson Prentice Hall.

Take Notes

English Language Development

In English, the prefix con-, com- means "with." A *constitution* is something set up or established with other people. What is a *confederacy?*

_____
_____

Literary Analysis

Circle two words that show the nature of the Great White Roots in this **origin myth**. What can _____ from this passage about the purpose of the alliance?

_____
_____

Culture Note

The speaker sometimes repeats words and concepts: for example, "seats," "feathery down of the globe thistle," and "Five Nations." The repetitions draw attention to the formal, serious nature of the speaker's words and actions. Write one other word or phrase that is repeated in this selection.

_____
_____

Take Notes
Side-column questions accompany the selections that appear in the Reader's Notebooks. These questions are a built-in tutor to help you practice the skills and understand what you read.

Mark the Text
Use write-on lines to answer questions in the side column. You may also want to use the lines for your own notes.

When you see a pencil, you should underline, circle, or mark the text as indicated.

APPLY THE SKILLS

The Earth on Turtle's Back • When Grizzlies Walked Upright • *from* The Navajo Origin Legend • *from* The Iroquois Constitution

1. **Infer:** Why do the Navajo people believe that spirits are kind?
_____
_____

2. **Infer:** Why do the Modoc people believe that spirits are mean?
_____
_____

3. **Literary Analysis:** Use this chart to list one aspect or part of nature. Write the role it plays in Native American life.

Aspect of Nature	Connection to Native American Life

4. **Reading Strategy:** Write one **cultural detail** that you recognize from "The Earth on Turtle's Back."
_____
_____

5. **Reading Strategy:** Write one **cultural detail** that you recognize from "The Navajo Origin Legend."
_____
_____

© Pearson Education, Inc., publishing as Pearson Prentice Hall.

Check Your Understanding
Questions after every selection help you think about the selection. You can use the write-on lines and charts to answer the questions. Then, share your ideas in class discussions.

The Earth on Turtle's Back • When Grizzlies Walked Upright • *from* The Navajo Origin Legend • *from* The Iroquois Constitution

LITERARY ANALYSIS

People often have a need to explain how life began. **Origin myths** tell how life started. Myths are stories passed down from one age group to the next. Animals often play a main role in Native American myths. These myths help explain parts of people's lives such as

- customs and religion
- natural objects and events, such as mountains or floods
- events people cannot control.

READING STRATEGY

Many stories are filled with details about the people who created the story. **Recognizing cultural details** will help you understand the culture that tells the story.

- Note objects, animals, or activities in the story. These items can tell you how the people of a culture live. They can also tell you what the people think and believe.
- Note whether a detail is repeated in a story. A repeated cultural detail often shows an important part of the culture.
- Use this chart to list the cultural details that you recognize in these four stories.

Details that signal how each group lives, thinks, or worships	
Onondaga	
Modoc	
Navajo	
Iroquois	

The Earth on Turtle's Back

from the Onondaga

Summary The Onondaga are one of the Iroquois tribes of the Northeast woodlands. They tell about a time before Earth was above water. A brave muskrat brings a tiny piece of earth out of the water to help a woman who falls from the sky. A turtle's back then becomes the base for Earth. Then, life on Earth begins. A story such as this helps the reader understand the beliefs and thinking of the Onondaga people.

Note-taking Guide

Use this diagram to record the events in the order in which they happen in this story.

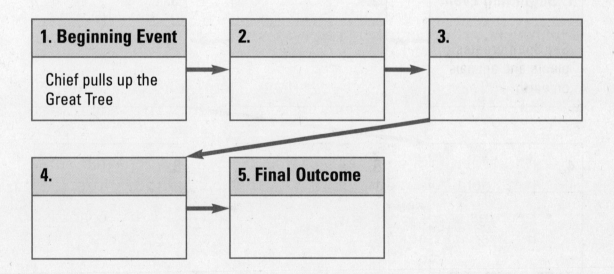

1. Beginning Event	2.	3.
Chief pulls up the Great Tree		

4.	5. Final Outcome

When Grizzlies Walked Upright

from the Modoc

Summary The Modoc lived in areas that became part of the western United States. They tell a story that explains where the first Native Americans come from. A daughter of the Chief of the Sky Spirits comes to Earth and marries a grizzly bear. Their children become the first Native Americans.

Note-taking Guide

Use this diagram to record the events in the order in which they happen in this story.

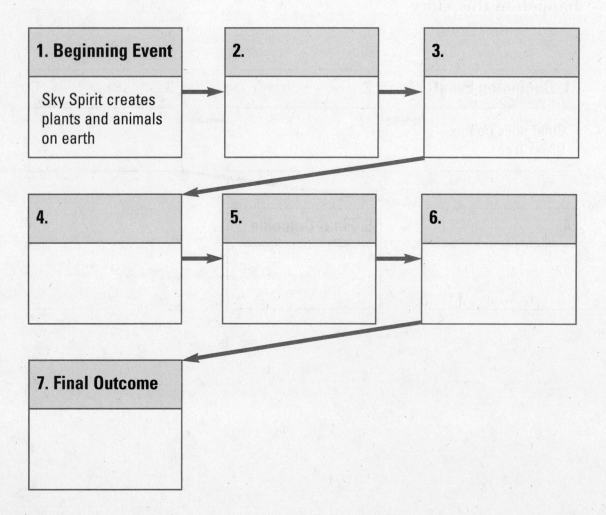

1. Beginning Event	2.	3.
Sky Spirit creates plants and animals on earth		

4.	5.	6.

7. Final Outcome

from The Navajo Origin Legend

Summary This part of the Navajo legend tells how the wind breathes life into corn to create the First Man and First Woman. This creation myth shows how important nature, corn, animal skins, feathers, and the wind are to the Navajo.

Note-taking Guide

Use this diagram to record the events in the order in which they happen in this story.

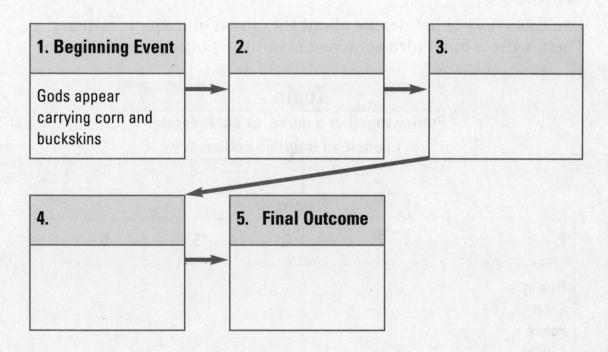

1. Beginning Event	2.	3.
Gods appear carrying corn and buckskins		

4.	5. Final Outcome

from The Iroquois Constitution

Translated by Arthur C. Parker

Red Jacket, George Catlin, The Thomas Gilcrease Institute of Art, Tulsa, Oklahoma

Summary This selection is an excerpt, or a section, from *The Iroquois Constitution.* Dekanawidah, who is an Iroquois prophet, speaks here of the Tree of Great Peace that gives shelter and protection to the Iroquois nations. He explains why and how the Five Nations, a group of five Iroquois tribes, should come together to form a union or confederacy for their common good.

Note-taking Guide

Use this chart to list details about the union of Iroquois nations. Then, write a main idea sentence about the purpose of the union.

Topic					
Putting together a union, or confederate council, of Iroquois nations					

Details					
1. →	2. →	3. →	4. →	5. →	6.
Tree of Great Peace = Tree of Great Leaves					

Main Idea Sentence

from The Iroquois Constitution
Translated by Arthur C. Parker

I am Dekanawidah and with the Five Nations[1] <u>confederate</u> lords I plant the Tree of the Great Peace. I name the tree the Tree of the Great Long Leaves. Under the shade of this Tree of the Great Peace we spread the soft white feathery down of the globe thistle as seats for you, Adodarhoh, and your cousin lords.

We place you upon those seats, spread soft with the feathery down of the globe thistle, there beneath the shade of the spreading branches of the Tree of Peace. There shall you sit and watch the council fire of the confederacy of the Five Nations, and all the affairs of the Five Nations shall be transacted[2] at this place before you.

Roots have spread out from the Tree of the Great Peace, one to the north, one to the east, one to the south and one to the west. The name of these roots is the Great White Roots and their nature is peace and strength.

♦ ♦ ♦

Other nations wishing to speak with the Five Nations will trace the roots to the tree. Peaceful and obedient people will be welcomed.

♦ ♦ ♦

Vocabulary Development

confederate (kon FED er it) *adj.* united with others for a common purpose

---

1. **Five Nations** the Mohawk, Oneida, Onondaga, Cayuga, and Seneca tribes. Together, these tribes formed the Iroquois Confederation.
2. **transacted** (trans ACT id) *v.* done.

TAKE NOTES

English Language Development

In English, the prefix *con-*, *com-* means "with." A *constitution* is something set up or established with other people. What is a *confederacy*?

_____

_____

Literary Analysis

Circle two words that show the nature of the Great White Roots in this **origin myth**. What can you tell from this passage about the purpose of the alliance?

_____

_____

Culture Note

The speaker sometimes repeats words and concepts: for example, "seats," "feathery down of the globe thistle," and "Five Nations." The repetitions draw attention to the formal, serious nature of the speaker's words and actions. Write one other word or phrase that is repeated in this selection.

_____

What role does the eagle play as a **cultural detail** for the Five Nations?

_____

_____

_____

Circle the **cultural details** in the under-lined passage that show why the smoke of the council fire will ascend to the sky. What is one requirement for all the lords of the Five Nations?

_____

_____

_____

Circle the **cultural details** in the underlined passage that show why the smoke of the council fire will ascend to the sky.

We place at the top of the Tree of the Long Leaves an eagle who is able to see afar. If he sees in the distance any evil approaching or danger threatening he will at once warn the people of the confederacy.

The smoke of the confederate council fire shall ever <u>ascend</u> and pierce the sky so that other nations who may be allies may see the council fire of the Great Peace . . .

◆ ◆ ◆

The Onondaga lords will open every council meeting by giving thanks to their cousin lords. They will also offer thanks to the earth, the waters, the crops, the trees, the animals, the sun, the moon, and the Great Creator.

◆ ◆ ◆

All lords of the Five Nations' Confederacy must be honest in all things . . . It shall be a serious wrong for anyone to lead a lord into trivial[3] affairs, for the people must ever hold their lords high in estimation[4] out of respect to their honorable positions.

◆ ◆ ◆

When a new lord joins the council, he must offer a pledge of four strings of shells. The speaker of the council will then welcome the new lord. The lords on the other side of the council fire will receive the pledge. Then they will speak these words to the new lord:

◆ ◆ ◆

Vocabulary Development

ascend (uh SEND) *v.* rise
deliberation (di lib er A shun) *n.* careful consideration

---

3. **trivial** (TRIV i al) *adj.* unimportant.
4. **estimation** (es ti MA shun) *n.* opinion, judgment.

"With endless patience you shall carry out your duty and your firmness shall be tempered[5] with tenderness for your people. Neither anger nor fury shall find lodgement in your mind and all your words and actions shall be marked with calm underline deliberation. In all your deliberations in the confederate council, in your efforts at law making, in all your official acts, self-interest shall be cast into oblivion.[6] Cast not over your shoulder behind you the warnings of the nephews and nieces should they chide[7] you for any error or wrong you may do, but return to the way of the Great Law which is just and right. Look and listen for the welfare of the whole people and have always in view not only the present but also the coming generations, even those whose faces are yet beneath the surface of the ground—the unborn of the future nation."

Read Fluently

Read the bracketed passage aloud. Circle three words that name qualities a new lord should have.

Vocabulary and Pronunciation

The expression *cast not over your shoulder behind you* means "don't discard or throw away." What does the underlined sentence mean?

_____

_____

_____

Reading Strategy

What attitude about the future do the members of the speaker's **culture** have?

_____

_____

_____

---

5. tempered (TEM perd) *v.* made more moderate.
6. oblivion (uh BLIV i un) *n.* forgetfulness.
7. chide (CHY D) *v.* criticize.

from The Iroquois Constitution **9**

The Earth on Turtle's Back • When Grizzlies Walked Upright • *from* The Navajo Origin Legend • *from* The Iroquois Constitution

1. **Infer:** Why do the Navajo people believe that spirits are kind?

   _____

   _____

2. **Infer:** Why do the Modoc people believe that spirits are mean?

   _____

   _____

3. **Literary Analysis:** Use this chart to list one aspect or part of nature. Write the role it plays in Native American life.

Aspect of Nature	Connection to Native American Life

4. **Reading Strategy:** Write one **cultural detail** that you recognize from "The Earth on Turtle's Back."

   _____

   _____

   _____

5. **Reading Strategy:** Write one **cultural detail** that you recognize from "The Navajo Origin Legend."

   _____

   _____

   _____

A Journey Through Texas • Boulders Taller Than the Great Tower of Seville

LITERARY ANALYSIS

Early European explorers often wrote about their travels in the Americas. These stories are called **exploration narratives.** Exploration narratives use details to describe the places explorers visit and the people they meet. Explorers write narratives to help people back home imagine what a place is like.

Authors write with different styles. An **author's style** is the author's choice of words, detail, and focus. For example, the authors of these two narratives provide different details to tell about their explorations. They focus on events, people, and places in different ways. Fill out this Venn diagram by writing down things that are similar about the two narratives in the center oval. Write down things that are different about the focus of each author in the proper place.

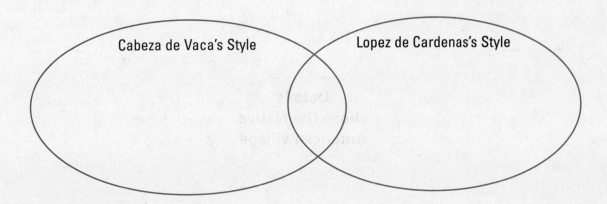

READING STRATEGY

Signal words connect or show relationships among ideas. They help you follow the order of events in a narrative.

- Some signal words show a relationship based on **time.** *We found water <u>after</u> searching for two days.*

- Some signal words show a **contrast.** *We were excited to see the canyon <u>but</u> worried about the terrain.*

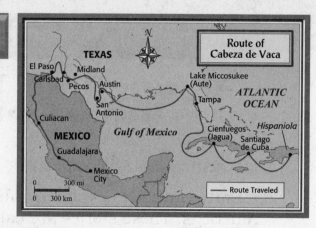

A Journey Through Texas

by Alvar Núñez Cabeza de Vaca

Summary In this narrative, the author describes his journey into what is now the state of Texas. There, he meets many Native Americans who help him on his journey. The Native Americans share food with him and help him find his way. The author learns to appreciate the different ways people have found to live.

Note-taking Guide

Use this diagram to record details about the author's experiences.

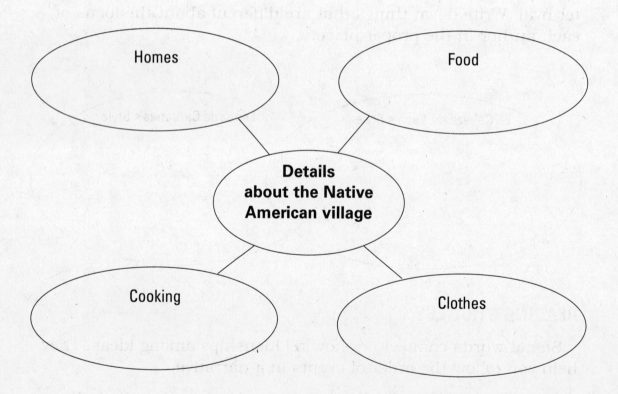

Boulders Taller Than the Great Tower of Seville

by García López de Cárdenas

Summary This narrative tells about the first time that Europeans come to the Grand Canyon. The author describes the canyon's vast size, difficult landscape, and cold weather. He explains what happens when his group tries to explore the canyon.

Note-taking Guide

Use this diagram to record details about the author's experiences.

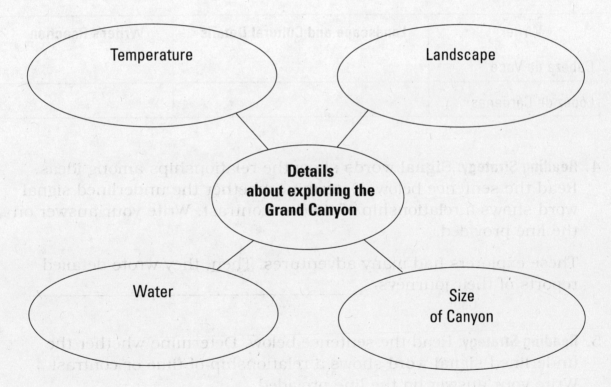

Temperature

Landscape

Details about exploring the Grand Canyon

Water

Size of Canyon

A Journey Through Texas • Boulders Taller Than the Great Tower of Seville

1. **Draw Conclusions:** Cabeza de Vaca explains that many Native Americans fell sick and eight of them died. What do the Native Americans believe caused the sickness? _____

2. **Infer:** Why does Coronado send López de Cárdenas and his group on a mission north? _____

3. **Literary Analysis: Compare and contrast** the way Cabeza de Vaca and López de Cárdenas react to the Native Americans. Use this chart to record your ideas.

Writer	Landscape and Cultural Details	Writer's Reaction
Cabeza de Vaca		
López de Cárdenas		

4. **Reading Strategy: Signal words** show the relationships among ideas. Read the sentence below. Determine whether the underlined signal word shows a relationship of time or contrast. Write your answer on the line provided.

   These explorers had many adventures. <u>Then</u>, they wrote detailed reports of their journeys. _____

5. **Reading Strategy:** Read the sentence below. Determine whether the underlined **signal word** shows a relationship of time or contrast. Write your answer on the line provided.

   The Native Americans sometimes had to deal with their enemies while helping the explorers, <u>but</u> they helped the explorers anyway.

   _____

from Journal of the First Voyage to America

LITERARY ANALYSIS

A **journal** is a written account of what happens in a person's life each day. European explorers who came to the Americas kept details of their travels in daily journals.

- Journals provide details from eyewitnesses, or spectators who can describe what actually happened.

- Journals are accounts of the writer's personal reactions. A journal can reveal much about the writer's feelings, thoughts, and values.

Irony and a surprise ending show the story's theme, or message.

READING STRATEGY

Authors have many different reasons for writing. **Recognizing the author's purpose** can help you understand why a work was written. If you know the author's purpose, you can also understand the word choices and ideas included in the written work.

Use this chart as you read Columbus's journal. List Columbus's favorable descriptions of objects, people, and events. Then, explain his purpose for writing those descriptions.

Favorable Descriptions	Author's Purpose

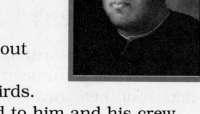

from Journal of the First Voyage to America

Summary Columbus writes in his journal about his exploration of a beautiful island. He describes spectacular trees, flowers, and birds. He also tells how the native people respond to him and his crew. Columbus wants to impress the people who are paying for his trip, so he describes the exotic objects he is bringing home.

Note-taking Guide

Use this diagram to record the events in the order in which they happen in this journal.

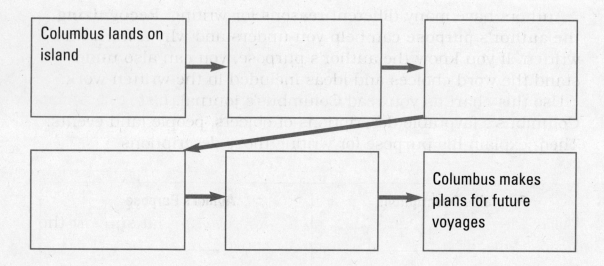

from Journal of the First Voyage to America

1. **Literary Analysis:** Identify three details from Columbus's **journal** that could only be provided by an eyewitness. List the details in a chart like this one.

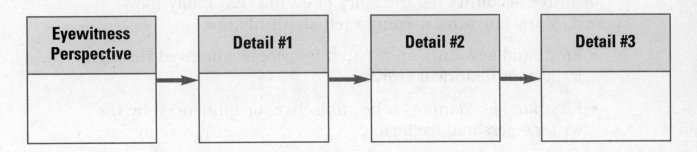

Eyewitness Perspective	→	Detail #1	→	Detail #2	→	Detail #3

2. **Literary Analysis:** What does Columbus think about each of the details you listed in the chart?

_____

_____

3. **Reading Strategy:** What is the **author's purpose** for writing this journal?

_____

_____

4. **Support:** Identify specific words, details, and events that support the purpose you identified in the question above.

_____

_____

5. **Hypothesize:** How would this journal be different if it had been written by a Native American who was there watching?

_____

_____

from The General History of Virginia • *from* Of Plymouth Plantation

LITERARY ANALYSIS

Narrative accounts tell the story of events that really happened. Many narrative accounts tell about history.

- Firsthand accounts are written by people who lived through important historical events.

- Firsthand accounts can be subjective, or influenced by the writer's personal feelings.

- Secondhand accounts are written by people who have gathered information about an event. However, these writers did not actually experience the events themselves.

John Smith and William Bradford both provide firsthand observations in their narrative accounts.

READING STRATEGY

Breaking down sentences can help you understand sentences that are long and complicated.

- Look at one section of the sentence at a time. Separate the most important parts of the sentence from any difficult language.

- Use punctuation to help you decide where to break sentences into smaller parts.

- Use a chart like this one to help you break down sentences and figure out their meaning.

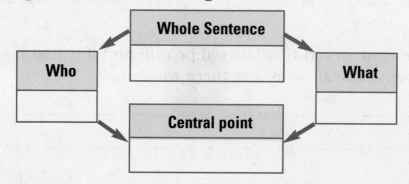

from The General History of Virginia

John Smith

Summary This excerpt tells of the hardships of the Jamestown colony. Fifty colonists die between May and September. When Captain John Smith goes on an expedition, he and his men are attacked by Indians. Smith's life is saved by Chief Powhatan's daughter. After six weeks as a captive, Smith is allowed to return to Jamestown. Pocahontas brings the settlers food, saving their lives.

Note-taking Guide

Use this chart to record four important events.

Topic			
The first months of the Jamestown settlement			
1. →	**2.** →	**3.** →	**4.** →
After the ship leaves, the settlers do not have enough food.	The settlers work so hard that they become weak.		

Main Idea Sentence
Despite great challenges, the settlement survives.

Read the bracketed passage aloud. How do things change after the ships leave?

_____

_____

_____

In the underlined clause, the word *if* has been omitted. Rewrite that part of the sentence using the word *if.*

_____

_____

_____

from The General History of Virginia
John Smith

What Happened Till the First Supply

Being thus left to our fortunes, it fortuned[1] that within ten days, scarce ten amongst us could either go[2] or well stand, such extreme weakness and sickness oppressed us. And thereat none need marvel if they consider the cause and reason, which was this: While the ships stayed, our allowance was somewhat bettered by a daily proportion of biscuit which the sailors would pilfer to sell, give, or exchange with us for money, sassafras,[3] or furs. But when they departed, there remained neither tavern, beer house, nor place of relief but the common kettle.[4] Had we been as free from all sins as gluttony and drunkenness we might have been canonized[5] for saints, but our President[6] would never have been admitted for engrossing to his private,[7] oatmeal, sack,[8] oil, aqua vitae,[9] beef, eggs, or what not but the kettle; that indeed he allowed equally to be distributed, and that was half a pint of wheat and as much barley boiled with water for a man a day, and this, having fried some twenty-six weeks in the ship's hold,[10] contained as many worms as grains so that

Vocabulary Development

pilfer (PIL fer) *v.* steal
gluttony (GLUT un ee) *n.* habit of eating too much

---

1. **fortuned** *v.* happened.
2. **go** *v.* be active.
3. **sassafras** (SAS uh fras) *n.* a tree, the root of which was valued for its use as medicine.
4. **common kettle** communal cooking pot.
5. **canonized** (KAN uh niyzd) *v.* made a saint.
6. **President Wingfield,** the leader of the colony.
7. **engrossing to his private** taking for his own use.
8. **sack** *n.* type of white wine.
9. **aqua vitae** (AK wuh VY tee) *n.* brandy.
10. **hold** *n.* storage area for a ship's cargo.

we might truly call it rather so much bran than corn; our drink was water, our lodgings castles in the air.

◆ ◆ ◆

That summer fifty colonists die, and another President is elected. Suddenly the fortunes of the settlers change. The Indians bring them food. Smith blames the hard times on the colonists' ignorance. They thought the sea journey would take two months and it took five. So supplies run short.

◆ ◆ ◆

Such actions have ever since the world's beginning been subject to such accidents, and everything of worth is found full of difficulties, but nothing so difficult as to establish a commonwealth so far remote from men and means and where men's minds are so untoward[11] as neither do well themselves nor suffer others. But to proceed.

The new President and Martin, being little beloved, of weak judgment in dangers, and less industry in peace, committed the managing of all things abroad[12] to Captain Smith, who, by his own example, good words, and fair promises, set some to mow, others to bind thatch, some to build houses, others to thatch them, himself always bearing the greatest task for his own share, so that in short time he provided most of them lodgings, neglecting any for himself. . . .

◆ ◆ ◆

Leading an expedition on the Chickahominy River, Smith and his men are attacked by Indians. Smith is held prisoner for six or seven weeks. Several times he is on the point of being killed. However, he

---

11. **untoward** adj. stubborn.
12. **abroad** adv. outside the perimeter fence.

TAKE NOTES

Reading Check

Why is the corn spoiled?

_____

_____

_____

Reading Strategy

Break down the underlined **long sentence.** Circle the part of the sentence that states the main idea.

English Language Development

"Castles in the air" is a phrase that has become a proverb in English, meaning "imaginary schemes." Give an example of a proverb or traditional saying in your native language.

_____

_____

_____

Literary Analysis

Circle two phrases in this part of Smith's **narrative account** that might be examples of reporting that is not objective.

Break down the bracketed **sentence**. List five factual details that Smith gives to describe this scene.

_____

_____

_____

_____

_____

Vocabulary and Pronunciation

Smith uses a number of archaic, or old-fashioned, words that are no longer current in English, such as *whereat*. Use the context to determine the meaning of this word and write the meaning below.

_____

_____

_____

Stop to Reflect

Why do you think Powhatan does not kill Smith?

_____

_____

_____

gains the favor of the Indian leader, who finally brings him to Powhatan.

◆ ◆ ◆

At last they brought him to Werowocomoco, where was Powhatan, their Emperor. Here more than two hundred of those grim courtiers stood wondering at him, as he had been a monster, till Powhatan and his train had put themselves in their greatest braveries.[13] Before a fire upon a seat like a bedstead, he sat covered with a great robe made of raccoon skins and all the tails hanging by. On either hand did sit a young wench[14] of sixteen or eighteen years and along on each side the house, two rows of men and behind them as many women, with all their heads and shoulders painted red, many of their heads bedecked[15] with the white down of birds, and a great chain of white beads about their necks.

At his entrance before the King, all the people gave a great shout. The queen of Appomattoc was appointed to bring him water to wash his hands, and another brought him a bunch of feathers, instead of a towel, to dry them; having feasted him after their best barbarous manner they could, a long consultation was held, but the conclusion was, two great stones were brought before Powhatan: then as many as could, laid hands on him, dragged him to them, and thereon laid his head and being ready with their clubs to beat out his brains, Pocahontas, the King's dearest daughter, when no <u>entreaty</u> could prevail, got his head in her arms and laid her own upon his to save him from death; <u>whereat</u> the Emperor was

---

Vocabulary Development

entreaty (en TREE tee) *n.* plea or prayer

---

13. **braveries** (BRAY vuh reez) *n.* fine dress.
14. **wench** *n.* young woman.
15. **bedecked** (bee DEKT) *v.* decorated.

contented he should live to make him hatchets, and her bells, beads, and copper, for they thought him as well of all occupations as themselves.[16]

♦ ♦ ♦

   Powhatan and Smith become friends. The Indian king offers to sell the colonists land in exchange for guns and a grindstone. Smith returns to Jamestown and sends cannons and a millstone back to Powhatan. When some of the colonists try to turn back to England, Smith prevents them by force. He is also able to defeat a plot against him by the President and some other settlers.

♦ ♦ ♦

   Now every once in four or five days, Pocahontas with her attendants brought him so much provision that saved many of their lives, that else for all this had starved with hunger.

   His <u>relation</u> of the plenty he had seen, especially at Werowocomoco, and of the state and bounty of Powhatan (which till that time was unknown), so revived their dead spirits (especially the love of Pocahontas) as all men's fear was abandoned.

   Thus you may see what difficulties still crossed any good endeavor; and the good success of the business being thus oft brought to the very period of destruction; yet you see by what strange means God hath still delivered it.

TAKE NOTES

Vocabulary and Pronunciation

In English, the word *relation* can mean "a person in the same family" or "an account or a telling." Which meaning of the word is used in the bracketed paragraph?

_____

_____

Reading Check

Underline two parts of the bracketed passage that explain why the colonists were no longer afraid.

Read Fluently

Read the last paragraph aloud. Who or what does Smith say is responsible for the "good success of the business"?

_____

_____

_____

16. **as well . . . themselves** capable of making them just as well as they could themselves.

from Of Plymouth Plantation

Summary This narrative account tells of the Puritans' first journey to the New World. The first part of the narrative describes their voyage. The second section describes the hardships of their first winter in Massachusetts. The third part tells how the Puritans received help from Native Americans and made a peace treaty with them.

The Coming of the Mayflower, N.C. Wyeth, from the Collection of Metropolitan Life Insurance Company, New York City, Photograph by Malcolm Varon

Note-taking Guide

Use this table to record how the settlers survived hardship and danger.

Section of text	Hardships the settlers faced	What the settlers did
Of Their Voyage		
The Starving Time		
Indian Relations		

from The General History of Virginia •
from Of Plymouth Plantation

1. **Literary Analysis:** Find examples in these selections of these important elements of **narrative accounts.** Write your answers in the chart.

What the Writer Saw

Factual Information

Selection

What the Writer Heard

Subjective Bias

2. **Literary Analysis:** What was Smith's purpose in writing his narrative account of exploring Virginia?

_____

_____

3. **Literary Analysis:** What was Bradford's purpose in writing his narrative account of Plymouth Plantation?

_____

_____

4. **Reading Strategy:** Choose a sentence in the narratives that you found difficult to understand. Try **breaking down the sentence.** Separate the hard language from the most important parts. Write what the sentence means using your own words.

Original sentence: _____

Your interpretation of the sentence: _____

5. **Hypothesize:** Explain how Bradford's account might have been different if the Pilgrims had successfully settled at their original destination farther south.

_____

_____

WEB SITES

About Web Sites

A **Web site** is a collection of Web pages—words and pictures on a topic that can be found on the Internet. Each page has its own URL, or "address." Web sites feature underlined words and icons that serve as links to other sites or pages. You can find more information by clicking on these words.

Reading Strategy

Learn how to **locate appropriate information** to get the most out of Internet research. Use a search engine. It will list any page on the Web that has words matching a search term you type in. Use specific words when you use a search engine. If you are looking for information on the Puritans who settled in America, search for the word *Pilgrim.* Too broad a term, such as *colony,* will give you a list that is too long.

Even a focused search term may bring you too many results. To further narrow down the list of sites, review the name of the sponsor that is listed on the search engine list. Also look at the description of the site.

The box below lists a few of the features found on Web sites.

Elements of Web Sites

- **Links, hotspotted text**, and other **navigation elements** help you move around the site quickly. Click on any area of the page over which your cursor changes to a hand.
- **A SEARCH function** helps you locate information on the site, using search terms.
- **Photos, videos, and audio clips** are added to many sites. You may need to download additional software to use these resources.
- **Links** connect you to other pages within the site and to other related Web sites.
- **Contact information** tells you who sponsored the site.

Build Understanding

Knowing this term will help you understand the information on this Web site.

virtual tour (VER choo uhl TOOR) tour that is taken through a computer

---

http://www.plimoth.org/

PLIMOTH PLANTATION

Living Breathing History

visit ⁞ learn ⁞ shop ⁞ participate   *plan your visit, get directions, take a virtual tour*

News & Events:

Winter Education Programs are here!

Apply to be an intern today

Subscribe to our e-newsletter

General Information:

Tickets and Hours

Directions to the Museum

Calendar of Events

Favorites:

Explore Plymouth, MA

Activities Just for Kids

Online Fun - Become a Historian!

foreign languages | e-news sign-up | press kit | privacy policy | terms & rights | employment | contact us

PLIMOTH PLANTATION *Living Breathing History*

virtual tour :: what to see & do :: plan your visit :: explore plymouth, ma :: calendar of events :: group tours :: functions

what to see & do

1627 pilgrim village

hobbamock's homesite

mayflower II

crafts center

nye barn

thanksgiving exhibit

dining

practical questions about visiting

Featured Item in
Our Shop :
Making of a Colony Video

*"Welcome to the town! How do you fare?
Are you just passing through, or mayhaps you are desiring to settle in this wilderness?"*

1627 Pilgrim Village

This is one of the ways you may be greeted in the 1627 Pilgrim Village, a re-creation of the small farming town built by English colorists in the midst of the Wampanoag homeland. Find yourself immersed in the year 1627, just seven years after the voyage of the Mayflower. In the village you will be surrounded by the modest timber-framed houses, fragrant raised-bed gardens, well-tended livestock and fascinating townspeople of Plymouth Colony, the first permanent English settlement in New England.

The people you will meet are costumed role players who have taken on the names, viewpoints and life histories of the people who actually lived in the colony in 1627, popularly known as the "Pilgrims" today. Each one has a unique story to tell. Learn about the colony's difficult beginnings or discover the gossip of the day. Ask about religious beliefs, medical practices or relations with the local Wampanoag People. Talk to a housewife and learn what a "pottage" is, or see how a duck or bluefish is cooked on the hearth. Help a young colonist pull up a few weeds in a cornfield, mix daub with your feet for a house under construction, or just relax on a bench enjoying the unique atmosphere of 17th-century New Plymouth.

THINKING ABOUT THE WEB SITE

1. What should you do to get the Web site's information in Spanish?

_____

2. Why are pictures on the home page used as links?

_____

READING STRATEGY

3. How can you use the Web site to buy books about seventeenth-century New England?

_____

4. On the home page, under what category do you find a link to Plimoth Plantation's calendar of events?

_____

TIMED WRITING: EVALUATION (20 minutes)

Use this cluster diagram to brainstorm the features of a well-organized Web site. Think about the features of a Web site, such as links, hotspotted text, photos, videos, and SEARCH functions. Does the Web site offer these things? Use the cluster diagram to write your evaluation.

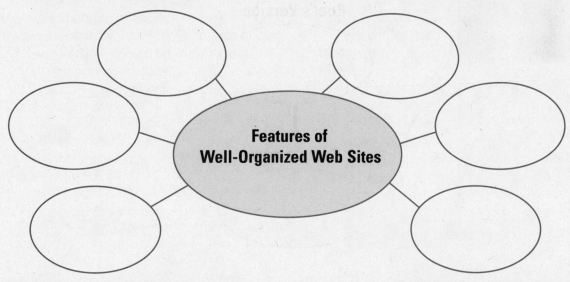

Features of Well-Organized Web Sites

Huswifery • To My Dear and Loving Husband

LITERARY ANALYSIS

Puritan Plain Style is a writing style used by many Puritan writers. This style reflects the simple Puritan lifestyle. Characteristics of Puritan Plain Style include

- short words
- direct statements
- references to everyday, ordinary objects.

Puritan believed that poetry should be written about religious subjects in order to serve God.

READING STRATEGY

- When you **paraphrase** a written work, you restate the main ideas in your own words. Paraphrasing is a good skill to use when reading poetry. For example, Puritan poetry may be written in a simple style, but it can still be difficult to understand. Paraphrasing can help you understand the difficult ideas expressed by these Puritan poets.

- When you read a line from these poems that you don't understand, try to paraphrase it. Use a diagram like this one to organize your paraphrases.

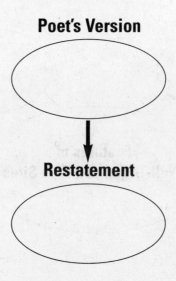

Poet's Version

Restatement

Huswifery • To My Dear and Loving Husband

Summaries Taylor's poem is addressed to God. The speaker in the poem compares himself to a spinning wheel that turns yarn into cloth. The speaker wants to be changed by God into a person who is worthy of being saved. In Bradstreet's poem, the speaker addresses her husband. She expresses her deep love for him, which will last even after their lives on earth are over.

Note-taking Guide

Use this chart to help you compare elements of these two poems.

Taylor		Bradstreet
	The poet is speaking to…?	
	Images in poem	
	Religious references	

Huswifery • To My Dear and Loving Husband

1. **Literary Analysis: Puritan Plain Style** reflects the Puritans' plain, simple lives. Use a chart like this one to list words, phrases, and references in each poem that represent Puritan Plain Style.

Concept		Perception
Thy spinning wheel complete.	→	References to household objects reflect plain lives.

2. **Analyze:** Analyze each poem to identify characteristics that are not typical of Puritan Plain Style.

   Taylor's poem: _____

   Bradstreet's poem: _____

3. **Reading Strategy: Paraphrase** this passage from "To My Dear and Loving Husband." Restate in your own words what the passage means.

   Lines 5–6: _____

4. **Reading Strategy: Paraphrase** this passage from "Huswifery." Restate in your own words what the passage means.

   Lines 13–16: _____

5. **Interpret:** What images in "To My Dear and Loving Husband" suggest the richness of the love that the speaker and her husband share?

   _____

   _____

from Sinners in the Hands of an Angry God

LITERARY ANALYSIS

A **sermon** is a speech given by a preacher in a house of worship. A sermon is a type of **oratory,** or formal public speaking. As you read, keep in mind these features of an oratory:

- It is persuasive.

- It appeals to the emotions of listeners.

- It addresses the needs of listeners.

- It calls for listeners to take action.

- It uses colorful language.

READING SKILL

Context clues help you understand the meanings of unfamiliar words. A word's context is its surrounding words, phrases, and sentences. Look for context clues to find the meaning of *abominable* in the following sentence:

> You are ten thousand times more abominable in his [God's] eyes than the most hateful venomous serpent is in ours. . . .

The context clue here is in the comparison. Edwards says that the way a sinner looks in God's eyes is like the way a hateful snake looks in our eyes. From this clue, you can guess that *abominable* must be close in meaning to *horrible* or *disgusting*.

Use this chart to help you find the meaning of unfamiliar words.

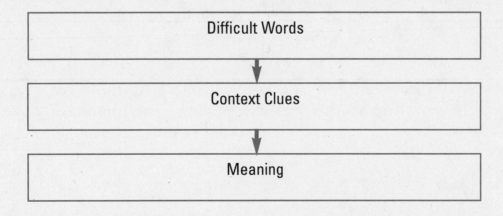

Difficult Words

↓

Context Clues

↓

Meaning

PREVIEW

from Sinners in the Hands of an Angry God

Jonathan Edwards

Summary Edwards's sermon tells about God's anger toward the sinners in his audience. He compares God's anger to floods and to a bow bent ready to shoot an arrow. The only thing that keeps God from dropping sinners into the fire is his mercy, according to Edwards. He tells the people that they can be reborn and save themselves from the anger.

Note-taking Guide

Use this chart to record details of what Edwards tells the sinners in his audience.

Purpose	Details to Achieve This Purpose
To motivate listeners to convert and save their souls	• Only the power of God holds you up.

from Sinners in the Hands of an Angry God

Jonathan Edwards

The author, Jonathan Edwards, directs his sermon toward those with whom God is not pleased. He talks about a world of misery for them.

◆   ◆   ◆

There is the dreadful pit of the glowing flames of the <u>wrath</u> of God; there is Hell's wide <u>gaping</u> mouth open; and you have nothing to stand upon, nor anything to take hold of; there is nothing between you and Hell but the air; it is only the power and mere pleasure of God that holds you up.

◆   ◆   ◆

Sinners may think they are kept out of Hell by their own life and strength, but they are wrong. Sinners are like heavy weights of lead. If God chose to let them go, they would sink straight to Hell. God's anger is like a terrible storm, held back for the moment.

God's wrath is like a stream that is dammed. The longer it is dammed, the stronger the waters will be once the dam is opened.

◆   ◆   ◆

It is true, that judgment against your evil works has not been executed hitherto;[1] the Hoods of God's vengeance have been withheld; but your guilt in the meantime is constantly increasing, and you are every day treasuring up more wrath; the waters are constantly rising, and <u>waxing</u> more and more mighty; and there is

---

Vocabulary Development

wrath (RATH) *n.* great anger

waxing (WAKS ing) *v.* increasing

---

1. **hitherto** (hi thuhr TOO) *adv.* up to now.

TAKE NOTES

Literary Analysis

Underline two words in the **sermon's** title that suggest the emotional focus of Edwards's message.

Reading Strategy

Circle the **context clues** that help you understand the meaning of *gaping*. What does *gaping* mean?

_____

_____

_____

English Language Development

Adjectives and adverbs in English have three forms: positive (*pretty, beautiful*), comparative (*prettier, more beautiful*), and superlative (*prettiest, most beautiful*). Adjectives and adverbs form the comparative by adding *-er* to the end of the word (*prettier*) or *more* at the beginning of the word (*more beautiful*). Comparative adjectives and adverbs in the bracketed section include *longer* and *stronger*. What is the superlative form of the adjectives *long* and *strong*?

_____

The word *inconceivable* contains the prefix *in-* meaning "not," and also the suffix *-able*, meaning "capable of." These word parts help you to determine the meaning: "not able to be imagined or conceived." What would the word *inseparable* mean?

_____

_____

_____

To what does Edwards compare the wrath of God?

_____

_____

_____

Read the bracketed paragraph aloud. Then fill in the blanks below.

1. The wrath of God is like a

_____

that is bent.

2. Justice directs the

_____

to the heart of the sinner.

nothing but the mere pleasure of God, that holds the waters back, that are unwilling to be stopped, and press hard to go forward.

◆ ◆ ◆

God's hand is holding the gate that controls the dam. If he should decide to move his hand, the flood of anger would be <u>inconceivable</u>. No human strength, or even the strength of the devil, could stop it.

◆ ◆ ◆

The bow of God's wrath is bent, and the arrow made ready on the string, and justice bends the arrow at your heart, and strains the bow, and it is nothing but the mere pleasure of God, and that of an angry God, without any promise or obligation at all, that keeps the arrow one moment from being made drunk with your blood.

◆ ◆ ◆

Everyone who does not repent risks being destroyed. Sinners may not believe that they are in danger now. There will come a time, though, when they will be convinced.

◆ ◆ ◆

The God that holds you over the pit of Hell, much as one holds a spider, or some loathsome insect over the fire, abhors you, and is dreadfully provoked: his wrath towards you burns like fire; he looks upon you as worthy of nothing else, but to be cast into the fire; he is of purer eyes than to bear to have you in his sight; you are ten thousand times more <u>abominable</u> in his eyes, than the most hateful <u>venomous</u> serpent is in ours. . . .

❖ ❖ ❖

Edwards warns sinners that they are in great danger. God is as angry with them as he is with those already in Hell.

❖ ❖ ❖

You hang by a slender thread, with the flames of divine wrath flashing about it, and ready every moment to singe it, and burn it <u>asunder</u>; and you have no interest in any mediator, and nothing to lay hold of to save yourself, nothing to keep off the flames of wrath, nothing of your own, nothing that you ever have done, nothing that you can do, to <u>induce</u> God to spare you one moment. . . .

❖ ❖ ❖

Edwards says that God will have no mercy on sinners who do not repent. However, the punishments of sinners will be just. If sinners repent now, God will show them mercy. If they refuse to repent, they will be tormented forever. Sinners who do not repent are in daily and hourly danger. Think of those who are now suffering endless misery in Hell. They have no more chances to obtain salvation. But those who are still alive may still be saved.

Vocabulary Development

abominable (uh BAHM uh nuh buhl) *adj.* hateful, disgusting

venomous (VEN uh muhs) *adj.* poisonous

asunder (a SUN duhr) *adv.* apart

induce (in DOOS) *v.* persuade

Reading Strategy

Circle the **context clues** that help you determine this meaning of *flocking*. What does *flocking* mean?

_____

_____

_____

English Language Development

Circle the punctuation marks on this page that show a quotation. What book is the quotation from

_____

_____

_____

Literary Analysis

In the bracketed summary of the passage of this persuasive **sermon**, what does Edwards want the congregation to do?

_____

_____

_____

Reading Check

Underline the quotation from the Bible in the last paragraph. Why is the Biblical quotation appropriate for Edwards's sermon?

Sinners now have a wonderful opportunity to gain forgiveness. They can save their souls from everlasting suffering. Many other sinners are flocking to him and entering his kingdom. They are coming from everywhere. These sinners had been miserable, but now God has washed their sins away and they are rejoicing. It would be awful to be left behind and not join in this joyful celebration. Edwards says all sinners in his congregation should escape God's wrath and experience the saving grace of conversion.

◆ ◆ ◆

"Haste and escape for your lives, look not behind you, escape to the mountain, lest you be consumed."[2]

Vocabulary Development

congregation (kahn gruh GAY shuhn) *n.* members of a place of worship

2. **"Haste . . . consumed"** from Genesis 19:17, the angels' warning to Lot, the only virtuous man in Sodom, to flee the city before they destroy it.

from Sinners in the Hands of an Angry God

1. **Literary Analysis:** In his **sermon,** Edwards tells his audience that they need to do something. What does he tell his audience that they need to do?

   _____

   _____

   _____

2. **Literary Analysis:** Edwards uses fear in his sermon to appeal his audience. Why does this strategy work well for his purpose?

   _____

   _____

   _____

3. **Connect:** A **symbol** is a person, place, or thing that has a broader meaning. Name two symbols that Edwards uses to describe God's Wrath. Complete this chart.

   | Wrath | → | Great waters | → | | → | |

4. **Reading Strategy: Context clues** are words and phrases near another word that gives clues to the word's meaning. Use context clues to define the underlined word: "you are every day treasuring up more wrath; the waters are constantly rising, and <u>waxing</u> more and more mighty . . ."

   _____

   _____

   _____

   _____

from Sinners in the Hands of an Angry God (cont'd)

5. **Evaluate:** Given his purpose and his audience, do you think Edwards's sermon was effective? Why or why not?

_____

_____

_____

_____

from The Autobiography • from Poor Richard's Almanack

LITERARY ANALYSIS

An **autobiography** is the story of a person's life. It is told by the person. Autobiography was a new form of literature when Benjamin Franklin wrote *The Autobiography*. His work helped set the rules for this new type of writing.

- An autobiography presents events in a person's life according to how that person sees them.
- An autobiography can give personal views of history.

Information about the politics, habits, ideas, and values of a society can be found in autobiographies.

Use this chart to record details from *The Autobiography*.

Details About Franklin's Life	Details About Franklin's Attitudes	Details About Franklin's Times

READING STRATEGY

Franklin tells readers details about his life. He explains his goals and his interests. You can **draw conclusions** about Franklin and his life. A conclusion is an opinion you reach by pulling together facts and details.

Use this pattern for drawing conclusions about Franklin's character while you read:

- **Details:** Franklin changes his plan when he sees he is not meeting his goals.
- **Personal Experience:** You also thought of a different way to meet a goal that was not being met.
- **Conclusion:** Franklin is someone who makes adjustments to meet his goals.

from The Autobiography

Benjamin Franklin

Summary Franklin is working on a plan to reach moral perfection. He will work on thirteen virtues, or qualities. Franklin writes the virtues in a notebook to see how well he is doing. He makes a black mark beside a virtue every time he forgets to follow it. He works on a different virtue each week. Franklin thinks his plan is helpful but not completely successful.

Note-taking Guide

Use this chart to keep track of the different virtues that Franklin works on. List the virtues in order from most important to least important.

Virtues to Help Franklin Reach His Goal
• Temperance
•
•
•
•
•
•
•
•
•
•
•

from The Autobiography

Benjamin Franklin

> Franklin decides to take up a difficult project. He will try to live a perfect life. He knows, or thinks he knows, what is right and wrong. He does not see why he cannot always do the one and avoid the other.

◆ ◆ ◆

But I soon found I had undertaken a task of more difficulty than I had imagined. While my care was employed in guarding against one fault, I was often surprised by another. . . .
I therefore contrived the following method.

◆ ◆ ◆

Franklin has read other people's lists of virtues in the past. These lists don't seem quite right to him. He writes his own list of thirteen virtues. He adds short notes. The notes explain what the virtue means to him. Here is his list.

◆ ◆ ◆

1. TEMPERANCE Eat not to dullness; drink not to elevation.
2. SILENCE Speak not but what may benefit others or yourself; avoid trifling conversation.
3. ORDER Let all your things have their places; let each part of your business have its time.
4. RESOLUTION Resolve to perform what you ought; perform without fail what you resolve.
5. FRUGALITY Make no expense but to do good to others or yourself; i.e., waste nothing.
6. INDUSTRY Lose no time; be always employed in something useful; cut off all unnecessary actions.
7. SINCERITY Use no hurtful deceit; think innocently and justly, and, if you speak, speak accordingly.

TAKE NOTES

Reading Strategy

Which phrases in the bracketed paragraph help you **draw conclusions** about Franklin's character? Circle them.

Stop to Reflect

Franklin makes a list to organize his plan. What does this show about his character?

English Language Development

Sometimes the *ee* sound in English is spelled *ie* or *ei*. How do you know when to use each spelling? There is a rule in English that goes like this: *i* before *e* except after *c*, or when sounded as *a* as in *neighbor* and *weigh*. Notice that in *deceit*, the *e* comes first. That's because a *c* is before the letters. Write *ei* or *ie* in each of the blanks in these words. Follow the rule to spell the words correctly.

1. rec_____pt
2. bel_____ve
3. _____ghteen
4. gr_____ve
5. ch___f
6. conc_____t

Reading Check

What is Franklin's attitude about wasting time? Circle the answer.

A suffix is a word part added to the end of a word. It changes the part of speech of the word. The word *frugal* is used to describe a person who does not waste things. When you add the suffix *-ity*, it means "the quality of not being wasteful." The suffix *-ity* means "quality, state, or condition of." Find two other words in Franklin's list that end in *-ity*. Write them here:

Reading Strategy

What might Franklin say to someone who was very upset about a minor traffic accident? **Draw conclusions** from the underlined text.

Reading Strategy

What **conclusion** can you **draw** from the bracketed text about the values of the time? Complete this sentence with your answer.

In Franklin's day, people thought virtues such as _____ and _____ were good to have.

Reading Strategy

How does Franklin think we add to our knowledge? Circle the answer.

8. JUSTICE Wrong none by doing injuries, or omitting the benefits that are your duty.
9. MODERATION Avoid extremes; forebear resenting injuries so much as you think they deserve.
10. CLEANLINESS Tolerate no uncleanliness in body, clothes, or habitation.
11. TRANQUILITY <u>Be not disturbed at trifles, or at accidents common or unavoidable.</u>
12. CHASTITY
13. HUMILITY Imitate Jesus and Socrates.

◆ ◆ ◆

Franklin's goal is to get into the habit of all these virtues. He tries one at a time, then goes on to the next. He thinks that some virtues might make other ones easier. That is why he lists *Temperance* first. Temperance helps you keep a clear head. A clear head helps you guard against bad habits. With the habit of temperance, *Silence* would be easier.

He also wants to gain knowledge. He knows that knowledge is obtained more by listening than by speaking. He gives *Silence* the second place. This virtue and the next, *Order,* would give him more time for his studies. *Resolution* is next. It will help Franklin stick to his plan. *Frugality* and *Industry* will help him pay all his debts. They will also help him add to his wealth. Then it will be easier to practice *Sincerity* and *Justice,* and so on. He decides to check his progress every day.

◆ ◆ ◆

I made a little book, in which I <u>allotted</u> a page for each of the virtues. I ruled each page with red ink, so as to have seven columns, one for each

Vocabulary Development

allotted (uh LOT ted) *v.* assigned, gave a part

day of the week, marking each column with a letter for the day. I crossed these columns with thirteen red lines, marking the beginning of each line with the first letter of one of the virtues, on which line and in its proper column I might mark, by a little black spot, every fault I found upon examination to have been committed respecting that virtue upon that day.

♦ ♦ ♦

He decides to spend a week on each virtue. In the first week, he practices Temperance. His goal the first week is to keep his first line, marked T, clear of spots. The next week, he might try the next virtue. He will try to keep both lines clear of spots. He can go through the whole list in thirteen weeks, and he repeats this process four times a year.

Franklin follows his plan for some time. One thing surprises him. He has more faults than he had imagined. But he is glad to see them become less and less. After a while, he goes through only one course in a year. Later, he goes through one in several years. At last, he stops doing it. He is too busy with trips and business in Europe. But he always carries his little book with him.

The virtue of Order gives him the most trouble. He just isn't used to putting papers and things in their places. He has a very good memory. He can always remember where he has left something.

♦ ♦ ♦

This article, therefore, cost me so much painful attention, and my faults in it <u>vexed</u> me so much, and I made so little progress in

---

Vocabulary Development

vexed (VEKST) *v.* annoyed, bothered

TAKE NOTES

Reading Strategy

Use separate paper to show what a page in Franklin's book would look like.

Background

Benjamin Franklin's "business in Europe" was to represent the United States there. He spent time in both England and France as a diplomat. In fact, while he was in France, he helped arrange the terms to end the Revolutionary War between England and the United States.

Literary Analysis

In this **autobiography,** Franklin mentions that he does other things besides keep a list of virtues. Underline the sentence in the bracketed passage that tells you what else Franklin is doing.

Here, Franklin tells a story about a man with an ax. What **conclusion** can you **draw** from this story about Franklin's sense of humor?

_____

_____

_____

Reading Check

Why does Franklin think a good man should keep a few faults?

_____

_____

_____

<u>amendment</u>, and had such frequent <u>relapses</u>, that I was almost ready to give up the attempt, and content myself with a faulty character in that respect, like the man who, in buying an ax of a smith,[1] my neighbor, desired to have the whole of its surface as bright as the edge. The smith consented to grind it bright for him if he would turn the wheel; he turned, while the smith pressed the broad face of the ax hard and heavily on the stone, which made the turning of it very <u>fatiguing</u>. The man came every now and then from the wheel to see how the work went on, and at length would take his ax as it was, without farther grinding. "No," said the smith, "turn on, turn on; we shall have it bright by and by; as yet, it is only <u>speckled</u>." "Yes," says the man, "*but I think I like a speckled ax best.*"

◆ ◆ ◆

Franklin believes that many people are like this man. Some people find it too difficult to form good habits. They just give up the struggle. They decide that "a speckled ax is best." Franklin is the same way about the virtue of Order. He thinks that other people might envy or hate him if he becomes perfect. He thinks that a good man should keep a few faults. This way, he can keep his friends.

◆ ◆ ◆

In truth, I found myself <u>incorrigible</u> with respect to Order; and now I am grown old, and

Vocabulary Development

amendment (uh MEND ment) *n.*   improvement, correction
relapses (REE lap ses) *n.*   slips back to a former state
fatiguing (fuh TEEG ing) *adj.*   tiring
speckled (SPEK uhld) *adj.*   covered with small spots
incorrigible (in KOR ij uh buhl) *adj.*   not able to be corrected

1. **smith** (SMITH) *n.* a person who works in metals.

my memory bad, I feel very sensibly the want of it. But, on the whole, though I never arrived at the perfection I had been so ambitious of obtaining, but fell far short of it, yet I was, by the <u>endeavor</u>, a better and a happier man than I otherwise should have been if I had not attempted it.

◆ ◆ ◆

Franklin wants his <u>descendants</u> to know about their <u>ancestor</u>. His list of virtues is important to him. In fact, he says he owes the constant happiness in his life to it. He is now seventy-nine years old. He owes his good health to *Temperance*. He owes his fortune to *Industry* and *Frugality*. To *Sincerity* and *Justice*, he owes the confidence his country has in him.

◆ ◆ ◆

<u>. . . and to the joint influence of the whole mass of the virtues, even in the imperfect state he was able to acquire them, [their ancestor ascribes] all that evenness of temper, and that cheerfulness in conversation, which makes his company still sought for, and agreeable even to his younger acquaintance.</u> I hope, therefore, that some of my descendants may follow the example and reap the benefit.

TAKE NOTES

Literary Analysis

An **autobiography** uses first-person pronouns like *I, me, my, we, us, mine, our,* and *ours*. Underline the words in the bracketed section that show that Franklin is writing an autobiography.

Stop to Reflect

Franklin tells us that he fell short of his goals. Does his attitude about this seem normal to you? Explain.

_____

_____

_____

_____

Read Fluently

Read aloud the underlined section. Then, circle the qualities that other people liked in Franklin.

Vocabulary Development

endeavor (en DEV er) *n.*   try, attempt

descendants (dee SEN dents) *n.*   people in one's family who come after

ancestor (AN ses ter) *n.*   a person in one's family who came before

___

from The Autobiography   **47**

from Poor Richard's Almanack

Benjamin Franklin

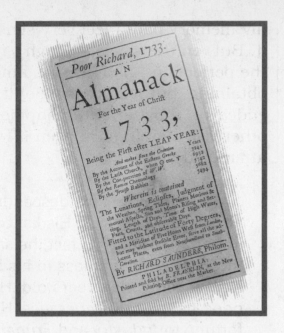

Summary Franklin gives advice about how people should behave. He presents his thoughts in **aphorisms**, or short sayings with a message. Many of his aphorisms come from traditional folk sayings. Sayings such as "Well done is better than well said" tell something about Franklin and what he values.

Note-taking Guide

Aphorisms can sometimes mean more than one thing. Use this chart to examine some of Franklin's sayings. Write down any second meanings.

Saying	Meaning
Keep thy shop, and thy shop will keep thee.	Work hard and your work will earn you money.

from The Autobiography • from Poor Richard's Almanack

1. **Generalize:** In what ways can analyzing one's own behavior contribute to personal growth?

_____

_____

2. **Literary Analysis:** Franklin's **autobiography** shows that he is concerned with improving his moral virtues. What does this concern tell you about the time period in which he lived?

_____

_____

3. **Connect:** Connect **aphorisms** from *Poor Richard's Almanack* to virtues listed in the *Autobiography*. Explain each connection you make. Use this chart to record your responses.

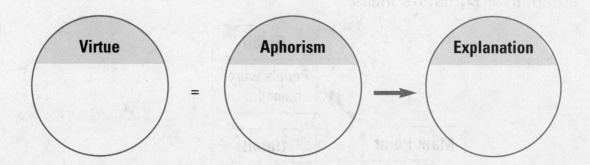

4. **Reading Strategy:** In the *Autobiography*, Franklin keeps track of how much he improves his moral virtues. He explains that he had to adjust his record-keeping system as his plan progressed. What **conclusion** can you draw about his character based on these adjustments?

_____

_____

from The Interesting Narrative of the Life of Olaudah Equiano

LITERARY ANALYSIS

In an autobiography, a person tells the story of his or her own life. A **slave narrative** is an autobiography written by a slave. It describes the horrors of slavery firsthand from the author's point of view. In the following example, Olaudah Equiano describes the conditions on the ship that brought him to Barbados. He uses **emotional appeals**, persuasive statements that inspire sympathy in his readers.

> The shrieks of the women, and the groans of the dying, rendered the whole a scene of horror almost inconceivable.

READING STRATEGY

It is helpful to **summarize** the main points of a challenging text. When you summarize, you use your own words to state the main ideas and details. A good summary is much shorter than the original text. The chart below summarizes Equiano's first paragraph. As you read, write notes in the boxes to help you summarize Equiano's ideas.

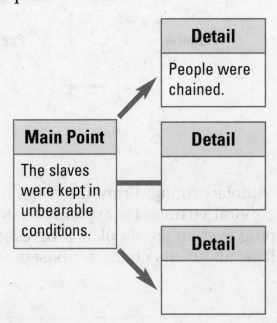

Detail

People were chained.

Main Point

The slaves were kept in unbearable conditions.

Detail

Detail

These chains were found at a Plantation Slave
Quarter site on Wadamalan Island, S.C.
approximately 25 miles from Charleston. They are
Blacksmith made.

PREVIEW

from The Interesting Narrative of the Life of Olaudah Equiano

Olaudah Equiano

Summary Olaudah Equiano tells what happened to him aboard a slave ship. He describes the crowded conditions and sickening smells. He also tells of the slaves' despair. He explains that the ship's crew chained, starved, and beat the slaves. Many people died during the terrible journey. Those who lived were examined and sold when they reached Barbados.

Note-taking Guide

Use this chart to describe the conditions on a slave ship.

Main Idea: Conditions on slave ships from Africa cause many slaves to die during the journey		
The smell inside the ship is terrible.	The ship's crew is cruel.	Many slaves die.
	Slaves are chained.	

In modern English, a comma almost never divides the subject of a sentence from the main verb. What verb goes with the subject *ship* in the first sentence?

Many words in English have multiple meanings. The word *hold*, for example, can be a verb meaning "to have in one's hands." It can also be a noun meaning "the inside of a ship." What is the meaning of *hold* in the first paragraph?

Underline three details in this **slave narrative** that show the horrible conditions for the slaves on board ship.

Why would it have been in the interest of the slave traders to treat the slaves better?

_____

_____

_____

from The Interesting Narrative of the Life of Olaudah Equiano
Olaudah Equiano

At last when the ship we were in, had got in all her cargo, they made ready with many fearful noises, and we were all put under deck, so that we could not see how they managed the vessel. But this disappointment was the least of my sorrow. The stench of the <u>hold</u> while we were on the coast was so intolerably <u>loathsome</u>, that it was dangerous to remain there for any time, and some of us had been permitted to stay on the deck for the fresh air; but now that the whole ship's cargo were confined together, it became absolutely <u>pestilential</u>. The closeness of the place, and the heat of the climate, added to the number in the ship, which was so crowded that each had scarcely room to turn himself, almost suffocated us. This produced <u>copious</u> perspirations, so that the air soon became unfit for respiration, from a variety of loathsome smells, and brought on a sickness among the slaves, of which many died—thus falling victims to the <u>improvident</u> <u>avarice</u>, as I may call it, of their purchasers. This wretched situation was again aggravated by the galling[1] of the chains, now become insupportable, and the filth of the necessary tubs, into which the children often fell, and were almost suffocated. The shrieks of the

---

Vocabulary Development

loathsome (LOHTH suhm) *adj.* hateful
pestilential (pes ti LEN shuhl) *adj.* likely to cause disease
copious (KO pee uhs) *adj.* plentiful
improvident (im PRAH vuh duhnt) *adj.* shortsighted
avarice (AV uh ris) *n.* greed for riches

---

1. galling (GAWL ing) *n.* the creation of sores by rubbing or chafing.

women, and the groans of the dying, rendered the whole a scene of horror almost inconceivable.

♦ ♦ ♦

Equiano envied the fish of the sea for their freedom. During the voyage, he grew more fearful of the white slavers' cruelty.

♦ ♦ ♦

One day they had taken a number of fishes; and when they had killed and satisfied themselves with as many as they thought fit, to our astonishment who were on deck, rather than give any of them to us to eat, as we expected, they tossed the remaining fish into the sea again, although we begged and prayed for some as well as we could, but in vain. . . .

♦ ♦ ♦

Some of the hungry slaves tried to get fish in secret. They were discovered and whipped. Then three desperate slaves jumped into the sea. The others were immediately put below deck. Two of the slaves drowned. The third was rescued and then beaten unmercifully.

♦ ♦ ♦

During our passage, I first saw flying fishes, which surprised me very much; they used frequently to fly across the ship, and many of them fell on the deck. I also now first saw the use of the quadrant;[2] I had often with astonishment seen the mariners make observations with it, and I could not think what it meant. They at last took notice of my surprise; and one of them, willing to increase it, as well as to gratify my curiosity, made me one day look through it. The clouds appeared to me to be land, which disappeared as they passed along. This heightened my wonder; and I was now more

2. quadrant (KWAH druhnt) n. an instrument used by navigators to dete mine a ship's position.

TAKE NOTES

Reading Strategy

Summarize the bracketed section in your own words.

_____

_____

_____

English Language Development

The normal plural of *fish* in modern English is *fish*, not *fishes*. Using a dictionary, identify the plurals of the following nouns:

deer _____

tiger _____

wolf _____

sheep _____

Reading Check

Underline the parts of the summary that show what some slaves do to escape the misery of the journey.

Read Fluently

Read the bracketed passage aloud. Circle the two sights that attract Equiano's curiosity.

persuaded than ever, that I was in another world, and that every thing about me was magic.

◆ ◆ ◆

The ship anchored off Bridgetown, the capital of the island of Barbados in the West Indies. Merchants and planters came on board to examine the slaves. The slaves on the ship were fearful, but some older slaves came from the land to reassure them. Finally, the slaves went ashore.

◆ ◆ ◆

We were <u>conducted</u> immediately to the merchant's yard, where we were all pent up together, like so many sheep in a fold, without regard to sex or age. . . . We were not many days in the merchant's <u>custody,</u> before we were sold after their usual manner, which is this: On a signal given (as the beat of a drum), the buyers rush at once into the yard where the slaves are confined, and make choice of that parcel[3] they like best. . . .

Stop to Reflect

In the last paragraph of this **slave narrative**, what is the effect of these details on the reader's emotions?

_____

_____

_____

_____

_____

_____

Vocabulary Development

conducted (kuhn DUHK tuhd) *v.* led
custody (KUHS tuh dee) *n.* keeping, possession

---

3. **parcel** (PAR suhl) *n.* group.

from The Interesting Narrative of the Life of Olaudah Equiano

1. **Draw Conclusions:** What does the treatment of the slaves show about the captors' attitudes toward human life?

_____

_____

2. **Literary Analysis:** Equiano describes the conditions aboard a slave ship in his **slave narrative**. How did the slaves feel about their situation?

_____

_____

3. **Literary Analysis:** Use the following chart to list two **emotional appeals** in Equiano's narrative. Then, tell the effect of each.

Emotional Appeal		
Effect on Reader		

4. **Reading Strategy:** Name two main ideas from Equiano's narrative.

_____

_____

5. **Reading Strategy: Summarize** what happened after the ship reached Barbados.

_____

_____

The Declaration of Independence • *from* The Crisis, Number 1

LITERARY ANALYSIS

Writers and speakers use **persuasion** when they want their audience to think or act in a certain way. A persuasive writer or speaker
- appeals to the audience's emotions, ethics, and reason
- offers opinions, as well as facts, about a subject
- gives evidence to support the argument
- suggests a course of action or solution to a problem

Thomas Jefferson and Thomas Paine use persuasion in their writing to support the Revolutionary cause. Both writers appeal to the colonists' emotions. Jefferson and Paine also offer logical arguments that appeal to their audience's sense of reason.

READING STRATEGY

Charged words are often found in persuasive writing and speeches. These words produce a strong emotional response. For example, the word *tyranny* means "unfair power." This word has negative **connotations**, which means that it suggests negative ideas.

Selection	Word	Connotation	Emotion
The Declaration of Independence			
from The Crisis, Number 1			

The Declaration of Independence

Thomas Jefferson

Summary Thomas Jefferson explains that it is important to state why America is separating from Britain. He claims certain basic rights for the colonists. He says that the English king abuses those rights. Based on these abuses, the colonies are independent of Britain and the colonists pledge their support of this declaration.

Note-taking Guide

Use this diagram to list Jefferson's main reasons for going to war with the British.

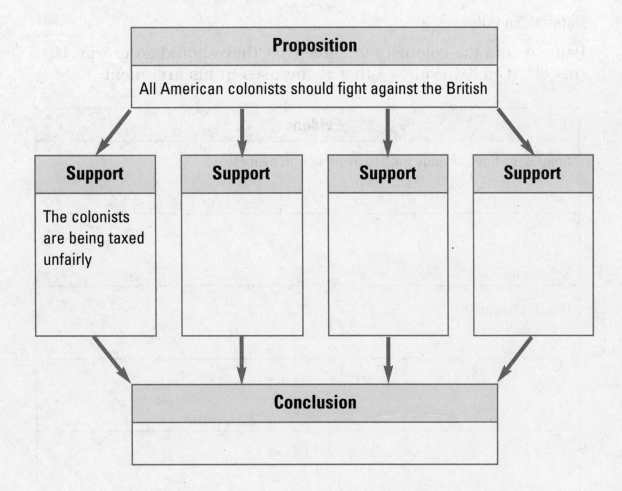

Proposition

All American colonists should fight against the British

Support

The colonists are being taxed unfairly

Support

Support

Support

Conclusion

PREVIEW

from The Crisis, Number 1

Thomas Paine

Summary Thomas Paine writes his essay to the American colonists. He wants to encourage them to fight against the British. Paine writes that God supports the American cause. He also argues that a good father will fight. If the fathers fight, their children may live in peace. Paine then asks Americans in every state to unite.

Note-taking Guide

Paine wants the colonists to agree that they should go to war. Use this chart to list evidence that Paine uses in his argument.

Evidence
Americans have already tried to avoid war in every way.

from The Crisis

Thomas Paine

Paine says that these are difficult times. He says that those who fight against the British deserve thanks from everyone. He knows that the summer soldier and sunshine patriot[1] will not serve their country in this crisis.

◆ ◆ ◆

Tyranny, like hell, is not easily conquered; yet we have this consolation with us, that the harder the conflict, the more glorious the triumph. What we obtain too cheap, we esteem too lightly; 'tis dearness only that gives everything its value. Heaven knows how to put a proper price upon its goods. . . .

◆ ◆ ◆

Paine goes on to say that Britain has a big army to stand behind her tyranny. She has said that she will keep on taxing the colonists and controlling them. Paine says this sounds like slavery. Britain has great power over America. Such power can belong only to God.

Paine believes that God Almighty will not give up on America. That is because America has tried so hard to avoid war. God would not give America up to the care of the devils. Paine says that the king of Britain is like a common murderer or robber. He has no grounds to look up to heaven for help against America.

Vocabulary Development

tyranny (TEER uh nee) *n.* oppressive or unfair power
consolation (kon suh LAY shuhn) *n.* comfort
esteem (es TEEM) *v.* value

---

1. **summer soldier and sunshine patriot** those who fight only when winning and those who are loyal only during good times.

TAKE NOTES

Reading Strategy

Paine uses **charged words** and phrases in the paragraph. Circle two that are positive. Underline four that are negative.

Literary Analysis

Paine uses facts and emotion to **persuade** his reader to agree with him. List four facts in the bracketed passage.

1. _____
2. _____
3. _____
4. _____

English Language Development

The apostrophe is used in English for two reasons. One is to show possession, as in the word *men's*. The second use of the apostrophe is to show that a letter or letters are missing, as in the word *'tis* in the first paragraph. The word *'tis* is not used much in modern English. In the past, it was used to mean *it is*. The apostrophe stands for the missing letter *i*. Write the complete meaning of each of the following words on the lines.

1. wasn't _____
2. aren't _____
3. couldn't _____
4. shouldn't _____

Read the underlined sentences. Do you agree with Paine's view here? Why, or why not?

_____

_____

_____

What will happen until America wins her freedom? Circle the sentence that answers this question.

I once felt all that kind of anger, which a man ought to feel, against the mean principles that are held by the Tories;[2] a noted one, who kept a tavern at Amboy, was standing at his door, with as pretty a child in his hand, about eight or nine years old, as I ever saw, and after speaking his mind as freely as he thought was <u>prudent</u>, finished with this unfatherly expression, "*Well! give me peace in my day.*"

◆   ◆   ◆

Paine says that <u>a generous parent should have said, "*If there must be a war, let it be in my day. That way, my child can have peace.*"</u> America could be the happiest place on earth. She is located far from all the <u>wrangling</u> world. All she has to do is trade with the other countries. Paine is sure that America will not be happy until she gets clear of foreign control. Wars, with no endings, will break out until that time comes. America must be the winner in the end.

Paine appeals to Americans in all states to unite. He feels that there cannot be too much strength for such an important mission. He wants those in the future to know that when danger arrived, the Americans joined together to fight.

Paine explains that British control will affect them all, no matter who they are or where they live.

◆   ◆   ◆

Vocabulary Development

prudent (PROO duhnt) *adj.*   wise
wrangling (RANG ling) *n.*   fighting, bickering, arguing

---

2. **Tories** colonists who were loyal to Britain.

The heart that feels not now, is dead: the blood of his children will curse his <u>cowardice</u>, who shrinks back at a time when a little might have saved the whole, and made *them* happy. (I love the man that can smile at trouble; that can gather strength from distress, and grow brave by reflection.)

◆ ◆ ◆

Paine says that only those with little minds will shrink back. <u>The strong of heart will fight unto death.</u> He would not support an offensive war for all the treasures in the world. Such a war is murder. Paine then asks an important question.

He wonders what the difference is between a thief breaking into his house and ordering him to obey and a king who orders him to obey. He finds no difference and feels that both deserve the same treatment.

◆ ◆ ◆

TAKE NOTES

Read Fluently

Read the bracketed sentences. What kind of man does Paine love?

_____

_____

Vocabulary and Pronunciation

When you see the letters *gh* together in English, they are often silent. For example, the word *right* is pronounced rīt. In the underlined sentence, circle the word that has silent *gh*.

Culture Note

The United States was not always free. It started out as a group of colonies under the rule of Britain. The Revolutionary War of 1775–1781 was fought to break free of Britain. Name one thing that the early colonists did not like about being under Britain's rule.

_____

_____

Vocabulary Development

cowardice (KOW uhr dis) *n.* lack of courage

The Declaration of Independence • *from* The Crisis, Number 1

1. **Evaluate:** Is Thomas Jefferson's argument effective? _____
   Why or why not?

   _____

   _____

2. **Literary Analysis:** Why does Jefferson present a long list of grievances, or
   complaints, as part of his **persuasive** writing?

   _____

   _____

3. **Analyze:** Paine uses **aphorisms** in his writing. Aphorisms are brief
   statements that express a wise observation. Use this chart to identify
   two aphorisms in Paine's essay. Analyze how each one contributes to
   his persuasive message.

Aphorism	Meaning	Purpose

4. **Reading Strategy:** Jefferson and Paine use **charged words** to stir
   readers' emotions. What is your emotional response to each of these
   words?

   a. liberty _____

   b. justice _____

5. **Reading Strategy:** Paine uses the word *thief* to refer to the British rulers
   who control the colonists. Would Paine have created a different
   response if he had used the word *supporters* instead? Explain.

   _____

An Hymn to the Evening • To His Excellency, General Washington

LITERARY ANALYSIS

Personification is a figure of speech that gives human qualities to something that is not human. For example, in the poem "To His Excellency, General Washington," Phillis Wheatley personifies the ocean. She gives the ocean human feelings by saying it is *astonish'd* and *feels the wild uproar*.

READING SKILL

When reading poetry, you may need to **clarify the meaning** of difficult passages. In these poems, Wheatley often reverses the usual order of sentences. She does this by placing a verb before its subject. Clarify meaning by restating unusual word order. Also, check the definitions of unfamiliar words. Use this chart to help you understand the poems.

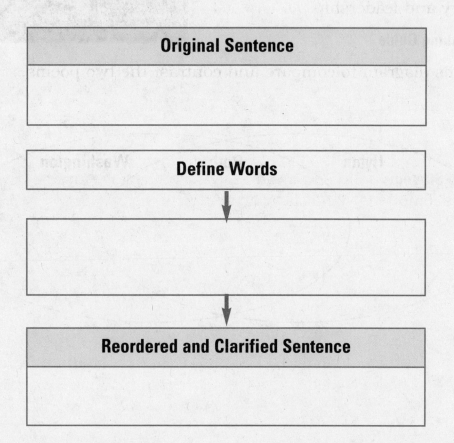

Original Sentence

Define Words

Reordered and Clarified Sentence

An Hymn to the Evening • To His Excellency, General Washington

Phillis Wheatley

Summaries In "Hymn to the Evening," the speaker sees a higher power in the beauty of the sunset. She hopes that virtue as bright as the sunset and peaceful sleep will cause people to wake up to the next day pure and safe from sin. "**To His Excellency, General Washington**" praises the revolutionary cause. The poem personifies America as the goddess Columbia. It also praises George Washington for his bravery and leadership.

Note-taking Guide

Use this diagram to compare and contrast the two poems.

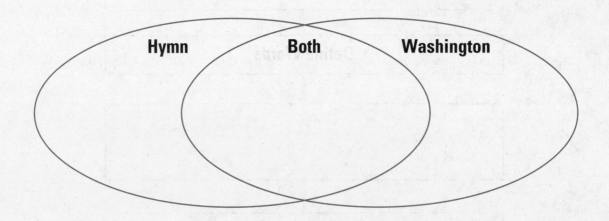

Hymn   Both   Washington

An Hymn to the Evening •
To His Excellency, General Washington

1. **Compare and Contrast:** In "An Hymn to the Evening," what mood or feeling does the poet connect with each time of day?

   _____

   _____

2. **Relate:** If you were going to write a poem of praise, how would you **personify** the spirit of the United States today?

   _____

   _____

3. **Literary Analysis:** Use this chart to analyze an example of **personification** that appears line 17 in "An Hymn to the Evening."

Object/Idea	Human Qualities	→	Poet's Meaning

4. **Literary Analysis:** Reread lines 9–12 of "To His Excellency, General Washington." What details does Wheatley use to describe the way Columbia looks?

   _____

   _____

5. **Reading Strategy:** Clarify lines 11–14 of "To His Excellency, General Washington" by defining *unnumber'd* and *graces* and reordering the sentence parts.

   _____

   _____

PRESS RELEASES

About Press Releases

A **press release** is a document that a company sends to give information to news organizations. It is sometimes known as a **news release**. A press release might announce

- an upcoming lecture, conference, or performance
- the winners of awards
- a change in leadership at an organization or a company

The purpose of a press release is to convince the media to report on the event. Sometimes a newspaper will use a press release as a short news article.

Reading Strategy

Distinguishing Between Fact and Opinion Journalists need to **distinguish between fact and opinion** when using press releases.

- A **fact** is a statement that can be proved true.
- An **opinion** is a judgment or viewpoint that can be supported by facts and well-reasoned arguments, but not proved.

Use the information in the chart to help you distinguish between facts and opinions as you read a press release.

Identifying Facts and Opinions
Facts
• can be proved true • can be verified with proof or experiment, or can be confirmed by an authority **Example:** "Professor Gates is coeditor . . . of the encyclopedia *Encarta Africana*."
Opinions
• cannot be proved true or false • are judgments or viewpoints • may be supported by facts and well-reasoned arguments **Example:** Gates is a "relentless and outspoken champion for tolerance through understanding."

NEWS RELEASE

The Echo Foundation *Voices Against Indifference Initiative*
The Henry Louise Gates, Jr., Project • November 11, 2003 • Charlottte, NC

THE ECHO FOUNDATION BRINGS
HENRY LOUIS GATES, JR., TO CHARLOTTE;
Noted Scholar, Literary Critic To Hold Public Lecture,
Student Dialogue Nov. 11th

September 26, 2003 (Charlotte, NC) - Henry Louis (Skip) Gates, Jr.,
chair of Harvard's African and Afro-American Studies department and
director of the W.E.B. Du Bois Institute, will be in Charlotte, Tues.,
Nov. 11 for a public lecture, student dialogue and an adult leadership
forum as part of The Echo Foundation's *Voices Against Indifference
Initiative*. Nobel Laureate for literature Wole Soyinka will introduce
Gates's lecture, "W.E.B. Du Bois and the *Encyclopedia Africana*," at
7 P.M. at Spirit Square's McGlohon Theatre, 345 N. College St. **Call
704. 372.1000 for reserved seats: individual ($20) and student
groups ($5). Call 704.347.3844 for patron tickets ($65),** which
include a pre-event reception with Gates and Soyinka at the Noel
Gallery, 401 N. Tryon St.

The *Voices Against Indifference Initiative* is an Echo Foundation
program that brings speakers to Charlotte whose personal experience
illuminates the power of the individual to have a positive impact on
humanity, through moral courage, action, and words.

Gates will share his story in several community venues, on Nov.
11. Some 400 students and teachers from Charlotte area private and
public high schools are studying curriculum materials to prepare for the
Gates dialogue at Providence Day School, from 11:15 - 12:30 P.M.
Plans are also underway for an adult leadership forum with Gates about
social capital issues, and he will be the featured guest on *Charlotte
Talks* with Mike Collins at 9 A.M. on WFAE Radio (90.7 FM).

TAKE NOTES

Reading Press Release

Press releases include
facts that tell who, what,
when, where, and why.
Underline this information in
the first paragraph.

TAKE NOTES

Reading Strategy

Readers of a press release must **distinguish between fact and opinion**. List two words that show a statement of opinion in the paragraph before NOTE TO THE EDITORS.

Culture Note

African Americans have been important in the history of the United States. Groups like the Echo Foundation share information and hold events. Their goal is to help people become more aware of the important contributions of African Americans.

Reading Check

Henry Louis Gates, Jr. will be speaking at a program. Underline the purpose of the program.

A relentless and outspoken champion for tolerance through understanding, Gates has earned numerous awards and accolades for broadening the discourse on African American literature and cultural tradition in his various roles as an educator, scholar, literary critic and writer. One recent accomplishment, the completion of *Encarta Africana*, is the result of his 25-year quest to realize the dream of W.E.B. Du Bois. The renowned early twentieth century black intellectual and civil rights leader envisioned a comprehensive encyclopedia about the entire black world that could be used as an instrument to fight racism by building greater awareness and understanding of the African culture. The 2.25 billion-word encyclopedia project, coedited by Gates and Princeton professor K. Anthony Appiah, and published in hardbound print and CD-ROM format, was dedicated in memory of Du Bois and in honor of Nelson Mandela on Martin Luther King's birthday, Jan. 19, 1999.

###

NOTE TO THE EDITORS: The following page includes more detailed information about Gates and The Echo Foundation. Photos are available through The Echo Foundation.

The Echo Foundation
926 Elizabeth Avenue • Suite 403 • Charlotte, NC 28204
www.echofoundation.org

ABOUT HENRY LOUIS GATES, JR.

W.E.B. Du Bois Professor of the Humanities,
Harvard University, Chair of Afro-American Studies
Director of the W.E.B. Du Bois Institute for Afro-American Research

Professor Gates is coeditor with K. Anthony Appiah of the encyclopedia *Encarta Africana* published on CD-ROM by Microsoft (1999), and in book form by Basic Civitas Books under the title *Africana: The Encyclopedia of the African and African American Experience* (1999). He is the author of *Wonders of the African World* (1999), the book companion to the six-hour BBC/PBS television series of the same name.

Professor Gates is the author of several works of literary criticism, including *Figures in Black: Words, Signs and the 'Racial' Self* (Oxford University Press, 1987); *The Signifying Monkey: A Theory of Afro-American Literary Criticism* (Oxford, 1988), 1989 winner of the American Book Award; and *Loose Canons: Notes on the Culture Wars* (Oxford, 1992.) He has also authored *Colored People: A Memoir* (Knopf, 1994), which traces his childhood experiences in a small West Virginia town in the 1950s and 1960s; *The Future of the Race* (Knopf, 1996), coauthored with Cornel West; and *Thirteen Ways of Looking at a Black Man* (Random House, 1997). Professor Gates has edited several anthologies, including *The Norton Anthology of African American Literature* (W. W. Norton, 1996); and *The Oxford-Schomburg Library of Nineteenth Century Black Women Writers* (Oxford, 1991). In addition, Professor Gates is coeditor of *Transition* magazine. An influential cultural critic, Professor Gates's publications include a 1994 cover story for *Time* magazine on the new black Renaissance in art, as well as numerous articles for *The New Yorker*.

Professor Gates earned his M.A. and Ph.D. in English Literature from Clare College at the University of Cambridge. He received a

---

TAKE NOTES

Reading Informational Materials

Press Releases give information on the organization that sponsors the event and the press release. Place a star next to the paragraph that has this information.

Stop to Reflect

Do you think this press release should be used for a newspaper article? [short WOL] Why or why not?

_____

_____

Read Fluently

Writers sometimes use semi-colons instead of commas to separate the different pieces of information. Circle the semicolons in the third paragraph.

The article includes information on accomplishments and education. Underline the sentences that tell about Gates's education.

Professor Gates earned his M.A. and Ph.D. in English Literature from Clare College at the University of Cambridge. He received a B.A. *summa cum laude* from Yale University in 1973 in English Language and Literature. Before joining the faculty of Harvard in 1991, he taught at Yale, Cornell, and Duke Universities. His honors and grants include a MacArthur Foundation "genius grant" (1981), the George Polk Award for Social Commentary (1993), Chicago Tribune Heartland Award (1994), the Golden Plate Achievement Award (1995), *Time* magazine's "25 Most Influential Americans" list (1997), a National Humanities Medal (1998), and election to the American Academy of Arts and Letters (1999).

ABOUT THE ECHO FOUNDATION

The Echo Foundation was founded in 1997 to carry on the message that Nobel Peace Prize winner Elie Wiesel brought to Charlotte that year—a call to action for human dignity, justice and moral courage. Its mission is "to sponsor and facilitate those voices which speak of human dignity, justice and moral courage in a way that will lead to positive action for humankind."

The Echo Foundation
926 Elizabeth Avenue • Suite 403 • Charlotte, NC 28204
www.echofoundation.org

THINKING ABOUT THE PRESS RELEASE

1. What is the topic of Henry Louis Gates's public lecture?

_____

2. Based on information in the **press release**, why do you think Gates is speaking on this topic?

_____

_____

Reading Strategy

3. Find two facts in the press release that support this opinion: Gates is an influential cultural critic.

_____

_____

4. Why do you think the Echo Foundation invited Gates to speak? Use at least two facts and one opinion from the press release in your response. Be sure to **distinguish between facts and opinion** in your response.

_____

_____

_____

TIMED WRITING: EXPLANATION (30 minutes)

Write a newspaper article that reports the event announced in this press release. Be sure to include the facts.
Answer these questions to get started.
- Who? _____
- What? _____
- When? _____
- Where? _____
- Why? _____

Speech in the Virginia Convention • Speech in the Convention

LITERARY ANALYSIS

Speeches are works that are written to be spoken to an audience. Effective speakers and writers both use persuasive techniques like these to emphasize their points:
- *Restatement*: repeating an idea in different ways
- *Repetition*: restating an idea using the same words
- *Parallelism*: repeating similar grammatical structures
- *Rhetorical questions*: questions whose answers are obvious

You will find examples of these techniques in the speeches by Patrick Henry and Benjamin Franklin.

READING STRATEGY

Speakers often appeal to people's emotions in order to make an impact. **Evaluating persuasive appeals** can help you when you read or hear a persuasive speech.
- Think about why the speaker appeals to the audience's emotions.
- Identify the speaker's arguments and supporting evidence.
- Decide whether the arguments and emotional appeals fit the occasion.

Use this diagram to record the persuasive appeals made by each speaker.

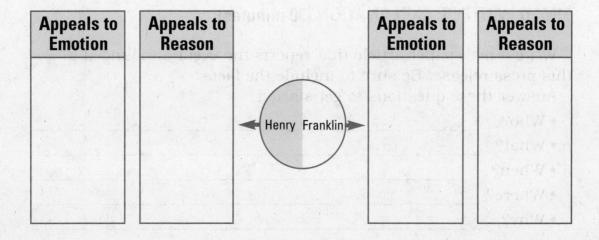

Appeals to Emotion	Appeals to Reason		Appeals to Emotion	Appeals to Reason
		Henry Franklin		

Speech in the Virginia Convention

Patrick Henry

Summary In this speech, Patrick Henry begins by saying that, without disrespect, he must disagree with the previous speeches. Judging by their conduct, he says, the British are preparing for war. We have tried discussing the problem. We are being ignored; there is no retreat except into slavery. The time for getting along peacefully is over. The war has already begun. "Give me liberty or give me death" is Henry's strong and well-known closing.

Note-taking Guide

Use this chart to compare the arguments for and against going to war.

Against	For
The colonists are too weak.	The colonists are as strong as they will ever be.

Do you agree that it is best to know the worst? Why, or why not?

_____

_____

_____

Read Fluently

Read aloud the underlined sentences. Then circle the words that tell how Patrick Henry judges the future.

English Language Development

In English, when we make words that end in *f* or *fe* plural, we change the ending to *ve* before adding *s*. For example, the word *yourself* become *your-selves* when it means more than one. Write the plural forms of these words:

shelf_____

knife_____

calf_____

elf_____

scarf_____

Speech in the Virginia Convention
Patrick Henry

Mr. President: No man thinks more highly than I do of the patriotism, as well as abilities, of the very worthy gentlemen who have just addressed the house. But different men often see the same subject in different lights . . . .

♦ ♦ ♦

Patrick Henry then says that the question before the house is very important. He cannot allow fear of offending someone to stop him from saying what he thinks.

He says it is natural for people to hold on to hope. But no matter how much it hurts, it is best to know the worst and to plan for it.

♦ ♦ ♦

I have but one lamp by which my feet are guided, and that is the lamp of experience. I know of no way of judging of the future but by the past. And judging by the past, I wish to know what there has been in the conduct of the British ministry for the last ten years to justify those hopes with which gentlemen have been pleased to solace themselves and the house? Is it that insidious smile with which our petition has been lately received? Trust it not, sir; it will prove a snare to your feet. Suffer not yourselves to be betrayed with a kiss.[1]

♦ ♦ ♦

Vocabulary Development

solace (SAHL uhs) *v.* comfort
insidious (in SID ee uhs) *adj.* waiting for a chance to harm
snare (SNAIR) *n.* a trap

---

1. betrayed with a kiss In the Bible, Judas betrays Jesus with a kiss. This is a signal to the people who want to arrest Jesus.

He then says that the British are using the tools of war. What else can the display of British force mean? Does Britain have any enemies in this area of the world? No, she has none. So the navies and armies are here for one reason only.

◆ ◆ ◆

They are meant for us: they can be meant for no other. They are sent over to bind and rivet upon us those chains which the British ministry have been so long forging.

And what have we to oppose to them? Shall we try argument? Sir, we have been trying that for the last ten years. Have we anything new to offer upon the subject? Nothing. We have held the subject up in every light of which it is capable; but it has been all in vain.

◆ ◆ ◆

Henry says that the colonists' petitions have been ignored. Their protests have met more violence. Their pleas have been set aside. They have been insulted from the foot of the throne.

◆ ◆ ◆

There is no longer any room for hope. If we wish to be free, if we mean to preserve inviolate those inestimable privileges for which we have been so long contending, if we mean not basely to abandon the noble struggle in which we have been so long engaged, and which we have pledged ourselves never to abandon until the glorious object of our contest shall be obtained— we must fight! I repeat it, sir, we must fight! An appeal to arms and the God of Hosts is all that is left us!

They tell us, sir, that we are weak—unable to cope with so <u>formidable</u> an <u>adversary</u>. But

---

Vocabulary Development

formidable (FOR mi duh buhl) *adj.*   inspiring fear or awe
adversary (AD ver sair ee) *n.*   enemy, opponent

TAKE NOTES

Reading Informational Materials

Reread the bracketed passage. Then, to **evaluate** Patrick Henry's **persuasive appeals**, check the answer that best completes the sentence.
When Patrick Henry refers to "those chains" that the British have been "forging," he wants his listeners to think that _____.
_____ the British want the colonists to buy new chains from them
_____ the British have put a new tax on chains
_____ the British want to treat the colonists like slaves
_____ the British want the colonists to make more chains

Reading Check

Underline the three sentences that tell how the colonists have been treated by Britain.

Literary Analysis

Underline the three **rhetorical questions** in the bracketed paragraph here and on page 76. Remember that a rhetorical question is one that has an obvious answer. What are the obvious answers to these questions?

question 1: _____

question 2: _____

question 3: _____

Henry tells us that the battle is "not to the strong alone." Then he uses **parallelism** to tell us who will fight the battle.

1. What three phrases tell who will fight the battle?

_____

_____

2. Later in this paragraph Henry uses **repetition**. What phrase does Henry repeat?

_____

_____

Vocabulary and Pronunciation

In English, the suffix -*ment* often means "action or process of." For example, the word *argument* means "the action or process of arguing." List two other English words that end in the suffix -*ment*, and give their meanings.

Word ending in -*ment*	Meaning

Reading Strategy

Evaluate the **persuasive appeals** made by Patrick Henry in the last paragraph.

1. How does this paragraph make you feel?

_____

2. Which sentences or phrases make you feel this way? Underline the three sentences or phrases that seem the most powerful to you. Number them 1, 2, 3 in the order of their importance to you.

when shall we be stronger? Will it be the next week, or the next year? Will it be when we are totally disarmed, and when a British guard shall be stationed in every house?

◆ ◆ ◆

He continues by saying that the colonists are not weak. There are three million of them. They are "armed in the holy cause of liberty." They cannot be beaten by any force the enemy might send.

◆ ◆ ◆

The battle, sir, is not to the strong alone; it is to the vigilant, the active, the brave. Besides, sir, we have no election; if we were base enough to desire it, it is now too late to retire from the contest. There is no retreat but in submission and slavery! Our chains are forged! Their clanging may be heard on the plains of Boston! The war is inevitable—and let it come! I repeat it, sir, let it come!

It is vain, sir, to extenuate the matter. Gentlemen may cry "Peace, peace"—but there is no peace. The war is actually begun! The next gale that sweeps from the north will bring to our ears the clash of resounding arms! Our brethren are already in the field! Why stand we here idle? What is it that gentlemen wish? What would they have? Is life so dear, or peace so sweet, as to be purchased at the price of chains and slavery? Forbid it, Almighty God! I know not what course others may take; but as for me, give me liberty or give me death!

Vocabulary Development

vigilant (VIJ uh luhnt) *adj.* watchful, alert
extenuate (ex TEN yoo ayt) *v.* to try to lessen how serious something is

Speech in the Convention

Benjamin Franklin

Summary Benjamin Franklin expresses his doubts about the Constitution. However, he still approves of the document. He supports his opinions with several reasons. Franklin feels that this Constitution is the best document that imperfect men can offer. He also thinks that it is important to show complete support for the Constitution.

Note-taking Guide

Franklin suggests that a perfect Constitution will never be created. Use this web to list his reasons why the delegates should support it even though it is not perfect.

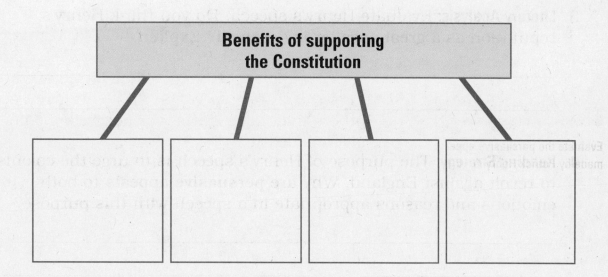

Benefits of supporting the Constitution

Speech in the Virginia Convention • Speech in the Convention

1. **Compare and Contrast:** Compare and contrast the endings of these two speeches. Why is each ending effective?

   _____

   _____

2. **Literary Analysis:** Use a chart like this one to identify the persuasive techniques used in each of these **speeches**.

	Example	Effect
Restatement		
Repetition		
Parallelism		

3. **Literary Analysis:** Evaluate Henry's speech. Do you think Henry's reputation as a great speaker is deserved? Explain.

   _____

   _____

4. **Reading Strategy:** The purpose of Henry's speech is to urge the colonists to revolt against England. Why are **persuasive appeals** to both emotions and reasons appropriate in a speech with this purpose?

   _____

   _____

Letter to Her Daughter From the New White House • *from* Letters From an American Farmer

LITERARY ANALYSIS

Personal, **private letters** usually have an informal style that sounds like conversation. Private letters are usually sent to close friends or family members. The writer of a private letter believes that the person to whom the letter is addressed is the only one who will read it. For example, when Abigail Adams writes to her daughter, she reminds her daughter to keep the letter to herself.

Public letters are often called **epistles**. They are essays written in the form of a letter. These letters are written for a wider audience. This form allows the writer to use an informal tone while discussing public ideas.

READING STRATEGY

Distinguishing between fact and opinion means telling the difference between the two. Keep these points in mind:

• A **fact** is something that can be proved.
• An **opinion** is a personal belief. Opinions can be supported but not proved.

Statement	Fact or Opinion?	Words Showing a Judgment If It Is an Opinion	How It Can Be Proved If It Is a Fact
The American ought therefore to love his country much better.	Opinion	Opinion	

Letter to Her Daughter From the New White House

Abigail Adams

Summary First Lady Abigail Adams' letter describes her journey to Washington, D.C. Washington is a new city with only a few public buildings. The White House is huge and filled with servants. The building and city, however, lack many conveniences. Adams tells her daughter to say that the house and city are beautiful if some-one asks. Adams also mentions that she has been invited to visit the homes of many famous people.

Note-taking Guide

Adams presents two different views of Washington, D.C. In one, she describes the enjoyable parts of living there. In the other, she talks about the inconveniences. Use this web to keep track of her remarks and decide whether Adams likes or dislikes her new surroundings.

What Adams likes	What Adams wants
a river view	firewood

Letter to Her Daughter from the New White House

Abigail Adams

Washington, 21 November, 1800

My Dear Child:

♦ ♦ ♦

Abigail Adams opens her letter by saying that she got to Washington on Sunday without accidents. But they did get lost outside of Baltimore. Adams says that woods are all you can see from Baltimore until you reach Washington. Here and there you see a small cottage, but you might travel miles without seeing a human being.

♦ ♦ ♦

In the city there are buildings enough, if they were <u>compact</u> and finished, to <u>accommodate</u> Congress and those attached to it; but as they are, and scattered as they are, I see no great comfort for them. The river,[1] which runs up to Alexandria,[2] is in full view of my window, and I see the <u>vessels</u> as they pass and repass. The house is upon a grand and superb scale, requiring about thirty servants to attend and keep the apartments in proper order, and perform the ordinary business of the house and stables; an establishment very well proportioned to the President's salary.

♦ ♦ ♦

Vocabulary Development

compact (KAHM pakt) *adj.* close together

accommodate (uh KAHM uh dayt) *v.* to provide with places to live

---

1. **river** the Potomac River, which runs through Washington, D.C.
2. **Alexandria** (al ex AN dree uh): a city in northeastern Virginia.

TAKE NOTES

Reading Check

How would you describe the land that Adams crosses on her trip to the White House?

_____

_____

_____

Culture Note

In the early years of the United States, it was easier for big cities to grow if they were located near rivers. The reason for this was that the rivers were used as trade routes. Ships carried goods needed by the settlers. Washington, D.C., is on the Potomac River. Name two other important rivers in the United States.

Vocabulary and Pronunciation

Many English words have multiple meanings. The word *vessels*, for example, can mean either "ships" or "hollow containers, such as bottles, cups, glasses, and bowls." Other multiple-meaning words in this paragraph include *scale* and *order*. Write two meanings for each of these words. Make the first meaning the one that Abigail Adams is using in her letter. If necessary, use a dictionary and separate paper.

scale: _____ _____

order: _____ _____

Adams's **private letter** tells us about the social custom of visiting people. Remember that telephones did not exist in those days. (1) How many visits did Abigail Adams make in one day?

_____

(2) Do you think those visits were short or long?

_____

(3) Explain your reasoning.

_____

Read this paragraph aloud. Then circle the answer to this question: Why isn't wood available?

Many words in English are spelled the same but are pronounced differently and have different meanings. When *content* is accented on the second syllable (kuhn TENT), it means "happy" or "to make oneself happy." When it is accented on the first syllable (KAHN tent), it means "something that is contained." Read the words below, along with their pronunciations. Write their meanings. If necessary, use a dictionary.

desert (dee ZERT) _____

_____

desert (DEZ ert)_____

_____

the apartments is a very difficult job. They also have to keep fires going to keep them from shivering. There are no bells anywhere in the building for calling the servants. Many of the ladies from Georgetown[3] and the city have visited her. Yesterday she returned fifteen visits. She starts to say something about Georgetown but doesn't finish her thought. Instead, she says "our Milton[4] is beautiful."

◆　◆　◆

But no comparisons—if they will put me up some bells and let me have wood enough to keep fires, I design to be pleased. I could content myself almost anywhere three months; but, surrounded with forests, can you believe that wood is not to be had because people cannot be found to cut and cart it?

◆　◆　◆

She then explains that Briesler was able to get only a few cords of wood. Most of that was used to dry the walls of the house before she and the President got there. Now they have to use coals instead, but they cannot get any grates for the coal.

◆　◆　◆

We have, indeed, come into a *new country*. You must keep all this to yourself, and, when asked how I like it, say that I write you the situation is beautiful, which is true. The house is made habitable, but there is not a single

Vocabulary Development

design (dee ZĪN) *v.*   intend, plan
habitable (HAB it uh buhl) *adj.*   able to be lived in

---

3. **Georgetown** (JAWRJ town): a section of Washington, D.C.
4. **Milton** (MIL tuhn): a town in eastern Massachusetts, south of Boston.

apartment finished, and all withinside,[5] except the plastering, has been done since Briesler came. We have not the least fence, yard, or other convenience without[6] and the great unfinished audience room I make a drying-room of, to hang up the clothes in. The principal stairs are not up, and will not be this winter.

◆ ◆ ◆

Six rooms are comfortable. Two are used by the President and Mr. Shaw. For the past twelve years, this house has been considered as the future headquarters of government. If it had been located in New England, it would have been fixed by now.

◆ ◆ ◆

It is a beautiful spot, capable of every improvement, and, the more I view it, the more I am delighted with it.

Since I sat down to write, I have been called down to a servant from Mount Vernon, with a <u>billet</u> from Major Custis, and a haunch of venison,[7] and a kind, congratulatory letter from Mrs. Lewis, upon my arrival in the city, with Mrs. Washington's love, inviting me to Mount Vernon,[8] where, health permitting, I will go before I leave this place.

Affectionately, your mother,
Abigail Adams

Vocabulary Development

billet (BIL uht) *n.*   a short letter, a note

---

5. **withinside** (with IN sīd): an old-fashioned way of saying "inside" or "indoors".
6. **without** (with OUT): an old-fashioned way of saying "outside".
7. **haunch of venison** (HAWNCH uv VEN uh suhn) *n.* a large piece of deer meat; half of the back side of a deer.
8. **Mount Vernon** (MOWNT VER nuhn) the estate in Virginia where George and Martha Washington lived.

from Letters From an American Farmer

Michel-Guillaume Jean de Crèvecoeur

Summary Crèvecoeur describes the situation of many American immigrants. In Europe, these people are starving and out of work. In America, laws protect them and help them succeed. As a result, people come to America from many different places. They come to start new lives where they can work for themselves and be free.

Note-taking Guide

Coming to America gives many immigrants things that they did not have in their former country. Use this chart to list the benefits that Crèvecoeur mentions.

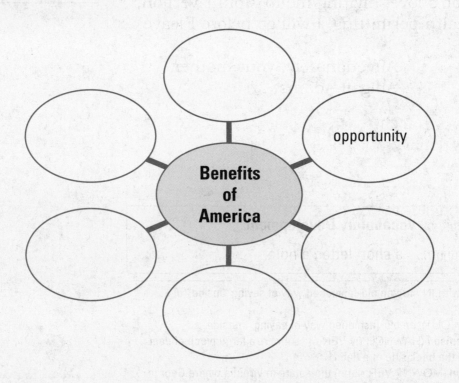

from Letters from an American Farmer

Michel-Guillaume Jean de Crèvecoeur

Crèvecoeur opens by saying that the poor of Europe have come to America for various reasons. He says that two thirds of them had no country. He explains it in this way.

◆ ◆ ◆

Can a wretch who wanders about, who works and starves, whose life is a continual scene of sore <u>affliction</u> or pinching <u>penury</u>, can that man call England or any other kingdom his country? A country that had no bread for him, whose fields <u>procured</u> him no harvest, who met with nothing but the frowns of the rich, the severity of the laws, with jails and punishments; who owned not a single foot of the extensive surface of this planet? No! Urged by a variety of motives, here they came.

◆ ◆ ◆

He goes on to say that everything in America has been better for the poor. <u>In Europe they were like useless plants, in need of rich soil and cool rains. They dried up. They were mowed down by poverty, hunger, and war. Now they have been transplanted here. They have taken root and done well.</u> Here, they are citizens. The laws and their hard work have done it.

◆ ◆ ◆

What attachment can a poor European emigrant have for a country where he had

---

Vocabulary Development

affliction (uh FLIK shuhn) *n.*   terrible troubles, state of distress

penury (PEN yuh ree) *n.*   extreme poverty

procured (proh KYOORD) *v.*   got, obtained

TAKE NOTES

Read Fluently

This **epistle**, or public letter, is a **primary source document**. It tells us about the time in which it was written. What does this paragraph tell you about living conditions for the poor in England at the time? List three facts that are suggested here.

1. _____
2. _____
3. _____

Vocabulary and Pronunciation

For words that end in *e,* we usually drop the *e* before adding *-ing*. Follow this rule to complete the chart below.

Base Word	+ *-ing* = New Word
live	living
leave	_____
come	_____
receive	_____
cause	_____

Vocabulary and Pronunciation

In the underlined section, to what natural object does Crèvecoeur compare the people who have left Europe?

_____
_____
_____

Read aloud the bracketed passage. Then count to find the answer to this question. How many different countries, including America, are represented in this family? _____

The suffix -*ment* changes a verb to a noun. The word *government* is an example of this. *Govern* means "to rule." *Government* means "the act of ruling." Complete this chart to learn other words that end in -*ment*.

Word	Meaning of Word
EX: allure	to tempt
entertain	
employ	
enjoy	

Word + -*ment*	Meaning of New Word
allurement	the act of tempting
entertain _____	
employ _____	
enjoy _____	

nothing? The knowledge of the language, the love of a few kindred as poor as himself, were the only cords that tied him; his country is now that which gives him land, bread, protection, and <u>consequence</u>: *Ubi panis ibi patria*[1] is the motto of all emigrants. What then is the American, this new man? He is either a European, or the descendant of a European, hence that strange mixture of blood, which you find in no other country. I could point out to you a family whose grandfather was an Englishman, whose wife was Dutch, whose son married a French woman, and whose present four sons have now four wives of different nations. *He* is an American, who, leaving behind him all his ancient prejudices and manners, receives new ones from the new mode of life he has embraced, the new <u>government</u> he obeys, and the new rank he holds.

◆ ◆ ◆

Crevecoeur goes on to say that the emigrant becomes an American by being received into America's broad lap. Here, persons from all nations are melted into a new race of people. The Americans came from all over Europe, and now they live together under the finest system that has ever appeared.

◆ ◆ ◆

Vocabulary Development

consequence (KAHN suh kwens) *n.* social importance

---

1. ***Ubi panis ibi patria:*** (OO bee PAH nis IB ee PAH tree uh): Latin for "Where there is bread, there is one's fatherland."

The American ought therefore love this country much better than that wherein either he or his forefathers were born. Here the rewards of his industry follow with equal steps the progress of his labor; his labor is founded on the basis of nature, *self-interest*; can it want a stronger allurement? Wives and children, who before in vain demanded of him a morsel of bread, now, fat and frolicsome, gladly help their father to clear those fields whence exuberant crops are to arise to feed and to clothe them all. . . .

❖ ❖ ❖

In America, the farmer does not have to pay large parts of his crop to any princes, abbots,[2] or lords. Here, religion demands little from him. All he has to do is give a small salary to the minister and thanks to God.

❖ ❖ ❖

The American is a new man, who acts upon new principles; he must therefore entertain new ideas, and form new opinions. From involuntary idleness, servile dependence, penury, and useless labor, he has passed to toils of a very different nature, rewarded by ample subsistence—This is an American.

Reading Strategy

Is the underlined sentence a **fact** or an **opinion**? _____ Circle the word that helped you figure out the answer.

Culture Note

Crèveceour points out the role of religion in American life. The separation of church and state is an important principle in America. What does he suggest about the role of religion in some other countries?

_____

_____

_____

Vocabulary Development

allurement (uh LOOR muhnt) *n.* attraction, charm
frolicsome (FRAH lik suhm) *adj.* full of fun
exuberant (ex OO buhr uhnt) *adj.* extreme in amount
subsistence (sub SIS tuhns) *n.* the means to obtain food, shelter, and clothing

---

2. abbots (A buhts) heads of small religious groups.

Letter to Her Daughter From the New White House • *from* Letters From an American Farmer

1. **Analyze:** Does Crèvecoeur present a realistic or an idealized view of America? Explain.

_____

_____

2. **Literary Analysis:** Use this chart to list words that show Adam's **private letter** is not meant for a public audience. Revise them for a public audience.

Letter	Words suggesting private purpose	Revision
Surrounded with forests, can you believe that wood is not to be had?	Can you believe	

3. **Literary Analysis:** What kinds of information would be appropriate in a private letter from Crèvecoeur to a friend, but not appropriate in an **epistle**?

_____

_____

4. **Reading Strategy:** Distinguish between the facts and opinions in this statement:

"Upstairs there is the oval room, which is designed for the drawing room, and has the crimson furniture in it. It is a very handsome room now; but, when completed, it will be beautiful."

What are the facts?

_____

_____

What are the opinions?

_____

_____

The Devil and Tom Walker

LITERARY ANALYSIS

Every story has a narrator or character who tells the story. The narrator tells the story from a particular **point of view.** Sometimes the narrator is not part of the story events. This type of narrator is **omniscient** (om NISH uhnt), or "all knowing." An omniscient narrator:

- tells the thoughts of many characters
- makes comments about story events and characters

As you read "The Devil and Tom Walker," look for details that reveal an omniscient point of view.

READING STRATEGY

Cultural attitudes are the opinions and values of a particular group of people at a particular time in history. "The Devil and Tom Walker" takes place in 1720s New England. You can **make inferences** about cultural attitudes of the time from the story's details. Use a chart like the following to make inferences.

Detail	Cultural Attitude

The Devil and Tom Walker

Washington Irving

Summary Tom Walker meets the Devil ("Old Scratch") in a swamp . The Devil offers the pirate Captain Kidd's treasure to Tom on certain conditions. Tom's wife encourages him to accept, but Tom refuses. She leaves to find the Devil and make her own bargain. After her second try, she doesn't come back. Later, Tom finds her apron with a heart and liver in it. He assumes that the Devil has killed her. Almost grateful, Tom looks for the Devil again. This time, he makes a deal. Tom will get Captain Kidd's treasure if he becomes a moneylender. Later, Tom regrets his deal and starts going to church often. But the Devil returns and sends Tom off on horseback into a storm. Tom never comes back, though his troubled spirit appears on stormy nights.

Note-taking Guide

Use this sequence chart to keep track of events in the story.

Event 1: Tom Walker takes a shortcut throught the swamp and finds a skull.
Event 2:
Event 3:
Event 4:
Event 5:
Event 6:
Event 7:
Event 8:
Event 9:
Event 10:

The Devil and Tom Walker
Washington Irving

Outside Boston, Massachusetts, in about 1727, Tom Walker lives near a swampy forest. Captain Kidd supposedly buried his pirate treasure in this forest. Tom and his wife are very stingy—so stingy that they even cheat each other. One day, Tom takes a shortcut through the forest. At an old fort that Native Americans had once used in fighting the colonists, Tom meets a mysterious stranger. The stranger, who carries an ax on his shoulder, is not Native American or African American, but he is still very dark, as if covered in soot.

♦ ♦ ♦

"What are you doing on my grounds?" said the black man, with a <u>hoarse</u> growling voice.

"Your grounds!" said Tom with a sneer, "no more your grounds than mine; they belong to Deacon Peabody."

"Deacon Peabody be d____d," said the stranger, "as I flatter myself[1] he will be, if he does not look more to his own sins and less to those of his neighbors. Look <u>yonder</u>, and see how Deacon Peabody is faring."[2]

♦ ♦ ♦

Tom looks at a tree and sees carved into it the name of Deacon Peabody, a local churchman grown rich through clever land deals. Other trees bear the names of other wealthy members of the community. The trees all have ax marks, and one with the name Crowninshield is completely chopped down.

♦ ♦ ♦

---

1. **as I flatter myself** as I am delighted to think.
2. **faring** (FAYR ing) *v.* doing.

TAKE NOTES

Culture Note

In 1727, there was no United States, and Massachusetts was still a British colony in North America. Circle two details here about life in colonial Massachusetts BEFORE Tom Walker's day.

Vocabulary and Pronunciation

The word *hoarse,* which means "a raspy, unclear way of speaking," is pronounced the same as the four-legged animal called a *horse.* The /ôrs/ sound in *hoarse* and *horse* has other spellings too. Say these words aloud. Circle the letters that spell /ôrs/.

coarse   force   horse
course   forcing   porcelain
divorce   hoarse   torso

Vocabulary and Pronunciation

Yonder was once used much more than it is in American English today, though it is still used in some regions. What do you think *yonder* means? Write your guess below.

yonder: _____

Vocabulary and Pronunciation

Firewood is a **compound word** formed by putting two smaller words together:

fire + wood = firewood

By studying the meaning of the smaller words, you can figure out that *firewood* means "wood to burn for a fire." Circle another compound word in the bracketed passage. Below, write the word and its meaning.

Compound Word:

_____

Meaning:

_____

_____

Literary Analysis

An **omniscient**, or all-knowing, **narrator** tells us the thoughts and attitudes of different characters. Circle Tom's wife's thoughts or attitudes about the treasure. Write one word to describe the wife.

_____

"He's just ready for burning!" said the black man, with a growl of triumph. "You see I am likely to have a good stock of <u>firewood</u> for winter."

"But what right have you," said Tom, "to cut down Deacon Peabody's timber?"

"The right of a <u>prior</u> claim," said the other. "This woodland belonged to me long before one of your white-faced race put foot upon the soil."

"And pray, who are you, if I may be so bold?" said Tom.

"Oh, I go by various names. I am the wild huntsman in some countries; the black miner in others. In this neighborhood I am known by the name of the black woodsman. . . . "

"The upshot of all which is, that, if I mistake not," said Tom, sturdily, "you are he commonly called Old Scratch."

"The same, at your service," replied the black man, with a half-civil nod.

♦ ♦ ♦

The Devil offers Tom Captain Kidd's pirate treasure if Tom agrees to his terms. Tom makes no decision. Instead he asks for proof that the Devil is who he says he is. So the Devil presses his finger to Tom's forehead and then goes off. When Tom gets home, he finds a black thumbprint burned into his forehead. He also learns of the sudden death of Absalom Crowninshield. Convinced he has met the Devil, he tells his wife all about it.

♦ ♦ ♦

All her <u>avarice</u> was awakened at the mention of hidden gold, and she urged her husband to <u>comply</u> with the black man's terms and

---

Vocabulary Development

prior (PRY uhr) *adj.* previous; from before
avarice (AV uh ris) *adj.* greed
comply (kum PLY) *v.* go along with; agree to

<u>secure</u> what would make them wealthy for life. However Tom might have felt <u>disposed</u> to sell himself to the Devil, he was determined not to do so to <u>oblige</u> his wife; so he flatly refused out of the mere spirit of contradiction. Many and bitter were the quarrels they had on the subject. . . .

At length she determined to drive the bargain on her own account, and if she succeeded, to keep all the gain to herself. Being of the same <u>fearless</u> temper as her husband, she set off for the old Indian fort at the close of a summer's day.

> To bargain with the Devil, Tom's wife takes the household silverware and other valuables, tying them up in her apron. She is never heard from again. According to one story, Tom goes hunting for her and finds nothing but her apron, with a heart and liver inside! Whatever happened, Tom seems more upset about losing his property than losing his wife. In fact, he decides that the Devil might have done him a favor. Soon he is again bargaining with the Devil to obtain the pirate's treasure.

♦ ♦ ♦

There was one condition which need not be mentioned, being generally understood in all cases where the Devil grants favors; but there were others about which, though of less importance, he was <u>inflexibly</u> <u>obstinate</u>. He insisted

---

Vocabulary Development

secure (se KYOOR) *v.* to make certain about; to guarantee

disposed (dis POHZD) *adj.* inclined; prone to

oblige (u BLYDG) *v.* do what someone else wants; please

inflexibly (in FLEKS uh blee) *adv.* completely unwilling to move or change

obstinate (AWB sti net) *adj.* stubborn

Vocabulary and Pronunciation

A **suffix** is a word part added to the end of a word to change its meaning. The *suffix -less* means "without." *Fearless* means "without fear." Think of another word that ends with *-less*. On the lines below, write the word and its meaning.

Word: _____

Meaning: _____

Stop to Reflect

What "one condition which need not be mentioned" is always involved when someone makes a deal with the Devil? Circle the letter of the correct answer below.

(a) person damned in the after-life

(b) person signs name in blood

(c) person becomes rich

(d) person gets revenge on enemies

What does the Devil want done with the money he gives Tom?

(a) spend it all

(b) bury it in the woods

(c) use it for evil purposes

(d) use it to fight slavery

English Language Development

In the bracketed passage, circle all the quotation marks that show when Tom and the Devil are speaking. Then show who is speaking by labeling each remark *Tom* or *Devil*. How does Irving show a change of speaker?

_____

_____

_____

Stop to Reflect

Do you think Tom will regret his decision? Circle your answer.

     yes   no

Why, or why not?

_____

_____

_____

_____

that money found through his means should be employed in his service. He proposed, therefore, that Tom should employ it in the black traffic; that is to say, that he should fit out a slave ship. This, however, Tom <u>resolutely</u> refused: he was bad enough in all conscience, but the Devil himself could not tempt him to turn slave-trader.

Finding Tom so squeamish on this point, he did not insist upon it, but proposed, instead, that he should turn usurer.[3] . . . To this no objections were made, for it was just to Tom's taste.

"You shall open a broker's shop[4] in Boston next month," said the black man.

"I'll do it tomorrow, if you wish," said Tom Walker.

"You shall lend money at two per cent a month."

"Egad, I'll charge four!" replied Tom Walker. . . .

"Done!" said the Devil.

"Done!" said Tom Walker. So they shook hands and struck a bargain.

So Tom becomes a cruel moneylender, charging his highest rates to his most desperate customers. He grows rich and powerful. He builds a large, showy house, though he is too stingy to furnish it well. He buys a fancy carriage but lets the horses nearly starve. Yet as he nears old age, he begins to worry.

Vocabulary Development

resolutely (REZ uh LOOT lee) *adv.* firmly

---

3. **usurer** (YOO zhur uhr) *n.* a moneylender who charges high interest rates.
4. **a broker's shop** a moneylending business.

Having secured the good things of this world, he began to feel anxious about those of the next. <u>He thought with regret on the bargain he had made with his black friend</u>, and set his wits to work to cheat him out of the conditions. He became, therefore, all of a sudden, a violent churchgoer. . . . Tom was as rigid in religious as in money matters; he was a stern supervisor and censurer[5] of his neighbors, and seemed to think every sin entered up to their account became a credit on his own side of the page.

◆ ◆ ◆

Frightened of the Devil, Tom keeps a small Bible in his coat pocket and a large one on his desk at work. One hot afternoon, while still in his bathrobe, Tom goes down to his office to demand repayment of a loan. The man who has taken the loan is a land jobber, or speculator who tried to make money by buying and selling land. In the past, Tom has acted as if this man were a good friend, but now Tom refuses to give him more time to repay his loan.

◆ ◆ ◆

"My family will be ruined and brought upon the parish," said the land jobber.

"Charity begins at home," replied Tom; "I must take care of myself in these hard times."

"You have made so much money out of me," said the speculator.

Tom lost his patience and his <u>piety</u>—"The Devil take me," said he, "if I have made a farthing!"[6]

Vocabulary Development

piety (PY uh tee) *n.* religious devotion

---

5. censurer (SEN sher rer) *n.* someone who criticizes the behavior of others.
6. farthing (FAHR thing) *n.* a small coin of little value.

English Language Development

The **past perfect tense** uses the helping verb *had* + the past participle of the main verb:

had lived   had done

It is used to show an action that happened before another action in the past. In this underlined part of a sentence, label the verbs "1-past" and "2-past perfect" to show which action came first.

Reading Check

As a result of worrying about his deal with the Devil, what does Tom become?

_____

_____

_____

_____

Culture Note

"Charity begins at home" is a common proverb or saying in English. It means that a person should first help family or others in his or her own household before going on to help outsiders. What is dishonest about Tom's use of this proverb to defend his behavior?

_____

_____

_____

Who is knocking on Tom's door?

_____

_____

Do you think Tom deserves this doom?

_____

Why, or why not?

_____

_____

_____

Circle the sentence in which the **omniscient narrator** gives advice directly to some of his readers. What does he want those readers to learn from the story?

_____

_____

_____

Just then there were three loud knocks at the street door. He stepped out to see who was there. A black man was holding a black horse, which neighed and stamped with impatience.

"Tom, you're come for," said the black fellow, <u>gruffly</u>. Tom shrunk back, but too late. He had left his little Bible at the bottom of his coat pocket, and his big Bible on the desk . . . never was a sinner taken more unawares.

◆ ◆ ◆

The Devil takes Tom up and rides off into a thunderstorm. They are said to have galloped like mad to the swamp by the old fort. Shortly afterward the forest is struck by lightning. The next day Tom's fancy new house catches fire and burns to the ground. Tom himself is never seen again. Those appointed to settle his affairs find nothing but ashes where his business papers should be and chests filled with worthless wood shavings instead of gold.

◆ ◆ ◆

Such was the end of Tom Walker and his ill-gotten wealth. Let all <u>griping</u> money brokers lay this story to heart. The truth of it is not to be doubted. The very hole under the oak trees, whence[7] he dug Kidd's money, is to be seen to this day; and the neighboring swamp and old Indian fort are often haunted in stormy nights by a figure on horseback, in morning gown and white cap, which is doubtless the troubled spirit of the usurer.

Vocabulary Development

gruffly (GRUHF lee) *adv.* abruptly
griping (GRYP ing) *adj.* complaining

---

7. **whence** (WENS) *prep.* from where.

The Devil and Tom Walker

1. **Evaluate:** What kind of people do you think Tom Walker and his wife are? Explain.

_____

_____

_____

2. **Literary Analysis:** The **omniscient point of view** narrator tells the thoughts of characters in a story. Give examples of what the narrator reveals about each character. Record your responses in this diagram.

```
┌──────────┐                              ┌──────────┐
│          │                              │          │
└────┬─────┘                              └────┬─────┘
     │                                         │
 ┌───┴────────┐   ┌────────────┐   ┌──────────┴──┐
 │ Tom Walker │───│ Omniscient │───│ Mrs. Walker │
 └───┬────────┘   │  Narrator  │   └──────────┬──┘
     │            └─────┬──────┘              │
┌────┴─────┐            │            ┌────────┴──┐
│          │      ┌─────┴─────┐      │           │
└──────────┘      │ The Devil │      └───────────┘
                  └───────────┘
```

3. **Reading Strategy:** People in Irving's story have **cultural attitudes** toward religion. What **inference** can you make about those attitudes?

_____

_____

_____

4. **Reading Strategy:** People in Irving's story have cultural attitudes toward moneylenders. What inference can you make about those attitudes?

_____

_____

_____

The Tide Rises, The Tide Falls • Thanatopsis • Old Ironsides • *from* Snowbound

LITERARY ANALYSIS

Meter is the pattern of syllables, or sounds, in poetry. Some syllables are stressed and some are unstressed. The meter is the placement of these stressed and unstressed syllables.

- The basic unit of meter is called the *foot.* The type and number of feet in a line of poetry determine the poem's meter.
- A foot usually has one stressed and one or more unstressed syllables.
- One type of foot is called the *iamb.* An iamb is one unstressed syllable followed by a stressed syllable.
- One pattern of iambs is *iambic tetrameter.* It has four iambs per line. The line from *Snowbound* is in iambic tetrameter. Count the four iambs. The stressed syllables are capitalized.

   The SUN that BRIEF DeCEMber DAY

READING STRATEGY

Summarizing helps you to check your understanding of what you have read. To summarize:

- State the main ideas and the supporting details.

- Use your own words.

Look at the chart below. Summarize each poem using this chart.

Poem	Main Idea	Supporting Details
The Tide Rises, The Tide Falls		
Thanatoposis		
Old Ironsides		
from Snowbound		

The Tide Rises, The Tide Falls

Henry Wadsworth Longfellow

Thanatopsis

William Cullen Bryant

Old Ironsides

Oliver Wendell Holmes

from Snowbound

John Greenleaf Whittier

Summaries The subjects of these poems connect to life in New England. Longfellow's **"The Tide Rises, The Tide Falls"** compares the cycle of tides in the ocean to the cycle of life and death. In **"Thanatopsis,"** Bryant also explores the theme of death through images from nature, such as the earth and ocean. Holmes celebrates a ship's history at sea in **"Old Ironsides."** Finally, Whittier describes the beauty of a world covered in snow in an excerpt from **Snowbound.**

Note-taking Guide

Use the chart below to record images of nature found in each of these poems.

The Tide Rises, The Tide Falls	Thanatopsis	Old Ironsides	*from* Snowbound

The Tide Rises, The Tide Falls • Thanatopsis • Old Ironsides • *from* Snowbound

1. **Assess:** (a) Choose one of these poems. (b) In what ways has life changed since the poem was written in the mid-1860s?

   (a) Name of Poem _____

   (b) _____

2. **Literary Analysis:** A poem's **meter** is the rhythm of stressed and unstressed syllables in a line. The first line below from "Thanatopsis" shows the stressed and unstressed syllables. Mark the stressed and unstressed syllables of the meter in the second line by circling the stressed syllables.

   > so SHALT thou REST, and WHAT if THOU withDRAW
   > In silence from the living, and no friend.

3. **Reading Strategy:** When you **summarize,** you briefly tell the main ideas and the most important details in your own words. Summarize the first stanza of the excerpt from Snowbound. Write the details and your summary in this chart.

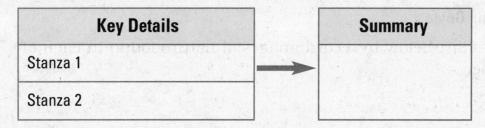

Key Details	Summary
Stanza 1	
Stanza 2	

4. **Reading Strategy:** Summarize the main idea of "Thanatopsis." Write the summary as though you are telling a friend or family member about the poem.

   _____

   _____

   _____

MEMORANDUMS

About Memorandums

A **memorandum** is a business document that tells employees about upcoming events, changes in policy, or other business-related matters. In today's workplace, the average memorandum is brief and informal. It usually contains a heading that indicates the sender, recipient, date, and subject of the memo. The body of the memo explains the subject in detail.

Historic memorandums are often more formal, more detailed, and longer than today's memorandums. Look for these qualities in this historic memorandum in which Thomas Jefferson assigned Meriwether Lewis the task of exploring the Missouri River in 1803.

Reading Strategy

Analyzing Text Structures: Patterns of Organization Informative writing can follow several different **patterns of organization.** Three patterns are described in the chart below.

Pattern of Organization	Structure	Type of Writing in Which It Is Found
Chronological Order	Step-by-step details are presented in time order.	Do-it-yourself instructions
Order of Importance	Ideas flow from most to least important or from least to most important.	Persuasive writing
Enumeration	Supportive details are provided in list form.	Brochure or sales documents

BUILD UNDERSTANDING

Knowing these words will help you read this historic memorandum.

commerce (KAHM ers) *n.* the buying and selling of goods

latitude and longitude east/west and north/south geographic lines that are used to pinpoint any location on Earth's surface

portage (POR tij) *n.* an area of land across which boats must be carried in order to reach the next stretch of open water

Commission of Meriwether Lewis
Thomas Jefferson

June 20, 1803

To Meriwether Lewis, esquire, captain of the first regiment of infantry of the United States of America: Your situation as secretary of the president of the United States, has made you acquainted with the objects of my confidential message of January 18, 1803, to the legislature; you have seen the act they passed, which, though expressed in general terms, was meant to sanction those objects, and you are appointed to carry them into execution.

. . .

The object of your mission is to explore the Missouri river, and such principal streams of it, as, by its course and communication[1] with the waters of the Pacific ocean, whether the Columbia, Oregan [sic], Colorado, or any other river, may offer the most direct and practicable[2] water-communication across the continent, for the purposes of commerce.

Beginning at the mouth of the Missouri, you will take observations of latitude and longitude, at all remarkable points on the river, and especially at the mouths of rivers, at rapids, at islands, and other places and objects distinguished by such natural marks and characters, of a durable kind, as that they may with certainty be recognized hereafter. The

1. **communication** (kuh MYOO ni KAY shun) *n.* the action of passing from one place to another.
2. **practicable** (PRAK ti kuh bul) *adj.* usable.

courses of the river between these points of observation may be supplied by the compass, the log-line, and by time, corrected by the observations themselves. The variations of the needle, too, in different places, should be noticed.

The interesting points of the portage between the heads of the Missouri,[3] and of the water offering the best communication with the Pacific Ocean, should also be fixed by observation;[4] and the course of that water to the ocean, in the same manner as that of the Missouri.

Your observations are to be taken with great pains and accuracy; to be entered distinctly and intelligibly for others as well as yourself; to comprehend all the elements necessary, with the aid of the usual tables, to fix the latitude and longitude of the places at which they were taken; and are to be rendered to the war-office, for the purpose of having the calculations made concurrently by proper persons within the United States. Several copies of these, as well as of your other notes, should be made at leisure times, and put into the care of the most trustworthy of your attendants to guard, by multiplying them against the accidental losses to which they will be exposed. A further guard would be, that one of these copies be on the cuticular membranes of the paper-birch, as less liable to injury from damp than common paper.

The commerce which may be carried on with the people inhabiting the line you will pursue, renders a knowledge of those people important. You will therefore endeavor to make yourself acquainted, as far as a diligent pursuit of your journey shall admit, with the names of the nations and their numbers;

3. **heads of the Missouri** the sources of the Missouri River.
4. **fixed by observation** established the position of a place based on measurements or surroundings.

TAKE NOTES

Stop to Reflect

List three things that Jefferson wants Lewis to observe.

1. _____

2. _____

3. _____

Why would Lewis's observations be important for future travel and trade?

_____

_____

_____

_____

Reading Check

What does Jefferson suggest that Lewis do when he has leisure time during the journey?

_____

_____

Circle the letter of the **pattern of organization** that Jefferson uses in the bracketed section.

a. chronological

b. order of importance

c. enumeration

Explain your answer.

_____

_____

_____

_____

In the bracketed section, Jefferson says Lewis should become familiar with the beliefs and values of native people, so later settlers can "civilize and instruct them." What is Jefferson assuming about native people?

_____

_____

_____

What advantages could Lewis gain from being friendly toward the native people?

_____

_____

_____

The extent and limits of their possessions;

Their relations with other tribes or nations;

Their language, traditions, monuments;

Their ordinary occupations in agriculture, fishing, hunting, war, arts, and the implements for these;

Their food, clothing, and domestic accommodations;

The diseases prevalent among them, and the remedies they use;

Moral and physical circumstances which distinguish them from the tribes we know;

Peculiarities in their laws, customs, and dispositions[5];

And articles of commerce they may need or furnish, and to what extent.

And, considering the interest which every nation has in extending and strengthening the authority of reason and justice among the people around them, it will be useful to acquire what knowledge you can of the state of morality, religion, and information among them; as it may better enable those who may endeavor to civilize and instruct them, to adapt their measures to the existing notions and practices of those on whom they are to operate. . . .

In all your [dealings] with the natives, treat them in the most friendly and conciliatory manner which their own conduct will admit; allay all jealousies as to the object of your journey; satisfy them of its innocence; make them acquainted with the position, extent, character, peaceable and commercial dispositions of the United States; of our wish to be neighborly, friendly, and useful to them, and of our dispositions to a commercial [relationship] with them; confer with them on the points most

5. **dispositions** (DIS puh ZI shunz) _n._ leanings.

convenient as mutual emporiums,[6] and the articles of most desirable interchange for them and us. If a few of their influential chiefs, within practicable distance, wish to visit us, arrange such a visit with them, and furnish them with authority to call on our officers on their entering the United States, to have them conveyed to this place at the public expense. If any of them should wish to have some of their young people brought up with us, and taught such arts as may be useful to them, we will receive, instruct, and take care of them. Such a mission, whether of influential chiefs, or of young people, would give some security to your own party. Carry with you some matter of the kine-pox; inform those of them with whom you may be of its efficacy as a preservative from the small-pox, and instruct and encourage them in the use of it. This may be especially done wherever you winter.

As it is impossible for us to foresee in what manner you will be received by those people, whether with hospitality or hostility, so is it impossible to prescribe the exact degree of perseverance with which you are to pursue your journey. We value too much the lives of citizens to offer them to probable destruction. Your numbers will be sufficient to secure you against the unauthorized opposition of individuals, or of small parties; but if a superior force, authorized, or not authorized, by a nation, should be arrayed against your further passage, and inflexibly determined to arrest it, you must decline its further pursuit and return. In the loss of yourselves we should lose also the information you will have acquired. By returning safely with that, you may enable us to renew the essay with better calculated means. To your own discretion, therefore, must be left the degree of danger you may risk, and the point at which you should decline, only saying, we wish you to err on the side of your safety, and to bring back your party safe, even if it be with less information. . . .

TAKE NOTES

Reading Informational Materials

A **memorandum** is often written using the imperative, or command, form. In the bracketed paragraph, underline three commands that Jefferson gives Lewis. Circle the verb in each example.

---

6. emporiums (em POR ee ums) *n.* trading centers.

THINKING ABOUT MEMORANDUMS

1. Why does Jefferson want Lewis to copy his observations multiple times?

_____

_____

2. What instructions does Jefferson give Lewis on how to treat the Native Americans he meets?

_____

_____

READING STRATEGY

3. Why do you think Jefferson starts his **memorandum** by stating Meriwether Lewis's mission?

_____

_____

4. Which **pattern of organization**—chronological order, order of importance, or enumeration—is **not** used in this memorandum?

_____

_____

TIMED WRITING: PERSUASION (25 minutes)

Identify one topic in Jefferson's memorandum. Write a brief summary of the topic. Remember to focus on key points. Answer the questions below to help you organize your writing.

• What is the topic? _____

• What details explain the topic? _____

_____

• Which pattern of organization—chronological order, order of importance, or enumeration—works best to present this information?

_____

_____

Crossing the Great Divide •
The Most Sublime Spectacle on Earth

LITERARY ANALYSIS

Description is writing that uses language to explain experiences with the five senses: sight, sound, smell, taste, and touch.

- Lewis relies on the senses of touch and sight when he describes the "level smooth bottom covered with a fine turf" of grass.
- Powell describes the sight of a rock "a mile in thickness."

Look for similar examples from Lewis's and Powell's reports. Use this chart to record descriptive details. These details should create vivid images in these selections.

Descriptions	
Sight	
Sound	
Taste	
Touch	

READING STRATEGY

Note spatial relationships when you read about landscapes. These details include the size, distance, and location of those features. Noting spatial details can help you visualize and understand the features being described.

Crossing the Great Divide

Meriwether Lewis

Summary Lewis reports on his early exploration of the American West. He speaks about the Native Americans he meets and how they helped him. He tells a positive story of American movement westward. Lewis tells the Native Americans that the United States government wishes to be friendly toward them. He also explains how new trade routes will help them.

Note-taking Guide

Use this diagram to record the main idea in Lewis's report. Then, list three details that support or illustrate this idea.

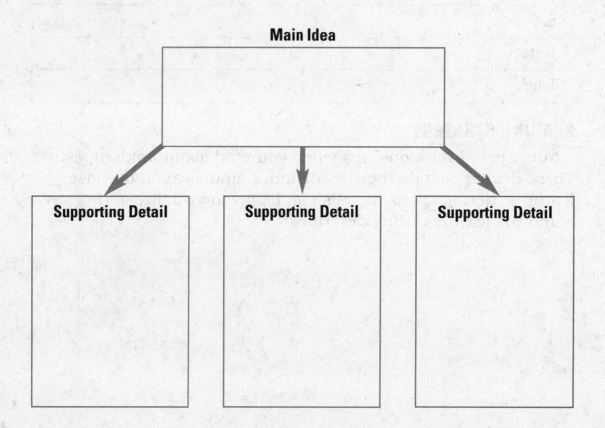

The Most Sublime Spectacle on Earth

by John Wesley Powell

Summary Powell speaks of the beauty of the Grand Canyon. He explains that rain and rivers formed the canyon over many centuries. He describes the complexity and depth of the canyon's history and beauty. Rather than speaking about himself, Powell focuses entirely on the magnificence of the Grand Canyon.

Note-taking Guide

Use this diagram to record the main idea in Powell's report. Then, list three details that support or illustrate this idea.

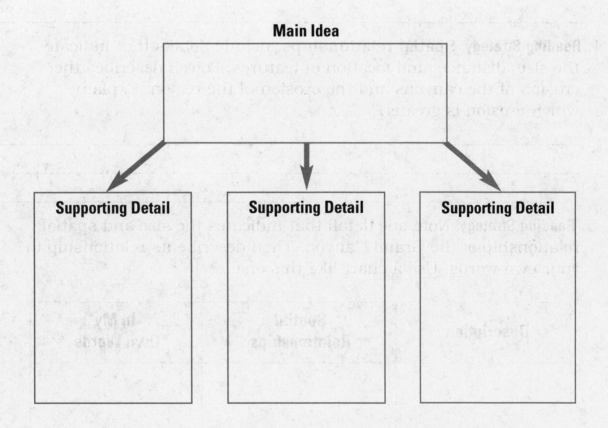

Main Idea

Supporting Detail

Supporting Detail

Supporting Detail

Crossing the Great Divide •
The Most Sublime Spectacle on Earth

1. **Compare and Contrast:** What might a painting of a scene from the American West show that these two written descriptions cannot?

   _____

   _____

2. **Literary Analysis:** Find one sentence that has **description** in "The Most Sublime Spectacle on Earth" and write it on the lines.

   _____

   _____

3. **Literary Analysis:** Explain what makes the sentence you identified above effective.

   _____

   _____

4. **Reading Strategy: Spatial relationships** include details that indicate the size, distance, and location of features. Powell describes the erosion of the canyons and the erosion of the region. Explain which erosion is greater.

   _____

   _____

   _____

5. **Reading Strategy:** Note one detail that indicates the size and spatial relationship of the Grand Canyon. Then describe its relationship in your own words. Use a chart like this one.

Description	Spatial Relationships	In My Own Words

The Fall of the House of Usher • The Raven

LITERARY ANALYSIS

Edgar Allan Poe believed that a good story should have a **single effect** on a reader. He thought that every character, event, and detail should work to create the single effect. As you read, look for the ways Poe tries to produce a single effect.

Although "The Fall of the House of Usher" is a short story and "The Raven" is a poem, both are examples of **Gothic** literature. Gothic style uses the following elements:

- dark and depressing settings
- grim or violent events
- tormented and disturbed characters
- supernatural events

Pay attention to how Poe uses different Gothic elements.

READING STRATEGY

Poems often contain long sentences with difficult words. It may help to **break down long sentences** into parts. Breaking a sentence into parts allows you to figure out how the parts work together.

Use this chart to break down Poe's long sentences. First, look for the subject and verb. Then, look for the object of the verb. Look for connecting words that pull the sentence together.

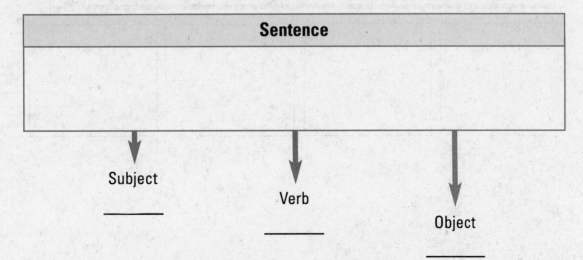

Sentence

Subject
_____

Verb
_____

Object
_____

The Fall of the House of Usher

Edgar Allan Poe

Summary Roderick Usher has asked the narrator to stay with him while he is ill. The narrator answers his old friend's request and travels to Usher's gloomy mansion. There, he learns that Usher is not well physically or mentally. The narrator also finds out that Usher's twin sister, Madeline, is ill. One evening, Usher tells the narrator that his sister has died. Usher and the narrator take her coffin to a vault within the mansion. After they seal her inside, strange things begin to happen.

Note-taking Guide

Complete the following timeline with events from the story.

1. Narrator comes to Usher's mansion.	3.	5.	7.
2.	4.	6.	8.

The Raven

Edgar Allan Poe

Summary The speaker in this poem sits alone reading at night. A mysterious raven comes knocking at his door. The speaker has been grieving for his lost love, Lenore. He begins to ask the raven questions, but the raven only has one response. Through the man's conversation with the raven, Poe explores a mind falling into madness.

Note-taking Guide

Complete the following chart by telling how the raven responds to the speaker.

What the speaker of the poem says	What the speaker hears the raven answer
• Excuse me, I was napping.	
• Lenore!	
• Tell me your name.	
• The bird will leave me tomorrow, as others have.	
• I need respite from my grief over Lenore.	
• "Is there balm in Gilead?"	
• Will I hold Lenore again?	

Adjectives in English usually come before the noun they modify. But here the adjective *dreary* comes after the noun it modifies, *midnight*. The unusual order sounds more poetic. How would you say "a midnight dreary" in usual spoken English?

_____

_____

Culture Note

December is the twelfth month of the year. It is a cold winter month in many parts of the United States. On the lines below, write all twelve months in English. One is done as an example. Remember that the English names of the months each start with a capital letter.

_____ _____

_____ _____

_____ _____

_____ _____

_____ _____

_____ December

Read Fluently

Read this underlined line aloud and circle the four /s/ sounds.
What sound do you think Poe is trying to capture?

(a) the curtains rustling

(b) the speaker's beating heart

(c) the speaker's terror

(d) a visitor knocking on the door

The Raven
Edgar Allan Poe

Once upon a <u>midnight dreary</u>, while I
    <u>pondered</u>, weak and weary,
Over many a quaint and curious volume of
    forgotten lore[1]—
While I nodded, nearly napping, suddenly there
    came a tapping,
As of some one gently rapping, rapping at my
    chamber door.
"'Tis some visitor," I muttered, "tapping at my
    chamber door—
        Only this, and nothing more."
Ah, distinctly I remember it was in the bleak
    <u>December</u>;
And each separate dying ember wrought its
    ghost upon the floor.
Eagerly I wished the morrow;[2]—vainly I had
    sought to borrow
From my books surcease[3] of sorrow—sorrow
    for the lost Lenore—
For the rare and radiant maiden whom the
    angels name Lenore—
        Nameless *here* for evermore.
<u>And the silken, sad, uncertain rustling of each
    purple curtain</u>
Thrilled me—filled me with fantastic terrors
    never felt before;
So that now, to still the beating of my heart, I
    stood repeating
"'Tis some visitor entreating entrance at my
    chamber door—

Vocabulary Development

pondered (PAHN derd) *v.* thought deeply
wrought (RAWT) *v.* carved

---

1. **quaint** (KWAYNT) **volume of forgotten lore** unusual book of forgotten knowledge.
2. **the morrow** the next day.
3. **surcease** (ser SEES) **of** relief from.

Some late visitor entreating entrance at my
    chamber door;—
               This it is and nothing more."
Presently my soul grew stronger; hesitating
    then no longer,
"Sir," said I, "or Madam, truly your forgiveness
    I implore;
But the fact is I was napping, and so gently
    you came rapping,
And so faintly you came tapping, tapping at my
    chamber door,
That I scarce was sure I heard you"—here I
    opened wide the door;—
            Darkness there and nothing more.

◆ ◆ ◆

The speaker searches the dark for the
source of the knocking, but he sees nothing.
When he calls out the name "Lenore," he
hears only an echo. Then he hears the
knocking again. This time he thinks it is
someone at the window.

◆ ◆ ◆

Open here I flung the shutter, when, with
    many a flirt and flutter,
In there stepped a <u>stately</u> Raven of the
    saintly days of yore;[4]
Not the least obeisance[5] made he; <u>not a
    minute stopped or stayed he</u>;
But, with mien[6] of lord or lady, perched above
    my chamber door—
Perched upon a bust of Pallas[7] just above my
    chamber door—
         Perched, and sat, and nothing more.

Vocabulary Development

stately (STAYT lee) *adj.* elegant; dignified

---

4. **days of yore** (YAWR) olden days; days of long ago.
5. **obeisance** (oh BAY suhns) *n.* show of respect, such as a bow or a
curtsy.
6. **mien** (MEEN) *n.* manner; way of conducting yourself.
7. **bust of Pallas** (PAL is) sculpture of the head and shoulders of Pallas
Athena (uh THEE nuh), the ancient Greek goddess of wisdom.

Reading Check

What does the speaker find
when he opens the door? Circle
your answer.

English Language Development

The **subject** is the noun or pronoun that performs
the action of the verb. In
English, the subject usually
comes before the verb. But
sometimes poetry inverts the
order, putting the verb first.
Circle the subject and verb in
this underlined clause, and label
them *S* or *V.*

Circle the speaker's request for information in the bracketed passage. Label it *Q.* Then circle the answer the Raven seems to give and label it *A.*

This stanza is one long sentence. Draw lines between words to **break up the long sentence** into manageable chunks. Circle the letter of the statement below that best sums up the meaning of the sentence.

(a) I was amazed by the bird and its speech, even if it made little sense.

(b) I was amazed that anything so ugly could have such a lovely voice.

(c) I chatted with the amazing bird, which sat on a bust labeled "Nevermore" over my door.

(d) I am the only human being who ever spoke with Nevermore.

Then this ebony bird beguiling my sad fancy[8] into smiling,
By the grave and stern decorum[9] of the countenance[10] it wore,
"Though thy crest be shorn and shaven,[11] thou," I said, "art sure no <u>craven</u>,
Ghastly grim and ancient Raven wandering from the Nightly shore—
Tell me what thy lordly name is on the Night's Plutonian[12] shore!"
        Quoth[13] the Raven, "Nevermore."

Much I marveled[14] this <u>ungainly</u> fowl to hear discourse[15] so plainly,
Though its answer little meaning—little relevancy bore;[16]
For we cannot help agreeing that no living human being
Ever yet was blessed with seeing bird above his chamber door—
Bird or beast upon the sculptured bust above his chamber door,
        With such name as "Nevermore."

Vocabulary Development

craven (KRAYV uhn) *n.* coward
ungainly (uhn GAYN lee) *adj.* awkward; clumsy

---

8. **ebony** (EB uh nee) **bird beguiling** (bi GYL ing) **my sad fancy** black bird charming my sad mood away.
9. **decorum** (duh KAWR uhm) *n.* act of polite behavior.
10. **countenance** (KOW tuh nuns) *n.* face.
11. **thy crest be shorn and shaven** The tuft of feathers on your head is clipped and shaved (by a previous owner).
12. **Plutonian** (ploo TOHN yuhn) *adj.* dark and evil; hellish (Pluto was the Roman god of the underworld).
13. **quoth** (KWOHTH) *v.* quoted; recited; said.
14. **marveled** found marvelous; felt awe or wonder about.
15. **discourse** (dis KAWRS) *v.* speak; talk.
16. **little relevancy** (REL uh vin see) **bore** had little meaning; did not make much sense.

But the Raven, sitting lonely on the placid[17]
   bust, spoke only
That one word, as if his soul in that one word
   he did outpour.
Nothing farther then he uttered—not a feather
   then he fluttered—
Till I scarcely more than muttered, "Other
   friends have flown before—
On the morrow *he* will leave me, as my Hopes
   have flown before."
                    Then the bird said, "Nevermore."

                   ◆   ◆   ◆

   The speaker worries about this
"Nevermore." This time it sounds like a real
answer to the question he asked. He tells
himself that maybe the Raven knows just this
one word. Yet he still keeps trying to find
some meaning in the word. No matter what
he asks the Raven, the bird says,
"Nevermore." By now the speaker is angry.

                   ◆   ◆   ◆

"Prophet!" said I, "thing of evil!—prophet still,
   if bird or devil!
By that Heaven that bends above us—by that
   God we both adore—
Tell this soul with sorrow laden[18] if, within the
   distant Aidenn,[19]
It shall clasp a sainted maiden whom the
   angels name Lenore—
Clasp a rare and radiant maiden whom the
   angels name Lenore."
                    Quoth the Raven, "Nevermore."

---
17. **placid** (PLA sid) *adj.* silent.
18. **this soul with sorrow laden** (LAY duhn) the speaker's own
    sorrowful soul.
19. **Aidenn** (AY den) Eden; heaven.

TAKE NOTES

Reading Check

What does the speaker think the Raven means when he says "Nevermore" in the underlined sentence?

_____

_____

_____

_____

Literary Analysis

How does repetition of "Nevermore" add to the **single effect** of horror?

_____

_____

_____

_____

Circle two more details on this page that add to the single effect of horror.

The /ee/ sound is often spelled *e, ea, ee, ie, ei,* and *y.* Circle six examples of the /ee/ sound in this bracketed stanza.

Reading Check

What is the situation at the end of the poem? Answer by completing this sentence:

The Raven is _____

_____,

and the speaker is _____

_____.

"Be that word our sign of parting, bird or fiend!" I shrieked, upstarting[20] —
"Get thee back into the tempest and the Night's Plutonian shore!
Leave no black plume as a token of that lie thy soul hath spoken!
Leave my loneliness unbroken!—quit the bust above my door!
Take thy beak from out my heart, and take thy form from off my door!"
　　　　　Quoth the Raven, "Nevermore."

And the Raven, never flitting, still is sitting, still is sitting
On the pallid bust of Pallas just above my chamber door;
And his eyes have all the seeming of a demon's that is dreaming;
And the lamp-light o'er him streaming throws his shadow on the floor;
And my soul from out that shadow that lies floating on the floor
　　　　　Shall be lifted—nevermore!

Vocabulary Development

fiend (FEEND) *n.* demon; devil
plume (PLOOM) *n.* feather
flitting (FLIT ing) *adj.* flying rapidly
pallid (PAL uhd) *adj.* pale; white

---

20. **upstarting** starting up; standing; moving.

The Fall of the House of Usher • The Raven

1. **Connect:** In what ways is the appearance of the interior of Usher's house related to the condition of Usher's mind?

   _____

   _____

2. **Literary Analysis:** How does the storm contribute to the **single effect** of a growing sense of terror in "The Fall of the House of Usher"?

   _____

   _____

3. **Literary Analysis:** Use this chart to compare the **Gothic** elements in the story and poem.

Gothic Element	House of Usher	Raven
Setting		
Violence		
Characterization		
The Supernatural		

4. **Reading Strategy:** Break down **this sentence** from the story and rewrite it in your own words.

   At times, again, I was obliged to resolve all into the mere inexplicable vagaries of madness, for I beheld him gazing upon vacancy for long hours, in an attitude of the profoundest attention, as if listening to some imaginary sound.

   _____

   _____

   _____

The Minister's Black Veil

LITERARY ANALYSIS

A **parable** is a simple story that teaches a moral lesson.
- Characters in a parable are human beings, not animals.
- A parable is a kind of **allegory**. An allegory is a story with more than one meaning.

The veil that Mr. Hooper vows never to remove is a **symbol**—something that stands for something greater than itself. To discover the veil's symbolic meaning, notice Hawthorne's descriptions of the veil and its effects on the characters in the story.

READING STRATEGY

Often, the message of a story is presented indirectly. To understand the message, you must **draw inferences**. Drawing inferences means you must read details carefully in order to figure out what they mean.

Many kinds of information can help you draw inferences:
- descriptions
- dialogue
- your own experiences
- symbols

Use this chart to draw inferences from the story. Write down descriptions or dialogue from the story. Then, write down an inference you can draw from that description or dialogue.

Description/Dialogue

Inference

The Minister's Black Veil

Nathaniel Hawthorne

Summary The parson, Mr. Hooper, arrives at church wearing a black veil over his face. He wears the veil without explanation through his sermon, through the following sermon, and then through a funeral and a wedding. The congregation whispers among themselves. They fear the veil. Only Mr. Hooper's fiancée has the courage to ask him why he wears the veil. She does not understand the answer and leaves him. Mr. Hooper wears the veil for the rest of his life. In fact, he offers no other explanation for it until his death.

Note-taking Guide

Use this character wheel to record information about Reverend Hooper.

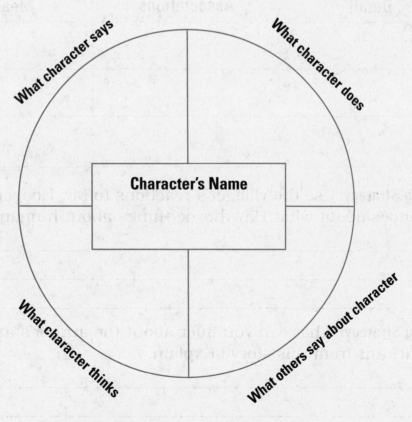

What character says

What character does

Character's Name

What character thinks

What others say about character

The Minister's Black Veil

1. **Interpret:** How does the veil affect Mr. Hooper's relationship with his congregation?

_____

_____

2. **Literary Analysis:** In what ways does this **parable** convey the message that people can be both good and evil?

_____

_____

3. **Literary Analysis:** A **symbol** is something that represents something else. In the first column of this chart, write down three descriptions of the veil. In the second column, describe the emotional associations of each description. In the third column, explain the symbolic meaning of each description.

Descriptive Detail	Emotional Associations	Symbolic Meaning

4. **Reading Strategy:** Use the villager's reactions to Mr. Hooper to **draw inferences** about what Hawthorne thinks about human nature.

_____

_____

_____

5. **Reading Strategy:** What can you infer about the author's attitude toward the Puritans from this story? Explain.

_____

_____

from Moby-Dick

LITERARY ANALYSIS

A **symbol** is a person, place, or thing that represents something else. Moby-Dick is a complex symbol. The white whale represents many ideas:

- Moby-Dick is huge, dangerous, and awful—but also beautiful.
- Moby-Dick's behavior seems unpredictable—but he is governed by nature's laws.
- He appears immortal, but he is subject to physical suffering.

To understand Moby-Dick's symbolic meaning, pay attention to details about his behavior and appearance.

READING STRATEGY

To **recognize symbols,** look for characters, places, and objects that are used repeatedly or are connected to larger ideas. Also read descriptions carefully. Descriptions often have symbolic meaning. Use this chart to record and interpret symbols.

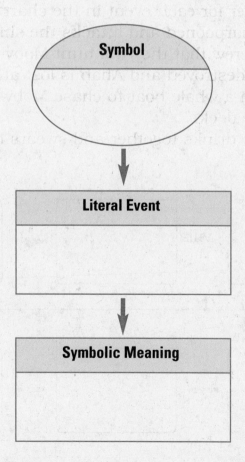

Symbol

↓

Literal Event

↓

Symbolic Meaning

from Moby-Dick

Herman Melville

Summary Captain Ahab has led the crew of the *Pequod* on a whale hunt. In the first excerpt from *Moby-Dick*, Ahab explains that they are not hunting for business. Instead, Ahab is looking for revenge. He wants to hunt and kill the great white whale called Moby-Dick. He blames the whale for the loss of his leg. The second excerpt is the final chapter. Here, the narrator tells what happens when Ahab and his crew finally catch up with the whale.

Note-taking Guide

Put the events in order according to when they happen in the story. Write the letter for each event in the chart.

A Moby-Dick is harpooned and attacks the ship.
B Ahab tells the crew that they will hunt Moby-Dick.
C Ahab's ship is destroyed and Ahab is lost at sea.
D Ahab sets off in a whale boat to chase Moby-Dick.
E Ahab paces the deck.
F The ship's crew drinks together and swears to kill the whale.

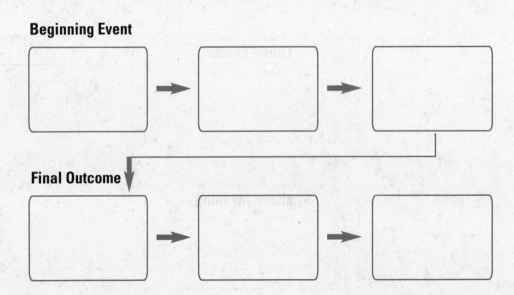

Beginning Event

Final Outcome

from Moby-Dick

1. **Compare and Contrast:** Moby-Dick surfaces and sees the ship. The whale then tries to head out to sea. What does Moby-Dick's reaction to the ship reveal about the difference between the real whale and the whale in Ahab's imagination?

   _____

   _____

2. **Literary Analysis:** Use this chart to identify the meaning of some of the **symbols** in this excerpt from *Moby-Dick*.

Symbol	Meaning
the color white	
the crew of the *Pequod*	
Moby-Dick	
the voyage of the *Pequod*	

3. **Reading Strategy:** What events, dialogue, or descriptions lead you to **recognize** Moby-Dick as a **symbol** of nature's power?

   _____

   _____

4. **Reading Strategy:** This novel has been called a symbolic "voyage of the soul." Would you agree or disagree with that assessment? Explain.

   _____

   _____

   _____

from Nature • from Self-Reliance • Concord Hymn • The Snowstorm

LITERARY ANALYSIS

Emerson and a group of his friends developed a system of beliefs called **Transcendentalism**. These are the key points of the Transcendentalist movement:

- Human senses, like sight or touch, only give you knowledge of the physical world. You must use your intuition to find deeper meaning and truth in life.
- Humans can learn about themselves through nature.
- God, nature, and humanity are connected. All living things share a universal soul called the Over-Soul.

As you read, pay attention to how Emerson's writing reflects these beliefs.

READING STRATEGY

You should never simply accept the ideas in a piece of writing. You should challenge them. The following are ways to **challenge a text**:

- question the author's ideas and explanations
- consider the author's supporting evidence
- think about what you have learned from your own experiences and other reading
- weigh the author's arguments against your opinions and other information
- decide if you agree with the author's ideas

Use this chart to record your thoughts about the selections.

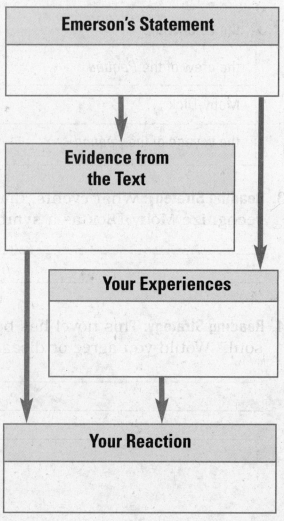

Emerson's Statement

Evidence from the Text

Your Experiences

Your Reaction

from Nature

Ralph Waldo Emerson

Summary In this selection, Emerson writes about the harmony between himself and nature. He believes all living things are connected and reflect each other. Emerson describes how beauty, peace, and spirituality can be found in the natural world.

Note-taking Guide

Read the selection. Using the chart, rewrite complicated or long sentences in your own words.

from Nature:	In your own words:
"In the woods, too, a man casts off his years, as the snake his slough, and at what period soever of life is always a child."	
"I become a transparent eyeball; I am nothing; I see all; the currents of the Universal Being circulate through me; I am part or parcel of God."	

from Self-Reliance

Ralph Waldo Emerson

Summary In this excerpt, Emerson speaks to the individual. He urges readers to avoid conforming to the standards of society. Instead, Emerson urges readers to think and act independently.

Note-taking Guide

Read the selection. Using the chart, rewrite complicated or long sentences in your own words.

from Self-Reliance:	In your own words:
"Trust thyself; every heart vibrates to that string"	
"Nothing is at last sacred but the integrity of your own mind. Absolve you to yourself,and you shall have the suffrage of the world . . ."	

Concord Hymn • The Snowstorm

Ralph Waldo Emerson

Summaries In these two poems, Emerson celebrates country and nature. **"Concord Hymn"** honors the Minutemen who fought at Lexington and Concord during the American Revolution. The poem suggests that those who make great sacrifices for others should not be forgotten. **"The Snowstorm"** wonders at the power of nature to create amazing beauty.

Note-taking Guide

Read each selection. Using the chart, rewrite complicated or long sentences in your own words.

Concord Hymn:	In your own words:
"On this green bank, by this soft stream, / We set today a votive stone; / That memory may their deed redeem, / When, like our sires, our sons are gone."	

The Snowstorm:	In your own words:
"Come see the north wind's masonry."	

from Nature • from Self-Reliance • Concord Hymn • The Snowstorm

1. **Infer:** What details in "Concord Hymn" reflect the Emerson's belief in an Over-Soul?

   _____

   _____

2. **Literary Analysis:** What does "Nature" tell you about the **Transcendentalist** attitude toward nature? Explain.

   _____

   _____

3. **Literary Analysis:** Use this chart to compare and contrast Emerson's descriptions of the relationship between people and society and the relationship between people and nature.

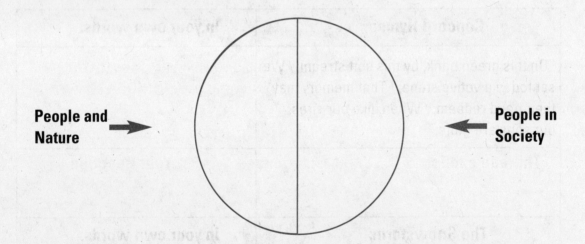

4. **Reading Strategy:** Emerson makes this claim in "Self-Reliance": "A foolish consistency is the hobgoblin of little minds." **Challenge the text** by noting evidence Emerson uses to support his position.

   _____

   _____

from Walden • from Civil Disobedience

LITERARY ANALYSIS

A writer puts his or her thoughts into words using a particular **style.** Thoreau's writing style has these characteristics:

- Sentences build to a climax in a paragraph.
- Important ideas are repeated to emphasize the work's message.

Thoreau often uses **metaphors.** Metaphors are figures of speech that compare two unlike things without using the words *like* or *as.* As you read, notice the metaphors that Thoreau uses.

READING STRATEGY

An essay can present many ideas, opinions, and arguments. It is important to **evaluate the writer's philosophy** when you are reading an essay. Ask these questions to decide whether you agree with a writer's position:

- How well does the writer support his or her argument?
- How do the writer's arguments compare to my thoughts, experiences, and knowledge?

Use this chart to evaluate Thoreau's ideas. Write down his ideas and any supporting details. Then, compare his ideas with your thoughts and experiences.

Thoreau's Ideas	Your Experiences	Your Reaction

from Walden

Henry David Thoreau

Summary For two years, Henry David Thoreau lived alone in a small cabin. He had built the cabin above Walden Pond. Seven years after he left the cabin, he used his journal to write *Walden*. In these selections, Thoreau shares his Transcendentalist vision. He believes human society has become too complex. He encourages people to simplify their lives, to slow down and do less, and to enjoy more.

Note-taking Guide

Use this table to keep track of Thoreau's statements and the details that support or clarify them.

Thoreau's Statement	Details
"The Holowell Farm has real attractions."	1. far from village 2. located on river

from Walden
Henry David Thoreau

When he was twenty-eight, Thoreau decided to leave the village of Concord, Massachusetts. He went to live several miles from town in the woods at Walden Pond. There he built a simple cabin that was little more than a shelter from the rain. He moved in on July 4, 1845—Independence Day. In a section of *Walden* called "Where I Lived and What I Lived For," he explains why he decided to live such a simple, rugged life, close to nature.

◆　◆　◆

I went to the woods because I wished to live <u>deliberately</u>, to front[1] only the <u>essential</u> facts of life, and see if I could not learn what it had to teach, and not, when I came to die, discover that I had not lived. I did not wish to live what was not life, living is so dear; nor did I wish to practice <u>resignation</u>, unless it was quite necessary.

◆　◆　◆

Thoreau went to the woods because he wanted to live life fully and find out what it was all about. If it was wonderful, he wanted to enjoy it. If it was awful, he wanted to face that too. He feels that too many people don't understand the meaning of life. Instead they live in a small way, like ants.

◆　◆　◆

Vocabulary Development

deliberately (duh LIB rit lee) *adv.* with thought and care
essential (uh SEN shuhl) *adj.* vital; necessary
resignation (re zig NAY shuhn) *n.* giving in to conditions beyond your control; hopelessness

---

1. front confront; face.

TAKE NOTES

Culture Note

July 4 celebrates the independence of the United States from Great Britain. It was an important holiday in Thoreau's time too. Why do you think he chose that day to go live alone in the woods?

_____

_____

_____

_____

_____

Reading Check

When he went to the woods, what kind of life experiences was Thoreau hoping to face? Circle the answer in the bracketed paragraph.

Stop to Reflect

How would living in the woods help Thoreau live life more fully?

_____

_____

_____

_____

_____

_____

English words change endings to change part of speech. The new word has a different but related meaning. For example, the adjective *pretty* adds *-ness* to become a noun and *-ify* to become a verb:

> pretty + -ness = prettiness, "the state of being pretty"
>
> pretty + -ify = prettify, "to make pretty"

In the bracketed paragraph, circle a noun and a verb formed from the adjective *simple*. Label the noun *N* and the verb *V*. On the lines below, write the words and their meanings.

noun: _____

meaning: _____

verb: _____

meaning: _____

What **statement of the writer's philosophy** does Thoreau make in the bracketed paragraph?

_____

_____

_____

_____

_____

Our life is <u>frittered away</u> by detail. An honest man has hardly need to count more than his ten fingers, or in extreme cases he may add his ten toes, and lump the rest. <u>Simplicity, simplicity, simplicity!</u> I say, let your affairs be as two or three, and not a hundred or a thousand; instead of a million count half a dozen, and keep your accounts on your thumbnail. In the midst of this chopping sea of civilized life, such are the clouds and storms and quicksands and thousand-and-one items to be allowed for, that a man has to live, if he would not founder[2] and go to the bottom and not make his port at all, by dead reckoning.[3] Simplify, simplify. Instead of three meals a day, if it be necessary eat but one; instead of a hundred dishes, five; and reduce other things in proportion.

◆ ◆ ◆

Thoreau complains that there is too much stress on business and commerce in the young American nation. To him, the focus on material things is shallow. It takes people away from the more important spiritual side of life. Instead of wasting time working on new inventions, like the telegraph and the railroad, Thoreau thinks people should work on their souls. He sees no need to travel farther and faster on the railroad. He thinks people should not be in such a hurry to get nowhere different in their lives.

◆ ◆ ◆

Vocabulary Development

frittered (FRIT erd) **away** wasted, bit by bit

---

2. **founder** (FOWN duhr) *v.* fill up with water and sink.
3. **dead reckoning** (REK uhn ing) sailing without using the stars to guide you.

Time is but the stream I go a-fishing in. I drink at it; but while I drink I see the sandy bottom and detect how shallow it is. Its thin current slides away, but eternity remains. I would drink deeper; fish in the sky, whose bottom is pebbly with stars. I cannot count one. I know not the first letter of the alphabet. I have always been regretting that I was not as wise as the day I was born. The intellect is a cleaver; it discerns and rifts[4] its way into the secret of things. I do not wish to be any more busy with my hands than is necessary. My head is hands and feet. I feel all my best faculties concentrated in it.

◆　◆　◆

Thoreau explains why he leaves his cabin on Walden Pond and returns to civilization.

◆　◆　◆

I left the woods for as good a reason as I went there. Perhaps it seemed to me that I had several more lives to live, and could not spare any more time for that one. It is remarkable how easily and insensibly[5] we fall into a particular route, and make a beaten track for ourselves. I had not lived there a week before my feet wore a path from my door to the pondside; and though it is five or six years since I trod[6] it, it is still quite distinct. It is true, I fear that others may have fallen into it, and so helped to keep it open. The surface

---

Vocabulary Development

cleaver (KLEE ver) n. a tool for cutting.
discerns (di SERNZ) v. recognizes separate ideas
faculties (FAK uhl teez) n. powers; abilities

---

4. **rifts** cuts through; divides.
5. **insensibly** (in SEN suh blee) adv. without noticing.
6. **trod** walked.

TAKE NOTES

English Language Development

Using an *a-* before an *-ing* verb form is not standard English, but it occurs in nonstandard spoken English:

Standard: I'm *going* now.
Nonstandard: I'm *a-going* now.

Circle the nonstandard word in the first underlined sentence, and show how it would appear in standard English.

Stop to Reflect

What does the second underlined statement mean? Circle the letter of the best answer below.

(a) It is important to keep busy.

(b) Being disabled need not prevent someone from leading a full life.

(c) Thinking is more important than physical action.

(d) The senses of sight, smell, taste, and hearing are more important than the sense of touch.

Vocabulary and Pronunciation

The word *route* has two pronunciations. Some people say it to rhyme with *spout*. Others say it the same as *root*. What does the word mean here?

TAKE NOTES

English Language Development

Circle the punctuation mark that tells you to pronounce this sentence with strong feeling.

Literary Analysis

Thoreau's **style** includes figurative language, or language not meant to be taken literally. Circle an example of figurative language in the bracketed paragraph.

English Language Development

Poorest is the **superlative form** of the adjective poor. You use the superlative to compare more than two people, groups, or things:

• They are *poor*.

• They are *poorer* than she is.

• Of all the people in town, they are the *poorest*.

Short adjectives, like *poor*, usually add *-est* to form the superlative. Longer ones usually use *most:*

• Of all the people in Concord, Thoreau was the *most unusual.*

Circle two more superlative adjectives in this selection.

---

of the earth is soft and impressible by the feet of men; and so with the paths which the mind travels. How worn and dusty, then, must be the highways of the world, how deep the ruts of tradition and conformity!

◆　◆　◆

Thoreau explains the things he learned from living in the woods. First, if a person follows his or her dreams, he or she will be rewarded in unexpected ways. Second, the more simply a person lives, the more rewarding his or her life will be. And last, there is no need to try to be like everyone else.

◆　◆　◆

Why should we be in such desperate <u>haste</u> to succeed, and in such desperate <u>enterprises</u>? If a man does not keep <u>pace</u> with his companions, perhaps it is because he hears a different drummer. Let him step to the music which he hears, however measured[7] or far away.

◆　◆　◆

To Thoreau, being alone is not the same as being lonely. And being poor does not stop you from enjoying the important things in life.

◆　◆　◆

However <u>mean</u> your life is, meet it and live it; do not <u>shun</u> it and call it hard names. It is not so bad as you are. It looks poorest when you are richest. The faultfinder will find faults even in paradise. Love your life, poor as it is. You may

---

Vocabulary Development

haste (HAYST) *n.* speed
enterprises (EN ter pry ziz) *n.* projects; undertakings
pace (PAYS) *n.* step
mean (MEEN) *adj.* low; petty
shun (SHUN) *v.* avoid

---

7. **measured** slow and steady.

perhaps have some pleasant, thrilling, glorious hours, even in a poorhouse. <u>The setting sun is reflected from the windows of the almshouse[8] as brightly as from the rich man's abode;[9] the snow melts before its door as early in the spring.</u> I do not see but a quiet mind may live as contentedly there, and have as cheering thoughts, as in a palace. The town's poor seem to me often to live the most independent lives of any. Maybe they are simply great enough to receive without misgiving. Most think that they are above being supported by the town; but it oftener happens that they are not above supporting themselves by dishonest means, which should be more <u>disreputable</u>. <u>Cultivate poverty like a garden herb, like sage. Do not trouble yourself much to get new things, whether clothes or friends. Turn the old;[10] return to them. Things do not change; we change. Sell your clothes and keep your thoughts.</u>

◆ ◆ ◆

Thoreau concludes with a story about a local farm family. They have a sixty-year-old kitchen table made from the wood of an apple tree. One day the family hears odd sounds from deep inside the table. Then, after several weeks, out comes a strong,

Stop to Reflect

What does the underlined statement literally mean? Circle the letter of the best answer.

(a) Rich and poor alike can enjoy love and friendship in life.

(b) Rich and poor alike can enjoy the wonders of nature.

(c) It is better to be rich than poor.

(d) The people who deserve to be rich are rich, and the people who deserve to be poor are poor.

Reading Check

What does Thoreau think is more important than clothes? Answer by circling a word in the underlined passage.

Reading Strategy

Below, **evaluate the writer's philosophy** about the poor by circling whether you agree or disagree. Then, use your own knowledge or experiences to support your opinion.

(1) I agree/disagree that the poor are more independent.

(2) Support: _____

_____

_____

_____

Vocabulary Development

contentedly (kuhn TEN tid lee) *adv.* with happy satisfaction

misgiving (mis GIV ing) *n.* regret

disreputable (dis REP yuh tuh buhl) *adj.* having a bad reputation; considered bad by society

cultivate (KUL tuh vayt) *v.* grow; encourage

---

8. **almshouse** (AHMZ HOWS) *n.* a homeless shelter for the poor.

9. **abode** (uh BOHD) *n.* home; residence.

10. **Turn the old** turn worn old clothes inside out so that you can keep wearing them.

Which elements of Thoreau's style are most clearly illustrated in the last two paragraphs? Check two.

____ simple language

____ images from nature

____ occasional short sentences

____ figurative language

Stop to Reflect

What does the underlined sentence mean?

_____

_____

_____

_____

_____

_____

beautiful bug. It hatched from an egg that had apparently been laid in the apple tree when it was still alive, sixty years before.

◆ ◆ ◆

Who knows what beautiful and winged life, whose egg has been buried for ages under many <u>concentric</u> layers of woodenness in the dead dry life of society, deposited at first in the alburnum[11] of the green and living tree, which has been gradually <u>converted</u> into the semblance of its well-seasoned tomb[12]—heard perchance[13] <u>gnawing</u> out now for years by the astonished family of man, as they sat round the festive board[14]—may unexpectedly come forth from amidst society's most trivial and handselled[15] furniture, to enjoy its perfect summer life at last!

I do not say that John or Jonathan[16] will realize all this; but such is the character of that morrow[17] which mere lapse of time can never make to dawn. The light which puts out our eyes is darkness to us. <u>Only that day dawns to which we are awake.</u> There is more day to dawn. The sun is but a morning star.

Vocabulary Development

concentric (kuhn SEN trik) *adj.*   with one circle inside another

converted (kuhn VER tid) *v.*   changed

gnawing (NAW ing) *adj.*   chewing

---

11. alburnum (al BUR nuhm) *n.* the soft wood between the bark and the core of the tree.

12. the semblance (SEM bluhns) **of its well-seasoned tomb** what seems like an aged tomb, or burial place.

13. perchance (puhr CHANS) *adv.* perhaps.

14. festive (FES tiv) **board** table.

15. handselled (HAN suhld) *adj.* handmade.

16. John or Jonathan average person.

17. the morrow (MAHR oh) the next day.

from Civil Disobedience

Henry David Thoreau

Summary In 1846, Henry David Thoreau spent a night in jail. He had refused to pay his taxes because he believed the tax money would support the war against Mexico. He opposed the war. After he was released, he wrote "Civil Disobedience." In this essay, Thoreau argues that people should oppose laws that violate their principles. In this excerpt, he explains his views on government.

Note-taking Guide

Use this chart to keep track of Thoreau's comments about the government.

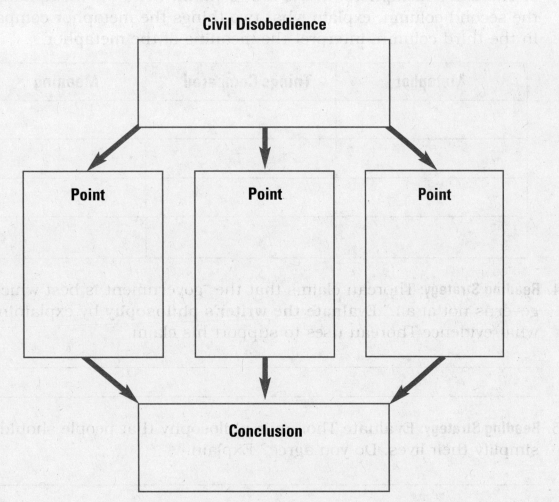

Civil Disobedience

Point

Point

Point

Conclusion

from Walden • from Civil Disobedience

1. **Deduce:** What did Thoreau hope to do by living at Walden Pond?

_____

_____

2. **Literary Analysis:** Thoreau's writing **style** uses sentences that build to a climax. Reread the paragraph in *Walden* that begins "Still we live meanly." How is this paragraph an example of Thoreau's style?

_____

_____

3. **Literary Analysis: Metaphors** are figures of speech that compare two unlike things without using *like* or *as*. Use this chart to identify two of Thoreau's metaphors. In the first column, write the metaphor. In the second column, explain what two things the metaphor compares. In the third column, interpret the meaning of the metaphor.

Metaphor	Things Compared	Meaning

4. **Reading Strategy:** Thoreau claims that the "government is best which governs not at all." **Evaluate the writer's philosophy** by explaining what evidence Thoreau uses to support his claim.

_____

_____

5. **Reading Strategy:** Evaluate Thoreau's philosophy that people should simplify their lives. Do you agree? Explain.

_____

_____

Emily Dickinson's Poetry

LITERARY ANALYSIS

Poets use rhyme in poetry to create musical sounds and to organize groups of lines, or stanzas.

- **Exact rhyme** occurs when two words have identical sounds in their final syllables. Example: *day* and *away*.
- **Slant rhyme** occurs when two words have final sounds that are similar but not identical. Example: *glove* and *prove*.

Dickinson creates effects in her poetry by using both exact rhyme and slant rhyme.

READING STRATEGY

Poets use figurative language to create **images,** or word pictures.

- Images help make abstract ideas about love, life, and death more concrete.
- When you **analyze images,** you use an image to figure out a poet's message.
- Use this chart to record your ideas about the images in Dickinson's poems.

Image	Abstract Idea

Emily Dickinson's Poetry

Summaries In "Because I could not stop for Death," the poet imagines that a carriage takes her to her grave after she dies. The poet also writes about her own death in "I heard a fly buzz—when I died." "There's a certain Slant of light" tells about the sad afternoon light of winter. In "My life closed twice before its close," the poet thinks about enduring a terrible event. The poet speaks of the soul's tendency to prefer one person over all others in "The Soul selects her own Society." "The Brain—is wider than the sky—" is a poem that claims that all of nature and even God can be contained in the mind. In "There is a solitude of space," the soul offers more solitude than any earthly place. The poet suggests that things can only be known through their opposites in "Water, is taught by thirst."

Note-taking Guide

Record references to nature found in Dickinson's poems in the diagram.

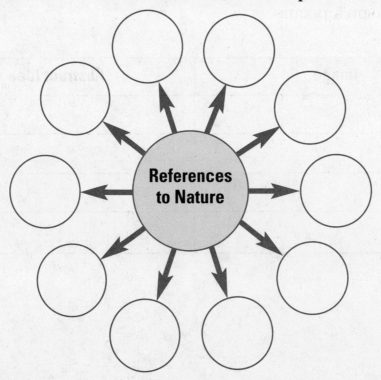

References to Nature

Emily Dickinson's Poetry

1. **Literary Analysis: Slant rhyme** occurs when lines end with sounds that are similar but not identical. Identify the words used to create **slant rhymes** for the words *Civility* and *Eternity* in "Because I could not stop for Death."

   _____

   _____

2. **Literary Analysis:** To identify rhyme scheme in a poem, use a system of letters. Give the same letter to each end word that contains an identical or similar sound. The chart below shows the *abc* rhyme scheme. Use the chart to describe the pattern of rhyme in "There's a certain slant of light."

	Stanza One	Two	Three	Four
Line 1	a			
Line 2	b			
Line 3	c			
Line 4	b			

3. **Reading Strategy: Analyze** the **image** Dickinson uses to represent a gravesite in "Because I could not stop for Death."

   _____

   _____

4. **Reading Strategy:** Identify two images in "The Brain—is wider than the Sky." Write them on the lines.

   _____

   _____

Walt Whitman's Poetry

LITERARY ANALYSIS

Some poetry is written with a fixed meter or line pattern. Other poetry is written in **free verse**.

- Free verse has irregular meter and varied line lengths.
- Free verse imitates the flow of natural speech.
- Walt Whitman was the first American poet to use free verse.
- Whitman used free verse because it allowed him to choose line lengths and rhythms that best fit his message:

"These are really the thoughts of all men in all ages and lands, they are not original with me . . ."

READING STRATEGY

You can **infer a poet's attitude** by looking at his or her choice of words and details. When you make an inference, you use details and your own knowledge to draw a conclusion.

Notice key words and images in Whitman's poetry:

"I jump from the crossbeams and seize the clover and timothy, And roll head over heels…"

Language and details such as "roll read over heels," "seize," and "jump" help you infer that the speaker likes rural life. Use this chart to makes inferences about Whitman's attitudes.

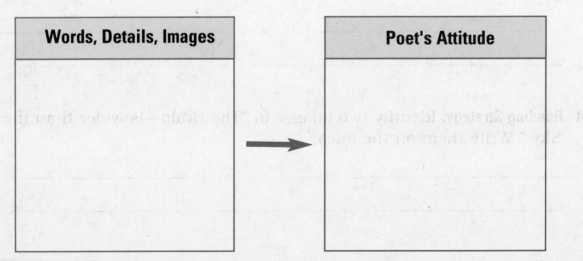

Words, Details, Images	Poet's Attitude

Walt Whitman's Poetry

Summaries In the Preface to the 1855 Edition of *Leaves of Grass*, the speaker says the United States is a great poem. In **"Song of Myself,"** he describes himself. Then, he considers the grass as a symbol of immortality. The speaker leaves a lecture on the stars to view the heavens in "perfect silence" in **"When I Heard the Learn'd Astronomer." "By the Bivouac's Fitful Flame"** is a poem that considers the army, life, and death. The speaker tells about carpenters, masons, and other workers in **"I Hear America Singing."** In **"A Noiseless Patient Spider,"** the speaker compares a spider's work to that of a soul trying to become attached to something.

Note-taking Guide

Write the main idea of each poem in this chart.

Poem	Main Idea
from Preface to the 1855 Edition of Leaves of Grass	
from Song of Myself	
When I Heard the Learn'd Astronomer	
By the Bivouac's Fitful Frame	
I Hear America Singing	
A Noiseless Patient Spider	

Walt Whitman's Poetry

1. **Synthesize:** Whitman believed that the world of nature mirrors the human spirit. What details in "A Noiseless Patient Spider" show this belief?

_____

_____

2. **Literary Analysis:** How does **free verse** allow Whitman to share his ideas in "Song of Myself"?

_____

_____

3. **Literary Analysis:** Catalogs are lists of things that poets use in their poems. Whitman uses catalogs in his poetry to make key points. Look for lists that Whitman uses in "When I Heard the Learn'd Astronomer." Use this chart to record what you find.

Poem	Cataloging	What the Details Share	Effect

4. **Reading Strategy:** In "When I Heard the Learn'd Astronomer." List three words that help you **infer the speaker's attitude**.

_____

_____

An Episode of War •
Willie Has Gone to the War

LITERARY ANALYSIS

Realism and **Naturalism** were literary movements that developed in the 1800s. A literary movement is a way of thinking and writing. These movements began as a reaction to Romanticism.

- Romanticism focuses on emotion, imagination, and nature.
- Realism tries to portray life as it really is. Writers of realism focus on ordinary people facing the challenges of everyday life.
- Naturalism also focuses on ordinary people. Writers of naturalism emphasize the power of nature, environment, and other forces over people.

READING SKILL

Recognizing historical details as you read gives historical context to a story. Context means the information and opinions that help you understand important ideas and events. Historical context includes the time, environment, culture, and political and social attitudes from a certain time period.

You can recognize historical details in several ways:

Authors use words, characters, and actions to provide context. Pay attention to what the author focuses on, what the characters say and think, and what happens to them.

Details about the landscape, time, and culture provide other important clues about the context. Notice how the author describes people, places, and things.

As you read, use this chart to record details in the selections that provide historical context.

Event	Historical Context
Battles	
Medical Practices	
Political Situations	
Social Attitudes	

An Episode of War

Stephen Crane

Summary A soldier fighting in the Civil War prepares the day's portions of coffee for his squad. As he measures the coffee, a bullet strikes him in the arm and changes his life. This story follows the soldier as he confronts the tragedy of war.

Note-taking Guide

Use this chart to record what happens to the lieutenant.

Beginning Event

> A lieutenant is shot in the arm while measuring coffee for his squad.

↓

>

↓

>

↓

>

Final Outcome

>

An Episode of War

Stephen Crane

The lieutenant's rubber blanket lay on the ground, and upon it he had poured the company's supply of coffee. Corporals and other representatives of the grimy and hot-throated men who lined the breast-work[1] had come for each squad's portion.

The lieutenant was frowning and serious at this task of division. His lips pursed as he drew with his sword various crevices in the heap, until brown squares of coffee, <u>astoundingly</u> equal in size, appeared on the blanket. He was on the verge of a great triumph in mathematics, and the corporals were thronging forward, each to reap a little square, when suddenly the lieutenant cried out and looked quickly at a man near him as if he suspected it was a case of personal assault. The others cried out also when they saw blood upon the lieutenant's sleeve.

♦ ♦ ♦

The lieutenant stares at the forest in the distance. He sees little puffs of smoke from the gunfire. The lieutenant holds his sword in his left hand. He struggles to put it in its scabbard, or holder. An orderly-sergeant helps him. The men stare thoughtfully at the wounded lieutenant.

♦ ♦ ♦

There were others who <u>proffered</u> assistance. One timidly presented his shoulder and asked the lieutenant if he cared to lean upon it, but the latter[2] waved him away mournfully.

Vocabulary Development

astoundingly (uh STOWN ding lee) *adv.* amazingly
proffered (PRAH ferd) *v.* offered

---

1. **breast-work** low wall put up quickly as a defense in battle.
2. **the latter** the second in a list of two people or things; here, "the latter" refers to the lieutenant.

TAKE NOTES

Reading Strategy

Circle two details in the first paragraph that reflect the **historical context** of the story.

Culture Note

During the Civil War, conditions in the army were very different from what they are today. In today's military, who would be responsible for handling food supplies?

_____

_____

_____

Stop to Reflect

How does one soldier offer to help the lieutenant?

_____

_____

_____

He wore the look of one who knows he is the victim of a terrible disease and understands his helplessness. He again stared over the breast-work at the forest, and then, turning, went slowly rearward. He held his right wrist tenderly in his left hand as if the wounded arm was made of very brittle glass.

And the men in silence stared at the wood, then at the departing lieutenant: then at the wood, then at the lieutenant.

As the wounded officer passed from the line of battle, he was enabled to see many things which as a participant in the fight were unknown to him. He saw a general on a black horse gazing over the lines of blue infantry at the green woods which veiled his problems. An aide galloped furiously, dragged his horse suddenly to a halt, saluted, and presented a paper. It was, for a wonder, precisely like a historical painting.

♦ ♦ ♦

The lieutenant observes the swirling movement of a crew of men with heavy guns. The shooting crackles like brush-fires. The lieutenant comes across some stragglers. They tell him how to find the field hospital. At the roadside, an officer uses his handkerchief to bandage the lieutenant's wound.

♦ ♦ ♦

The low white tents of the hospital were grouped around an old schoolhouse. There was here a singular[3] commotion.

Vocabulary Development

brittle (BRIT tuhl) *adj.* stiff and easily broken

---

3. **singular** (SING yoo ler) *adj.* remarkable, noticeable.

In the foreground two ambulances interlocked wheels in the deep mud. The drivers were tossing the blame of it back and forth, gesticulating[4] and berating,[5] while from the ambulances, both crammed with wounded, there came an occasional groan. An interminable crowd of bandaged men were coming and going. Great numbers sat under the trees nursing heads or arms or legs. There was a dispute of some kind raging on the steps of the schoolhouse. Sitting with his back against a tree a man with a face as grey as a new army blanket was serenely smoking a corncob pipe. The lieutenant wished to rush forward and inform him that he was dying.

◆ ◆ ◆

A doctor greets the lieutenant and notices his wounded arm. The doctor looks at the wound.

◆ ◆ ◆

The doctor cried out impatiently, "What mutton-head had tied it up that way anyhow?" The lieutenant answered, "Oh, a man."

When the wound was disclosed the doctor fingered it disdainfully. "Humph," he said. "You come along with me and I'll 'tend to you." His voice contained the same scorn as if he were saying: "You will have to go to jail."

Vocabulary Development

interminable (in TERM uh nuh buhl) *adj.* endless
dispute (dis PYOOT) *n.* disagreement
serenely (suh REEN lee) *adv.* calmly
disdainfully (dis DAYN fuh lee) *adv.* scornfully

---

4. **gesticulating** (jes TIK yoo layt ing) *v.* making vigorous gestures.
5. **berating** (bee RAYT ing) *v.* criticizing harshly.

TAKE NOTES

Read Fluently

Read the bracketed passage aloud. What impression does the passage give you of conditions at the field hospital?

_____

_____

_____

Vocabulary and Pronunciation

Notice that the verb *gesticulate* has the same root as the noun *gesture*. What verb that has the same root as the adjective *interminable*? Hint: Say the word to yourself without its prefix, *-in*.

_____

Vocabulary and Pronunciation

The word *mutton-head,* meaning "stupid person" or "fool," is an example of slang or informal English. Give two examples of slang expressions in your native language.

1. _____
2. _____

Stop to Reflect

What does the doctor's attitude toward the lieutenant show about the doctor?

_____

_____

_____

TAKE NOTES

Reading Strategy

How is the end of the story an example of **Naturalistic** writing, or writing that assumes that people are influenced by forces they cannot control?

_____

_____

_____

The lieutenant had been very <u>meek</u>, but now his face was flushed, and he looked into the doctor's eyes. "I guess I won't have it <u>amputated</u>," he said.

"Nonsense, man! Nonsense! Nonsense!" cried the doctor. "Come along, now. I won't amputate it. Come along. Don't be a baby."

"Let go of me," said the lieutenant, holding back <u>wrathfully</u>, his glance fixed upon the door of the old schoolhouse, as sinister to him as the portals[6] of death.

And this is the story of how the lieutenant lost his arm. When he reached home, his sisters, his mother, his wife, sobbed for a long time at the sight of the flat sleeve. "Oh, well," he said, standing shamefaced in the midst of these tears, "I don't suppose it matters so much as all that."

Vocabulary Development

meek (MEEK) *adj.* humble, mild-mannered
amputated (AMP yoo tay tuhd) *v.* cut off
wrathfully (RATH fuh lee) *adv.* angrily

---

6. **portals** (PORT uhlz) *n.* doors.

152 English Learner's Notebook

© Pearson Education, Inc., publishing as Pearson Prentice Hall.

Willie Has Gone to the War

George Cooper

Summary These song lyrics show another side to the Civil War. The speaker of the poem is a woman who waits by a brook. That is where she last saw the man she loves before he went to fight in the war. Her words speak of her sadness and how she misses him.

Note-taking Guide

Use this character wheel to record what you learn about Willie.

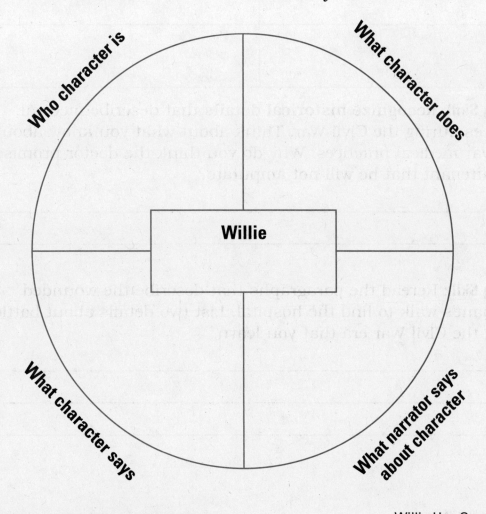

An Episode of War • Willie Has Gone to the War

1. **Apply:** According to the Naturalists, humans are weak beings subject to mysterious forces. How might this idea apply to "An Episode of War"?

_____

_____

2. **Literary Analysis:** Use this chart to record examples of **Realism** and **Naturalism** from the story.

Realism	Naturalism

3. **Reading Skill: Recognize historical details** that describe medical practices during the Civil War. Think about what you know about Civil War medical practices. Why do you think the doctor promises the lieutenant that he will not amputate?

_____

_____

4. **Reading Skill:** Reread the paragraphs that describe the wounded lieutenant's walk to find the hospital. List two details about battle during the Civil War era that you learn.

_____

_____

_____

Swing Low, Sweet Chariot • Go Down, Moses

LITERARY ANALYSIS

A **refrain** is part of a song or poem.

- A refrain can be a word, phrase, line, or group of lines.
- A refrain is repeated throughout a poem or song.
- A refrain emphasizes the main ideas of a poem or song.
- A refrain helps form a poem or song's rhythm.

Spirituals usually have at least one refrain. Some spirituals have more than one refrain. "Coming for to carry me home" is a refrain in "Swing Low, Sweet Chariot."

As you read these spirituals, look for one or more refrains. Think about what each refrain means.

READING STRATEGY

People write songs to be heard, not to be read. This means that listening is an important skill for appreciating lyrics.

- Read each spiritual aloud.
- Listen to the rhythm of the lyrics
- Pay attention to rhymes and other repeated sounds. For example, the opening line in "Go Down, Moses" contains three stressed, or emphasized, syllables in a row.

Often, rhythms and sounds suggest specific moods. As you read the spirituals, think about what moods the sounds suggest. Use this chart to record the moods you feel in the lyrics.

Song Text
Go down Moses, /Way down in Egypt land /Tell old Pharoah /To let my people go.

Mood Conveyed

Swing Low, Sweet Chariot
• Go Down, Moses

Summaries In the spiritual "**Swing Low, Sweet Chariot**," the chorus describes a chariot coming to take the singer home to heaven. The singer also describes crossing the river Jordan with a band of angels. If listeners get to heaven first, they are encouraged to tell everyone that the singer is on the way. In "**Go Down, Moses**," the singer tells the story of Moses following God's command to free the Israelites from Egypt. Moses tells the Pharaoh to "let my people go!" or God will punish the Egyptians.

Note-taking Guide

Write down the **symbols** that you see in these spirituals. Symbols are words that stand for something else. Write a brief phrase that explains what you think the symbol stands for. Use your prior knowledge of slavery in the American South.

Symbols	Possible Meaning
chariot	way to escape from slavery; Underground Railroad

Swing Low, Sweet Chariot • Go Down, Moses

1. **Interpret:** Spirituals were often used as "code" songs for escape. What hidden message do you see in "Swing Low, Sweet Chariot"?

_____

_____

2. **Literary Analysis:** A **refrain** can be just one line. What key idea or message is conveyed in the single-line refrain in "Go Down, Moses"?

_____

_____

3. **Reading Strategy: Listening** to a song's rhyme, rhythm, and repetition can help you understand the song's message and mood. Read the songs aloud. Then, identify how rhythm, rhyme, and repetition reinforce the meaning of these spirituals.

_____

_____

4. **Reading Strategy:** Rhythm, rhyme, and repetition are called sound elements. Use this diagram to compare the sound elements in the two spirituals.

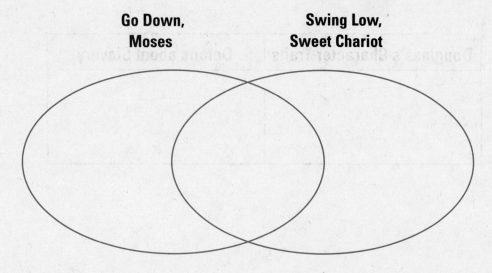

Go Down,
Moses

Swing Low,
Sweet Chariot

from My Bondage and My Freedom

LITERARY ANALYSIS

An **autobiography** is a person's written account of his or her life. Authors of autobiographies often believe that their lives are important in some way. They write about their lives for the following reasons:

- They think the events of their lives are interesting.
- They want people to learn something from their lives.

For example, Frederick Douglass believed that his life proved blacks were as capable, smart, and human as free whites. He wrote his autobiography to share this belief.

As you read about Douglass, notice how the events in his life demonstrate the equality of blacks and whites.

READING SKILL

Establishing a purpose for reading helps you focus on an important idea. Establishing a purpose means telling yourself what to look for as you read. For example, as you read from Douglass's autobiography, establish the purpose of learning about his special qualities. Also, read to learn about what it was like to be a slave. Use this chart to record details that support your purpose for reading.

Douglass's Character Traits	Details about Slavery

from My Bondage and My Freedom

Frederick Douglass

Summary Frederick Douglass learns to read from his mistress. As he reads, he learns that he has the same abilities and the same rights to freedom as white children. Soon, his mistress begins to act differently toward Douglass. The change in his mistress teaches Douglass that slavery makes both slaves and slave-owners less human. His autobiography tells about his struggle to gain knowledge and freedom.

Note-taking Guide

As you read, use this diagram to keep track of the events that occur in this section of Douglass's autobiography.

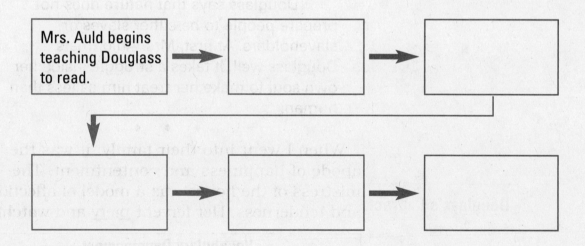

Mrs. Auld begins teaching Douglass to read.

from My Bondage and My Freedom

Frederick Douglass

Did Douglass have an easy or a hard time learning to read? Circle the phrase that serves as a clue to the answer.

English Language Development

A *flint* is a piece of hard, firm stone. What does this comparison suggest about Mrs. Auld's attitude?

_____

_____

_____

I lived in the family of Master Hugh, at Baltimore, seven years, during which time— as the almanac makers say of the weather—my condition was variable. The most interesting feature of my history here, was my learning to read and write, under somewhat marked disadvantages. In attaining this knowledge, I was compelled to resort to indirections by no means <u>congenial</u> to my nature, and which were really humiliating to me. My mistress—who had begun to teach me—was suddenly checked[1] in her <u>benevolent</u> design, by the strong advice of her husband. In faithful compliance with this advice, the good lady had not only ceased to instruct me, herself, but had set her face as a flint against my learning to read by any means.

◆　◆　◆

Douglass says that nature does not prepare people to be either slaves or slaveholders. At first, Mrs. Auld treats Douglass well. It takes a struggle inside her own soul to make her treat him as less than human.

◆　◆　◆

When I went into their family, it was the <u>abode</u> of happiness and contentment. The mistress of the house was a model of affection and tenderness. Her fervent <u>piety</u> and watchful

---

Vocabulary Development

congenial (kuhn JEEN yuhl) *adj.* agreeable
benevolent (buh NEV uh luhnt) *adj.* kindly, charitable
abode (uh BOHD) *n.* home
piety (PY uh tee) *n.* devotion to religious beliefs or practices

---

1. **checked** stopped, prevented.

uprightness made it impossible to see her without thinking and feeling—"that woman is a Christian." There was no sorrow nor suffering for which she had not a tear, and there was no innocent joy for which she did not [have] a smile. She had bread for the hungry, clothes for the naked, and comfort for every mourner that came within her reach. Slavery soon proved its ability to divest[2] her of these excellent qualities, and her home of its early happiness.

◆ ◆ ◆

Mrs. Auld stops teaching Douglass. Then she becomes even more opposed than her husband to his learning to read. She angrily snatches a book or a newspaper from his hand.

◆ ◆ ◆

Mrs. Auld was an apt[3] woman, and the advice of her husband, and her own experience, soon demonstrated, to her entire satisfaction, that education and slavery are incompatible with each other. When this conviction was thoroughly established, I was most narrowly watched in all my movements. If I remained in a separate room from the family for any considerable length of time, I was sure to be suspected of having a book, and was at once called upon to give an account of myself.

◆ ◆ ◆

However, these efforts come too late to stop Douglass from learning to read.

◆ ◆ ◆

Vocabulary Development

incompatible (in kuhm PAT uh buhl) *adj.* not able to exist together with

---

2. **divest** (duh VEST) *v.* strip, remove from.
3. **apt** (APT) *adj.* quick to learn.

TAKE NOTES

English Language Development

In English, two negative words cancel each other out, producing a positive. Try rewriting the underlined sentence without using the words "no," "nor," or "not." Be sure that your sentence has the same meaning as the original sentence.

Stop to Reflect

Underline two phrases that show the effects on Mrs. Auld of being a slaveholder.

Literary Analysis

According to Douglass in this **autobiography,** why were his owners suspicious of him?

_____

_____

_____

Read Fluently

Read the bracketed passage aloud. How did Douglass accomplish his goal of learning to read?

_____

_____

_____

Reading Strategy

One **purpose** for reading Douglass's account is to understand what it was like to be a slave. How does Douglass think his future will be different from the future of his white playmates?

_____

_____

_____

Reading Check

How do human beings react by nature to slavery? Underline the phrase that gives Douglass's opinion.

Seized with a determination to learn to read, at any cost, I hit upon many expedients[4] to accomplish the desired end. The plea which I mainly adopted, and the one by which I was most successful, was that of using my young white playmates, with whom I met in the street, as teachers. I used to carry, almost constantly, a copy of Webster's spelling book in my pocket; and, when sent on errands, or when play time was allowed me, I would step, with my young friends, aside, and take a lesson in spelling. I generally paid my *tuition fee* to the boys, with bread, which I also carried in my pocket.

◆ ◆

Douglass feels grateful to the boys, but he does not want to identify his teachers by name. They might get into trouble for helping him.

◆ ◆ ◆

Although slavery was a delicate subject, and very cautiously talked about among grownup people in Maryland, I frequently talked about it—and that very freely—with the white boys. I would, sometimes, say to them, while seated on a curbstone or a cellar door, "I wish I could be free, as you will be when you get to be men." "You will be free, you know, as soon as you are twenty-one, and can go where you like, but I am a slave for life. Have I not as good a right to be free as you have?" Words like these, I observed, always troubled them; and I had no small satisfaction in wringing from the boys, occasionally, that fresh and bitter condemnation of slavery, that springs from nature, unseared and unperverted.[5]

◆ ◆ ◆

---

4. **expedients** (ek SPEE dee uhnts) *n.* ways of getting things done.
5. **unperverted** (un puhr VERT id) *adj.* uncorrupted, pure.

Douglass never meets a boy who defends slavery. His love of liberty grows steadily. By age thirteen, he has learned to read. He buys a schoolbook. But the praise of liberty in what he reads makes him feel unhappy and depressed. He cannot bear the idea that he will be a slave all his life.

◆ ◆ ◆

Once awakened by the silver trump[6] of knowledge, my spirit was roused to eternal wakefulness. Liberty! the inestimable[7] birthright of every man, had, for me, converted every object into an asserter of this great right. It was heard in every sound, and beheld in every object. It was ever present, to torment me with a sense of my wretched condition. The more beautiful and charming were the smiles of nature, the more horrible and desolate was my condition. I saw nothing without seeing it, and I heard nothing without hearing it. I do not exaggerate, when I say, that it looked from every star, smiled in every calm, breathed in every wind, and moved in every storm.

◆ ◆ ◆

Douglass has no doubt that Mrs. Auld notices his attitude. While nature has made them friends, slavery has made them enemies. Douglass is not cruelly treated, but he still hates the condition of slavery.

◆ ◆ ◆

I had been cheated. I saw through the attempt to keep me in ignorance . . . The feeding and clothing me well, could not atone for taking my liberty from me. The smiles of

---

Vocabulary Development

atone (uh TOHN) *v.* make up for

---

6. **trump** trumpet.
7. **inestimable** (in ES tuh muh buhl) *adj.* priceless.

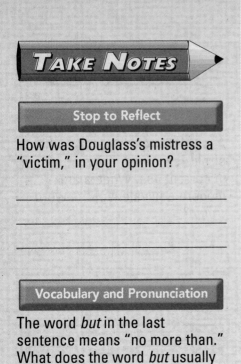

Stop to Reflect

How was Douglass's mistress a "victim," in your opinion?

_____

_____

_____

Vocabulary and Pronunciation

The word *but* in the last sentence means "no more than." What does the word *but* usually mean when it joins two ideas?

_____

_____

_____

my mistress could not remove the deep sorrow that dwelt in my young bosom. Indeed, these, in time, came only to deepen my sorrow. She had changed; and the reader will see that I had changed, too. We were both victims of the same overshadowing evil—*she*, as mistress, *I*, as slave. I will not <u>censure</u> her harshly; she cannot censure me, for she knows I speak but the truth, and have acted in my opposition to slavery, just as she herself would have acted, in a reverse of circumstances.

◆   ◆   ◆

Vocabulary Development

censure (SEN shuhr) *v.* condemn as wrong

---

from My Bondage and My Freedom

1. **Connect:** How does gaining knowledge change Douglass's attitude?

   _____

   _____

   _____

2. **Literary Analysis:** How does Douglass use his **autobiography** to make a case against slavery?

   _____

   _____

   _____

3. **Literary Analysis:** An autobiography is shaped by the author's own feelings, beliefs, and experiences. In what ways would the selection be different if it were Mrs. Auld's autobiography?

   _____

   _____

   _____

4. **Reading Strategy:** After **establishing a purpose** to learn more about slavery, tell what you learned from Douglass's autobiography. Use this chart.

Douglass's Account	Effects of Slavery
_____	_____

An Occurrence at Owl Creek Bridge

LITERARY ANALYSIS

A story's **point of view** depends on who is telling the story.

- A story with an *omniscient point of view* means that the narrator is an "all-knowing" observer. The narrator is not personally or emotionally involved in the events.

- A story with a *limited third-person point of view* means that the narrator writes about events as a character experiences them. The narrator tells the personal thoughts and feelings of one character.

The emotion and sense of time in a story can shift when the point of view changes. The main character in Bierce's story has an unreal sense of time. The character's unusual sense of time changes how the reader experiences time in the story.

READING SKILL

In Bierce's story, the action moves back and forth in time. He does not write events in **chronological order**. Chronological order means the order in which events take place. Use the chart below to put events in chronological order.

Event

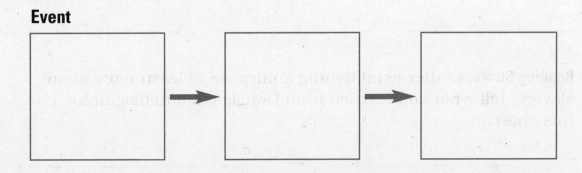

An Occurrence at Owl Creek Bridge

Ambrose Bierce

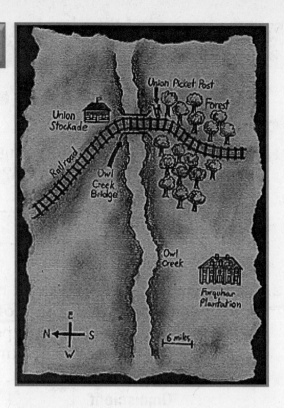

Summary A southern plantation owner is about to be hanged. He stands at the edge of the Owl Creek Bridge. Union soldiers prepare to put him to death for trying to burn down the bridge. A sergeant releases the plank that supports the plantation owner, and the author describes what happens as the man falls.

Note-taking Guide

Make a story map by completing the chart below. Record your responses in the second column.

Setting	
Characters	
Main Events	
High Point of Story	
Conclusion	

An Occurrence at Owl Creek Bridge

1. **Extend:** What does this story suggest about the mind of a person facing a life or death situation?

   _____

   _____

2. **Literary Analysis:** A story's point of view depends on who is telling the story. Bierce uses two **points of view** in this story. Analyze the story to identify these two different points of view. Determine the effects created by each one. Write your responses in a chart like this one.

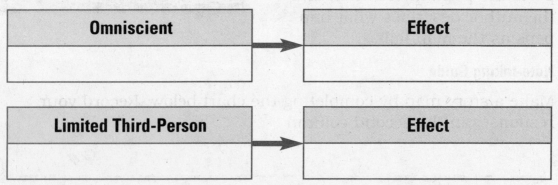

Omniscient	→	Effect

Limited Third-Person	→	Effect

3. **Literary Analysis:** The point of view shifts in the last paragraph of the story. What effect does that shift have on you?

   _____

   _____

4. **Reading Skill: Identify the chronological order** in the story by deciding which happened first: Farquhar's encounter with the Federal scout or his preoccupation with his ticking watch.

   _____

   _____

5. **Reading Skill:** How much real time probably passes between the opening scene of the story and the last scene of the story? Explain your answer.

   _____

   _____

The Gettysburg Address • Second Inaugural Address • Letter to His Son

LITERARY ANALYSIS

The words a writer uses and the way he or she arranges them is called **diction**.

- Diction can be formal or informal. It can be casual or serious.
- Diction can be direct, or it can be vague and symbolic.

A writer uses diction to suggest feelings about the information he or she is presenting. A writer adjusts diction to suit the audience and purpose for writing. Look at these examples of formal and informal diction from the selections:

Lincoln: "Four score and seven years ago our fathers brought forth . . ."

Lee: ". . . I must try and be patient and await the end . . ."

As you read, pay attention to how each writer uses words differently.

READING STRATEGY

It is helpful to know background information about a historical event when reading a historical document. Use background knowledge to better understand an author's purpose and meaning. For example, **background knowledge** about the Civil War will help you understand the ideas and feelings in these selections. Use this chart to organize your ideas.

	Concept in the Text	Background Knowledge	What Text Means
The Gettysburg Address			
Second Inaugural Address			
Letter to His Son			

The Gettysburg Address • Second Inaugural Address
Abraham Lincoln

Letter to His Son
Robert E. Lee

Summaries Lincoln delivers a brief speech to honor those who died at the battle of Gettysburg, Pennsylvania. In **"The Gettysburg Address,"** he calls on people to continue fighting to preserve the Union.

Lincoln delivers his **"Second Inaugural Address"** while the Civil War continues. He urges citizens to work for peace.

Robert E. Lee writes this **"Letter to His Son"** shortly before the Civil War starts. Lee discusses the conflict he feels over his belief in the Union and his commitment to his home state of Virginia.

Note-taking Guide

Use this chart to write down the main points from the selections.

	The Gettysburg Address	Second Inaugural Address	Letter to His Son
Point 1	The nation was formed around the idea that all men are created equal.	The Civil War began because the nation was divided on the issue of slavery.	Washington would be sad to see what happened to the nation he fought hard to form.
Point 2			
Point 3			
Point 4			

The Gettysburg Address • Second Inaugural Address • Letter to His Son

1. **Apply:** In what ways are Lincoln's addresses similar to and different from modern presidential addresses?

   _____

   _____

   _____

2. **Literary Analysis:** Analyze the **diction** of Lincoln and Lee. Use the chart to provide examples. Then, explain why each writer's diction is appropriate for his audience and purpose.

   _____

	Examples of Diction	Audience	Purpose
Lincoln			
Lee			

3. **Reading Strategy:** Use **background knowledge** to explain why Lincoln's speech at Gettysburg is so short.

   _____

   _____

   _____

4. **Reading Strategy:** Before the Civil War, Robert E. Lee had a long career in the United States Army. Why do you think Lee was so opposed to states seceding from the Union?

   _____

   _____

   _____

PUBLIC DOCUMENTS

About Public Documents

A **public document** is an official government paper. A law is an example of a public document. All citizens have the right to read, analyze, and discuss public documents.

This public document is the text of an official announcement. President Lincoln signed this announcement on January 1, 1863. The announcement says that "all persons held as slaves" in those states in rebellion against the Union are freed. Many historians believe that this document changed the course of the Civil War.

Reading Strategy

Some public documents are **objective**. This means that they present factual information and do not support a point of view or an opinion. Other public documents are **subjective**. These documents include opinions and express a particular point of view.

Read subjective public documents critically to **analyze an author's beliefs**. To analyze an author's beliefs, you must find the author's opinions. Then, you should look at the beliefs and assumptions the author uses to support his or her opinions. Assumptions are claims that must be true if the opinion or belief is true.

As you read, keep these points in mind:
- Writers can state their assumptions *explicitly*. This means that an author tells you exactly what he or she thinks.
- Often, writers state their assumptions *implicitly*. This means that an author does not tell you his or her assumptions directly. They are implied in the author's arguments.

Step One	Step Two	Step Three
Look for opinion phrases such as *I think, I believe,* or *in my opinion*. These phrases signal explicit beliefs.	Look for words that suggest opinions. These words might be adjectives that have clear opposites. For example, one writer might say that an action is *just*; another might say that it is *unfair*.	Look for details that suggest a specific point of view. Read the document sentence by sentence. Think about whether each sentence is factual or whether someone can make an argument against it.

By the President of the United States of America:

A Proclamation.

Whereas, on the twenty-second day of September, in the year of our Lord one thousand eight hundred and sixty-two, a proclamation was issued by the President of the United States, containing, among other things, the following, to wit:

"That on the first day of January, in the year of our Lord one thousand eight hundred and sixty-three, all persons held as slaves within any State or designated part of a State, the people whereof shall then be in rebellion against the United States, shall be then, thenceforward, and forever free; and the Executive Government of the United States, including the military and naval authority thereof, will recognize and maintain the freedom of such persons, and will do no act or acts to repress such persons, or any of them, in any efforts they may make for their actual freedom"

"That the Executive will, on the first day of January aforesaid, by proclamation, designate the States and parts of States, if any, in which the people thereof, respectively, shall then be in rebellion against the United States; and the fact that any State, or the people thereof, shall on that day be, in good faith, represented in the Congress of the United States by members chosen thereto at elections wherein a majority of the qualified voters of such State shall have participated, shall, in the absence of strong countervailing testimony, be deemed conclusive evidence that such State, and the people thereof, are not then in rebellion against the United States."

One way to **analyze an author's beliefs** is to look for words that suggest an opinion. Look at the underlined passage. What belief about war do Lincoln's words express?

_____

_____

_____

Stop to Reflect

The Emancipation Proclamation declared that all slaves in states waging war against the Union would be free as of January 1, 1863. However, the slave states still at war with the Union were not yet under the control of Union armies. As a result, few slaves were actually set free that day. The proclamation, however, became a powerful symbol of hope for African Americans still in slavery.

Now, therefore I, Abraham Lincoln, President of the United States, by virtue of the power in me vested as Commander-in-Chief, of the Army and Navy of the United States in time of actual armed rebellion against the authority and government of the United States, and as a <u>fit and necessary war measure for suppressing said rebellion</u>, do, on this first day of January, in the year of our Lord one thousand eight hundred and sixty-three, and in accordance with my purpose so to do publicly proclaimed for the full period of one hundred days, from the day first above mentioned, order and designate as the States and parts of States wherein the people thereof respectively, are this day in rebellion against the United States, the following, to wit:

Arkansas, Texas, Louisiana, (except the Parishes of St. Bernard, Plaquemines, Jefferson, St. John, St. Charles, St. James Ascension, Assumption, Terrebonne, Lafourche, St. Mary, St. Martin, and Orleans, including the City of New Orleans) Mississippi, Alabama, Florida, Georgia, South Carolina, North Carolina, and Virginia, (except the forty-eight counties designated as West Virginia, and also the counties of Berkley, Accomac, Northampton, Elizabeth City, York, Princess Ann, and Norfolk, including the cities of Norfolk and Portsmouth[)], and which excepted parts, are for the present, left precisely as if this proclamation were not issued.

And by virtue of the power, and for the purpose aforesaid, I do order and declare that all persons held as slaves within said designated States, and parts of States, are, and henceforward shall be free; and that the Executive government of the United States, including the military and naval authorities thereof, will recognize and maintain the freedom of said persons.

And I hereby enjoin upon the people so declared to be free to abstain from all violence, unless in necessary self-defence; and I recommend to them that, in all cases when allowed, they labor faithfully for reasonable wages.

And I further declare and make known, that such persons of suitable condition, will be received into the armed service of the United States to garrison forts, positions, stations, and other places, and to man vessels of all sorts in said service.

And upon this act, sincerely believed to be an act of justice, warranted by the Constitution, upon military necessity, I invoke the considerate judgment of mankind, and the gracious favor of Almighty God.

In witness whereof, I have hereunto set my hand and caused the seal of the United States to be affixed.

Done at the City of Washington, this first day of January, in the year of our Lord one thousand eight hundred and sixty three, and of the Independence of the United States of America the eighty-seventh.

By the President: *Abraham Lincoln*
Secretary of State.   *William H. Seward*

Reading Strategy

What **belief** is explicitly stated by Lincoln in the bracketed paragraph?

_____

_____

_____

Reading Informational Materials

Place and date are key elements of a **public document**. When and where was the Emancipation Proclamation signed?

_____

_____

Why do you think this information is important?

_____

_____

Thinking About Public Documents

1. Why does Lincoln decide to issue the Emancipation Proclamation?

_____

_____

2. Which parts of the United States are not included in the proclamation?

_____

Reading Strategy: Analyzing an Author's Beliefs

3. Think about the implicit and explicit beliefs expressed by Lincoln in the Emancipation Proclamation. What does Lincoln believe about the Constitution's authority, or power?

_____

_____

4. What does Lincoln believe about the need for emancipation?

_____

_____

Timed Writing: Proclamation (25 minutes)

Write a public document to announce a new national holiday or tradition. Select an important event, person, or cause to honor.

_____

Choose a date for your new holiday or tradition. Be sure to tell about the manner in which people will celebrate.

_____

Use your notes to write your proclamation.

Civil War Diaries, Journals, and Letters

LITERARY ANALYSIS

Writers often use **diaries, journals,** and **letters** to record what they think and feel about events in their lives. People may write about what they see, what happens to them, and what they do.

Diaries and journals are usually private. Often, the writer uses an informal, or personal, style of writing. The writer shares his or her thoughts and feelings.

Letters can also be personal. However, they are not as private as diaries and journals. Personal letters are written to a specific person.

You can learn about a historical era by reading diaries, journals, and letters. As you read these selections, use this chart to record details provided by the authors.

Title	Statement From Writer	What It Reveals
Civil War	There may be a chance for peace, after all.	Chestnut doesn't want the country to fight a civil war.

READING STRATEGY

A *fact* is a statement that can be proved to be true. An *opinion* is a judgment that cannot be proved to be true. It is important to **distinguish fact from opinion** in diaries, journals, and letters. As you read, identify statements as fact or opinion. Pay attention to what can be proved true and what can only be supported by arguments.

PREVIEW

Civil War Diaries, Journals, and Letters

Summaries The writers of these selections describe their personal experiences during the Civil War. In **"Civil War,"** Mary Chestnut writes about the tension and excitement in the days before the bombing of Fort Sumter in South Carolina. In **"Recollections of a Private,"** Warren Lee Goss describes the excitement and nervousness he feels when he enlists in the Union army. **"A Confederate Account of the Battle of Gettysburg"** is Randolph McKim's description of the South's costly defeat at the Battle of Gettysburg. In **"An Account of the Battle of Bull Run,"** Stonewall Jackson writes to his wife about his role in the South's first victory. In **"Reaction to the Emancipation Proclamation,"** Reverend Henry M. Turner records the excitement that surrounds the first issuance of the proclamation in September 1862. Finally, in **"An Account of an Experience With Discrimination,"** Sojourner Truth tells about the discrimination she experiences six months after the end of the Civil War.

Note-taking Guide

Use this table to record the main idea of each selection.

Title	Main Idea

Civil War Diaries, Journals, and Letters

1. **Compare and Contrast:** What can you learn from reading these diaries, journals, and letters that you cannot learn from reading a textbook account of the Civil War?

   _____

   _____

2. **Literary Analysis:** Identify one detail from Mary Chesnut's **diary** that shows her dislike of war.

   _____

   _____

3. **Literary Analysis:** What do details in Sojourner Truth's **letter** tell you about her personality?

   _____

   _____

4. **Reading Skill:** Underline the **facts** and draw a circle around the **opinions** in the following passage.

   The forage cap was an ungainly bag with pasteboard top and leather visor; the blouse was the only part which seemed decent; while the overcoat made me feel like a little nubbin of corn in a large preponderance of husk.

5. **Reading Skill:** Record one fact and one opinion from Stonewall Jackson's account in the following chart.

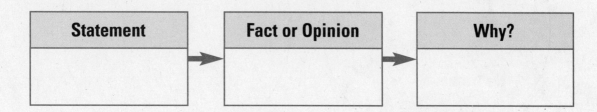

Statement	Fact or Opinion	Why?

The Boys' Ambition *from* Life on the Mississippi • The Notorious Jumping Frog of Calaveras County

LITERARY ANALYSIS

Humor causes people to laugh. Writers who like to use humor in their works are called humorists. Humorists use different techniques to build humor in a story. In the 1800s, many humorists used these comic techniques:

- They exaggerated events.
- They gave their stories narrators with funny qualities but serious tones. The idea that the narrator was not aware of his or her funny qualities made the tone and events humorous.

As you read, pay attention to the details that make these stories funny.

READING STRATEGY

Regional dialect is the way language is used in a specific area or by a particular group of people. Twain liked to use regional dialect in his stories. He was very skilled at using this dialect to build humor.

It takes practice to understand an unfamiliar dialect. Read unfamiliar words or phrases aloud. Reading aloud will help you recognize regional pronunciations of words you already know. Use this chart to write examples of regional dialect from the stories. Rewrite these examples in your own words.

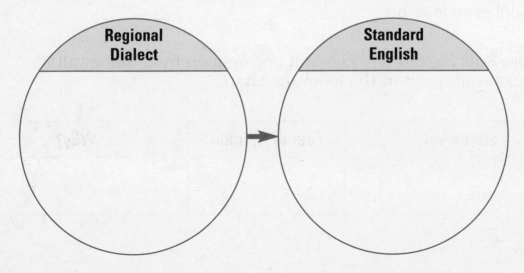

PREVIEW

The Boys' Ambition *from* Life on the Mississippi • The Notorious Jumping Frog of Calaveras County

Mark Twain

Summaries In "The Boys' Ambition," a boy dreams of becoming a steamboat captain. This selection comes from the book *Life on the Mississippi*. In that book Mark Twain shares the thoughts and hopes of a young boy who grows up along the Mississippi River. "**The Notorious Jumping Frog of Calaveras County**" is a humorous tale about a betting man and his frog.

Note-taking Guide

As you read, use this chart to explore Twain's purposes, or reasons, for writing in each selection.

The Boys' Ambition

Author's Purpose	Examples From Text
To inform	
To entertain	
To persuade	
To reflect	

The Notorious Jumping Frog of Calaveras County

Author's Purpose	Examples From Text
To inform	
To entertain	
To persuade	
To reflect	

The Notorious Jumping Frog of Calaveras County

Mark Twain

A friend of the narrator's asks him to call on talkative old Simon Wheeler. The friend says he wants news of his friend Reverend Leonidas W. Smiley. Instead, Wheeler tells the narrator a long-drawn-out story about Jim Smiley. As he tells the story, Wheeler never smiles, and he never frowns.

◆ ◆ ◆

Reading Check

According to Wheeler, what was Jim Smiley's outstanding personality trait? Underline the part of the bracketed passage that gives the answer.

"Rev. Leonidas W. H'm, Reverend Le—well, there was a feller here once by the name of Jim Smiley, in the winter of '49—or maybe it was the spring of '50—I don't <u>recollect</u> exactly, somehow, though what makes me think it was one or the other is because I remember the big flume[1] warn't finished when he first come to the camp; but anyway, he was the curiousest man about always betting on anything that turned up you ever see, if he could get anybody to bet on the other side; and if he couldn't he'd change sides.

◆ ◆ ◆

Literary Analysis

Humor often involves exaggeration, or overstatement. Identify two ways that Wheeler exaggerates.

1. _____

_____

2. _____

_____

Wheeler says Smiley was lucky. He almost always won his bets. He'd bet on horse races, dog fights, cat fights, and chicken fights. If he saw two birds sitting on a fence, he'd bet on which bird would fly first. He had several animals he'd bet on: a mare, a small bull-pup named Andrew Jackson, and lots of others. One day he caught a frog, taught him to catch flies, and named him Dan'l Webster.

◆ ◆ ◆

Vocabulary Development

recollect (rek uh LEKT) *v.* remember

1. **flume** (FLOOM) *n.* artificial channel for carrying water to provide power and transport objects

Well Smiley kep' the beast in a little lattice box and he used to fetch him downtown sometimes and lay for a bet. One day a feller—a stranger in the camp, he was—come acrost him with his box, and says:

"What might it be that you've got in the box?"

And Smiley says, sorter indifferent-like, "It might be a parrot, or it might be a canary, maybe, but it ain't—it's only just a frog."

And the feller took it, and looked at it careful, and turned it round this way and that, and says, "H'm—so 'tis. Well, what's *he* good for?"

"Well," Smiley says, easy and careless, "he's good enough for *one* thing, I should judge—he can outjump any frog in Calaveras county."

The feller took the box again, and took another long, particular look, and gave it back to Smiley, and says, very deliberate, "Well," he says, "I don't see no p'ints[2] about that frog that's any better'n any other frog."

"Maybe you don't," Smiley says. "Maybe you understand frogs and maybe you don't understand 'em; maybe you've had experience, and maybe you ain't only a amature,[3] as it were. Anyways, I've got *my* opinion, and I'll resk forty dollars that he can outjump any frog in Calaveras county."

And the feller studied a minute, and then says, kinder sad like, "Well, I'm only a stranger here, and I ain't got no frog; but if I had a frog, I'd bet you."

◆ ◆ ◆

TAKE NOTES

Reading Strategy

Rewrite the underlined passage of **regional dialect** in standard English.

_____

_____

English Language Development

In English, adverbs modify verbs. Twain uses the adjective form *careful* for the sake of the regional dialect. What adverb can you form from *careful*?

_____

Read Fluently

Read the bracketed paragraph aloud. What does this description of the stranger suggest about his personality?

_____

_____

_____

Literary Analysis

Smiley's long-drawn-out answer adds to the **humor**. Underline the word he repeats several times in order to spin out his answer to the stranger.

Vocabulary Development

deliberate (di LIB rit) *adj.* carefully thought out

---

2. **p'ints** dialect for *points,* meaning fine points or advantages.
3. **amature** dialect for *amateur* (AM uh chuhr) *n.* unskillful person.

Reading Strategy

Circle two words in the bracketed passage that are examples of **regional dialect**

Literary Analysis

How do these details about what the stranger does to Smiley's frog add to the story's **humor**?

_____

_____

_____

English Language Development

Because of the **regional dialect**, Twain uses a double negative: "I don't see no p'ints about that frog that's any better'n any other frog." Rewrite this sentence in standard English.

_____

_____

_____

Smiley offers to get the stranger a frog. Smiley leaves his own frog with the stranger while he looks for another frog. The stranger waits.

◆ ◆ ◆

So he set there a good while thinking and thinking to hisself, and then he got the frog out and prized his mouth open and took a teaspoon and filled him full of quailshot[4]—filled him pretty near up to his chin—and set him on the floor. Smiley he went to the swamp and slopped around in the mud for a long time, and finally he ketched a frog, and fetched him in, and give him to this feller, and says:

"Now, if you're ready, set him alongside of Dan'l, with his forepaws just even with Dan'l's, and I'll give the word." Then he says, "One—two—three—_git!_" and him and the feller touched up the frogs from behind, and the new frog hopped off lively, but Dan'l give a heave, and hysted[5] up his shoulders—so—like a Frenchman, but it warn't no use—he couldn't budge; he was planted as solid as a church, and he couldn't no more stir than if he was anchored out. Smiley was a good deal surprised, and he was disgusted too, but he didn't have no idea what the matter was, of course.

The feller took the money and started away, and when he was going out at the door, he sorter jerked his thumb over his shoulder—so—at Dan'l, and says again, very deliberate, "Well," he says, "I don't see no p'ints about that frog that's any better'n any other frog."

Smiley he stood scratching his head and looking down at Dan'l a long time, and at last he says, "I do wonder what in the nation that frog throw'd off for—I wonder if there ain't something the matter with him—he 'pears to

---

4. **quailshot** small lead pellets used for shooting quail.
5. **hysted** dialect for _hoisted,_ meaning raised.

look mighty baggy, somehow." And he ketched Dan'l by the nap of the neck, and hefted him, and says, "Why blame my cats if he don't weigh five pound!" and turned him upside down and he belched out a double handful of shot. And then he see how it was, and he was the maddest man—he set the frog down and took out after that feller, but he never ketched him. And—

◆   ◆   ◆

At this point someone calls Wheeler from the front yard. The narrator knows that Wheeler has no information about the Rev. Leonidas W. Smiley, so he starts to leave. He meets Wheeler at the door, and Wheeler says:

◆   ◆   ◆

"Well, thish-yer Smiley had a yaller one-eyed cow that didn't have no tail, only just a short stump like a bannanner, and—"

However, lacking both time and <u>inclination</u>, I did not wait to hear about the afflicted cow, but took my leave.

English Language Development

The phrase "what in the nation" on page 184 has more familiar equivalents: "what on earth" and "what in the world." These phrases are *idioms*, or informal expressions that are not intended literally. What would be another way of saying, "How on earth did you get here"?

_____

_____

_____

Culture Note

A tall tale is an exaggerated story told for entertainment. Telling tall tales like this one was a common form of entertainment on the western frontier. What does such a tale suggest about the character of the developing West?

_____

_____

_____

_____

Literary Analysis

What do you think Wheeler is about to do now? How does that contribute to the **humor** of the story?

_____

_____

_____

Vocabulary Development

inclination (in kluh NAY shuhn) *n.* liking or preference

The Boys' Ambition *from* Life on the Mississippi • The Notorious Jumping Frog of Calaveras County

1. **Evaluate:** If Mark Twain were alive today, do you think he would make a good stand-up comic? Explain.

   _____

   _____

2. **Literary Analysis: Humor** is writing meant to make people laugh. In "The Boys' Ambition," Twain uses the word "heavenly" to describe jobs, such as shaking out a tablecloth or holding a rope. Why does Twain's use of language like "heavenly" create humor in the story?

   _____

   _____

3. **Literary Analysis:** Writers use exaggeration to create humor in a story. Identify an example of exaggeration in "The Notorious Jumping Frog of Calaveras County." Explain why it is funny.

   _____

   _____

   _____

4. **Reading Strategy:** You can recognize what the words mean in Standard English if you say them aloud. Read the examples of **regional dialect** in the chart. Then write what each one means in Standard English.

Regional Dialect	St. Looey	reg'lar	warn't	thish-yer	feller
Standard English					

The Outcasts of Poker Flat

LITERARY ANALYSIS

Regionalism is a literary movement. Writers in this movement try to show the special qualities of a specific area and people.

- Regionalism uses description, dialogue, and other details to help the reader experience a place and time.
- "The Outcasts of Poker Flat" is an example of regionalism. This story shows what life was like on the western frontier in the 1800s.

As you read, pay attention to how Harte uses details and dialogue to portray the western frontier.

Regionalism relates the **local color** of an area. Local color shows how the environment, mood, language, and values of a place are unique. Use this chart to note how Harte shows the local color of Poker Flat and the Sierra Nevadas.

Language	
Setting in Town	
Setting Outside Town	
Local Color	
Attitude Towards Vices	
Attitude Towards Religion	

READING SKILL

When you read, you should **question the text** to better understand it. Questions like these can help you connect with the story:

- What is happening?
- What is the author's purpose, or reason, for writing?
- Why do the characters do the things they do?

As you read, look for answers to these questions.

The Outcasts of Poker Flat

Bret Harte

Summary The town of Poker Flat rids itself of four "undesirable characters": a gambler, two prostitutes, and a thief. The group travels into the foothills of the Sierra Nevada Mountains. There, they befriend two young travelers. As the story unfolds, the characters turn out to be more complex than the author originally presents them.

Note-taking Guide

In the chart, record an action taken by each of the characters that reveals some aspect of that character's personality.

Character	Action	What It Reveals
Mr. Oakhurst		
Duchess		
Mother Shipton		
Uncle Billy		
Tom Simson		
Piney Woods		

The Outcasts of Poker Flat

1. **Interpret:** What does the rescue party discover?

_____

What message might this discovery—and the story—convey?

_____

_____

2. **Literary Analysis: Regionalism** is a literary movement that focuses on the qualities of a region and its people. Identify two details that contribute to the regionalism of the story.

_____

_____

3. **Reading Strategy:** **Question the text** to understand the events and characters. Harte's closing lines claim that Oakhurst "was at once the strongest and yet the weakest of the outcasts of Poker Flat." Question the text by asking what Harte means by those lines.

_____

_____

4. **Reading Strategy:** Find one passage from the story. Ask a question about that passage. Record your answers in this chart.

Passage From Story	Question	Answer

Heading West • I Will Fight No More Forever

LITERARY ANALYSIS

Tone is a quality of language you encounter every day in speech. Two people might say the exact same words, but differences in tone reveal their individual emotions. In the same way, a writer's attitude emerges in his or her tone. Consider the optimistic, or positive, tone in this passage from Colt's diary:

> Full of hope, as we leave the smoking embers of our campfire this morning. Expect tonight to arrive at our new home.

As you read, pay attention to the words Colt uses and the details she provides. Use this chart to write down examples and interpret their tones

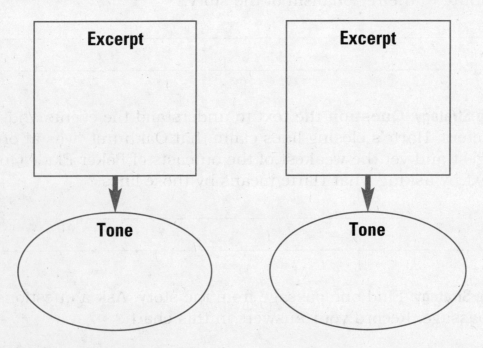

READING STRATEGY

The selections you are about to read describe life-changing events. Reading about life-changing events can produce strong emotions. As you read, pay attention to how you **respond** to the literature.

- How does the writing make you feel?
- What images do you see as you read?
- What is your opinion about the writer or the writing?

Heading West

Miriam Davis Colt

Summary Miriam Davis Colt and her husband have decided to leave New York and settle in the Kansas Territory. They plan to join a community of vegetarians. Colt writes about her experiences as she journeys west. She is full of excitement and looks forward to beginning a new life in a new home.

Note-taking Guide

Colt uses vivid language to help the reader see what she experiences. Use this diagram to record the images Colt uses to describe what she sees and feels.

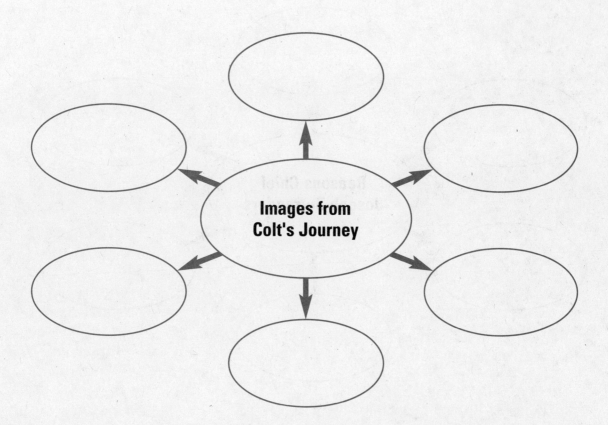

Images from Colt's Journey

I Will Fight No More Forever

Chief Joseph

Summary Chief Joseph has decided to stop fighting. He grieves for his people who have died during their flight from the United States Army. Those who remain are cold and starving. Chief Joseph speaks beautifully and painfully of his sadness and of his decision to surrender.

Note-taking Guide

Chief Joseph uses vivid details to explain why he has decided to stop running from the United States Army. Use this diagram to record the reasons he lists.

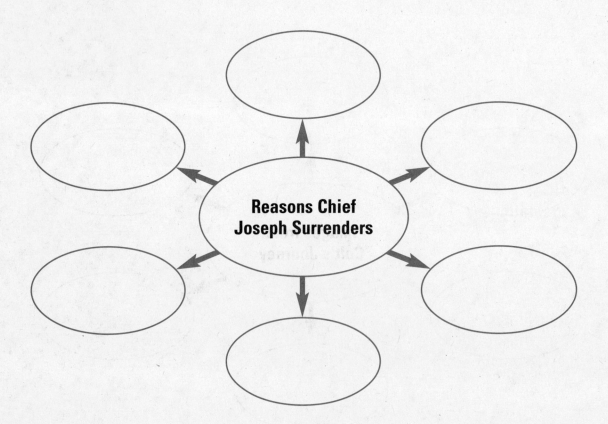

Heading West • I Will Fight No More Forever

1. **Literary Analysis: Tone** is the writer's attitude toward his or her subject. Miriam Davis Colt often adopts a positive tone in her diary. Identify an example of her upbeat tone.

   _____

   _____

2. **Literary Analysis:** Colt sometimes conveys a negative, downcast tone. Find an example of this discouraged tone.

   _____

   _____

3. **Literary Analysis:** Chief Joseph admits defeat in his speech. What is Chief Joseph's overall tone as he offers his surrender?

   _____

   _____

4. **Compare and Contrast:** Octagon City does not turn out to be like Colt thought it would. Fill in the following chart to show the differences.

Colt's Expectations	
Reality	

5. **Reading Strategy:** When you **respond** to literature, pay attention to how the writing makes you feel. Identify a passage from Chief Joseph's speech that makes you respond in a powerful way. Explain your responses.

   _____

   _____

To Build a Fire

LITERARY ANALYSIS

Conflict is a struggle between two opposing forces. In literature, conflict can take two forms:

- **Internal conflict** is a struggle that occurs within the mind of a character.
- **External conflict** is a struggle between a character and society, nature, another character, or an opposing force.

During a story, the character tries to resolve a conflict. The character's efforts to resolve the conflict make up the plot of the story. In "To Build a Fire," a man faces a deadly conflict with the cold Alaskan wilderness. His main conflict is an external conflict with nature.

READING STRATEGY

Predicting means guessing what will happen next. As you read, you can make predictions based on clues from what you have already read. The man in this story was not good at predicting what would happen. He did not pay attention to clues such as the weather and his dog's unease.

Use this chart to make your own predictions as you read this story. Write down clues from the story that support your predictions.

Clues	Predictions

To Build a Fire

Jack London

Summary This story focuses on a man who has been searching for gold in the Yukon, a frozen wilderness in Alaska. The man and his dog are walking toward a camp. The man does not recognize the danger of his journey. He does not realize that the temperature is far too cold for him to be traveling alone. Then he builds his fire in the wrong place. The man's terrible mistakes turn out to be deadly.

Note-taking Guide

Writers use sensory language to help readers experience a story. Sensory language includes details that relate to the five senses— sight, sound, smell, taste, and touch. Use this diagram to show how London uses sensory language in "To Build a Fire."

Sights	Sounds	Smells	Tastes	Feelings

To Build a Fire

1. **Draw Conclusions:** What message does this story present about human strength in the face of nature's power?

_____

_____

_____

2. **Literary Analysis:** Analyze the details London uses to develop the central **external conflict**. Record two details in the chart.

The man versus nature	
Detail 1	
Detail 2	

3. **Literary Analysis:** An **internal conflict** develops within the mind of the man during the story. What is the conflict?

_____

_____

4. **Reading Strategy:** As you read the story, when did you make your first **prediction** that the man would die before he reached his friends?

_____

_____

5. **Reading Strategy:** What clues in the text helped you make your prediction about the man's death?

_____

_____

The Story of an Hour

LITERARY ANALYSIS

Irony is a type of contradiction. A contradiction is something that is the opposite of what it should be. There are three kinds of irony in literature:

- **Verbal irony** is when a character says something that is different from what he or she means.
- **Situational irony** occurs when something happens that contradicts what the reader expects.
- **Dramatic irony** means the reader or audience knows something that a character does not know.

As you read, watch for different kinds of irony in "The Story of an Hour."

READING STRATEGY

To understand irony, readers must **recognize ironic details**. These details cause the reader to expect things to happen a certain way. When those expectations are not met, the reader experiences the irony of the situation.

- Pay attention to details in "The Story of an Hour." Details create expectations about feelings and events.
- As you read, note details that might suggest that circumstances that are not what they appear to be.

Use this chart to record details, expected outcomes, and actual oucomes.

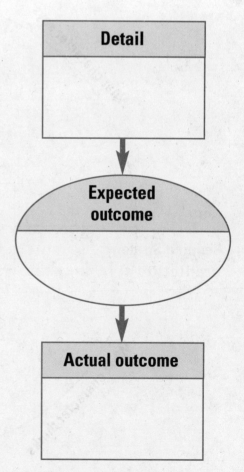

The Story of an Hour

Kate Chopin

Summary Mrs. Mallard has just learned that her husband has died in a train accident. She goes to her room, sits in a comfortable armchair, and looks out her window. She feels something she does not understand. She cries for her lost husband but she feels something else she has never felt before—freedom.

Note-taking Guide

Use this chart to make notes about the character of Mrs. Mallard.

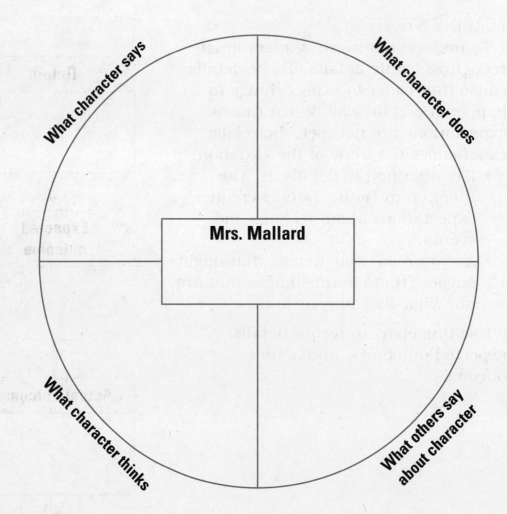

What character says

What character does

Mrs. Mallard

What character thinks

What others say about character

The Story of an Hour
Kate Chopin

Knowing that Mrs. Mallard was afflicted[1] with a heart trouble, great care was taken to break to her as gently as possible the news of her husband's death.

It was her sister Josephine who told her, in broken sentences; veiled hints that revealed in half concealing. Her husband's friend Richards was there too, near her. It was he who had been in the newspaper office when intelligence[2] of the railroad disaster was received, with Brently Mallard's name leading the list of "killed." He had only taken the time to assure himself of its truth by a second telegram, and had hastened to forestall any less careful, less tender friend in bearing the sad message.

◆ ◆ ◆

Mrs. Mallard bursts out weeping in her sister's arms. She goes to her room alone. There she sits in a chair facing the open window.

◆ ◆ ◆

She could see in the open square before her house the tops of trees that were all aquiver with the new spring life. The delicious breath of rain was in the air. In the street below a peddler was crying his wares.[3] The notes of a distant song which someone was singing reached her faintly, and countless sparrows were twittering in the eaves.

Vocabulary Development

forestall (fawr STAWL) *v.* prevent by acting ahead of time

---

1. **afflicted** (uh FLIK ted) *adj.* suffering from.
2. **intelligence** (in TEL i juhnts) *n.* news.
3. **wares** (wayrz) *n.* merchandise.

TAKE NOTES

Vocabulary and Pronunciation

The word *intelligence* can mean either "mental ability" or "news." Which meaning is used in the underlined sentence?

_____

_____

Stop to Reflect

Why is Richards careful to be sure that the message is true?

_____

_____

_____

Reading Strategy

Mrs. Mallard has just received news of her husband's death. Circle three **details** in the bracketed passage that you recognize as **ironic** under the circumstances.

Read the underlined paragraph aloud. What might the "patches of blue sky" showing through the clouds suggest about a change in Mrs. Mallard's mood?

_____

_____

_____

English Language Development

In English, the most common way to form a plural noun is to add *–s* to the singular form. A noun adds *–es* to form the plural if ends in *s, x, ch, or sh,* like patches. What are two other nouns in English that have *–es* in the plural?

1. _____

2. _____

Literary Analysis

What **irony**, or contrast, does the bracketed passage reveal between what was expected and what actually happens?

_____

_____

There were patches of blue sky showing here and there through the clouds that had met and piled one above the other in the west facing her window.

◆ ◆ ◆

Mrs. Mallard still sobs occasionally. She stares dully at the sky. Then, she senses a new emotion coming over her. She tries to fight her new feelings, but her effort is not successful.

◆ ◆ ◆

When she abandoned herself,[4] a little whispered word escaped her slightly parted lips. She said it over and over under her breath: "free, free, free!" The vacant stare and the look of terror that had followed it went from her eyes. They stayed keen and bright. Her pulses beat fast, and the coursing blood warmed and relaxed every inch of her body.

She did not stop to ask if it were or were not a monstrous joy that held her. A clear and exalted perception enabled her to dismiss the suggestion as trivial.

She knew that she would weep again when she saw the kind, tender hands folded in death; the face that had never looked save with love upon her, fixed and gray and dead. But she saw beyond that bitter moment a long procession of years to come that would belong to her absolutely. And she opened and spread her arms out to them in welcome.

There would be no one to live for her during those coming years; she would live for herself. There would be no powerful will bending hers in that blind persistence with which men and women believe they have a right to impose a private will upon a fellow creature.

◆ ◆ ◆

Vocabulary Development

trivial (TRIV i uhl) *adj.* unimportant

---

4. **abandoned herself** surrendered or gave herself up.

Mrs. Mallard reflects on her new-found freedom. Compared to the future, the past matters little. Suddenly she hears her sister Josephine begging her to open the door. Mrs. Mallard dreams of her future life a little longer. She prays for a long life. Then, she opens the door and puts her arm around her sister. They go down the stairs together. At the bottom, Richards stands waiting for them.

♦ ♦ ♦

Someone was opening the front door with a latchkey. It was Brently Mallard who entered, a little travel-stained, composedly[5] carrying his gripsack[6] and umbrella. He had been far from the scene of the accident, and did not know there had been one. He stood amazed at Josephine's piercing cry; at Richards's quick motion to screen him from the view of his wife.

But Richards was too late.

When the doctors came they said she had died of heart disease—of joy that kills.

5. **composedly** (kum POHZ uhd le) *adj.* calmly.
6. **gripsack** (GRIP sak) *n.* small bag for holding clothes.

The Story of an Hour

1. **Interpret:** Mrs. Mallard whispers "free" over and over as she sits in her room. What has she apparently resented about her marriage?

   _____

   _____

2. **Literary Analysis:** Mrs. Mallard's death is a surprising event. Explain why Mrs. Mallard's death is an example of **situational irony**.

   _____

   _____

3. **Literary Analysis:** Readers know something that the doctors in the story do not. Why is the diagnosis of Mrs. Mallard's cause of death an example of **dramatic irony**?

   _____

   _____

4. **Literary Analysis:** Find one passage from the story that contains irony. Ask a question about that passage. Record your answers in this chart.

Passage	Ironic Elements

5. **Reading Strategy:** Which **detail** in the second paragraph do you recognize that makes Mr. Mallard's arrival at the end all the more **ironic**?

   _____

   _____

Douglass • We Wear the Mask

LITERARY ANALYSIS

Rhyme is the repetition of sounds. Poets use rhyme and rhythm to make lines of poetry sound musical. There are different ways to use rhyme in poems:

- **Exact rhyme:** Vowel sounds and the consonants that come after them sound exactly the same *(boxes* and *foxes).*
- **Slant rhymes:** Two sounds are similar but not exactly the same *(prove* and *love).*
- **End rhymes:** Rhymes occur at the ends of two or more lines of poetry.
- **Internal rhymes:** Rhymes appear within one poetic line.

As you read, pay attention to how Dunbar uses rhymes.

READING STRATEGY

Poets often intend more than one meaning for their words. To find these "hidden" ideas means to interpret. To **interpret** poetry, you must look beyond a poet's words to find deeper meanings.

- Figure out the meaning of unfamiliar or unclear words.
- Learn the background or historical context of a work.
- Notice images described by the poet. A poem's imagery can carry an important message. For example, what might a mask mean?

Use this chart to help interpret and understand these two poems.

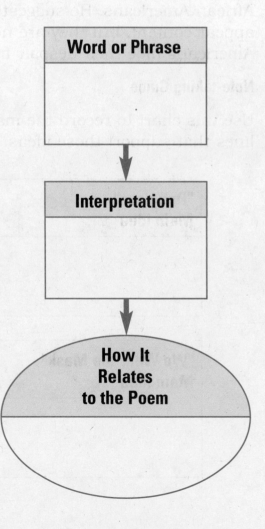

Douglass • We Wear the Mask

Paul Laurence Dunbar

Summaries In "Douglass," Dunbar appeals to Frederick Douglass. Douglass was a nineteenth-century abolitionist known for his strong speeches and writing. He worked to gain equal rights for African Americans. In his sonnet to Douglass, Dunbar writes that the fight for equality is not over.

In "We Wear the Mask," Dunbar describes the daily struggles of African Americans. He suggests that African Americans may appear content, but they are not. Dunbar describes how African Americans hide their despair from the eyes of white America.

Note-taking Guide

Use this chart to record the main ideas from each poem and the lines that support those ideas.

"Douglass" Main Idea	Lines that support the main idea

"We Wear the Mask" Main Idea	Lines that support the main idea

Douglass • We Wear the Mask

1. **Compare and Contrast:** Which poem most closely reflects the poet's daily struggles and feelings?

   _____

2. **Analyze:** In "We Wear the Mask," Dunbar speaks for African Americans. What struggles do African Americans face?

   _____

   _____

3. **Literary Analysis:** List all the words in "We Wear the Mask" that are **exact rhymes** with _lies_.

   _____

   _____

4. **Literary Analysis:** In your opinion, what is the effect of rhyme in these poems?

   _____

   _____

5. **Reading Strategy:** Poets use symbolic language to explain feelings and ideas. Identify and **interpret** four examples of symbolic language that you find in the poems. Record your responses in the chart.

	Symbolic language	Interpretation
"Douglass"		
"We Wear the Mask"		

Luke Havergal • Richard Cory • Lucinda Matlock • Richard Bone

LITERARY ANALYSIS

The **speaker** is the voice that is speaking in the poem. The speaker may be the poet or a fictional character.

For example, the speakers in Edgar Lee Masters's *Spoon River Anthology* are characters buried in a cemetery. Masters uses the characters' voices to help make them real. Instead of using a neutral speaker, Masters allows characters to speak for themselves. In this way, the poet can get into the minds and hearts of Spoon River's former citizens.

READING STRATEGY

A poem's speaker uses different tones and words. These tones and words show the speaker's **attitude**. A speaker's attitude tells the reader how the speaker feels about a topic. You can learn to **recognize the attitudes** of a poem's speaker by noticing details in the poem.

Use this chart to record the speakers' attitudes in these poems. Provide evidence to support your ideas.

Speaker's Attitude	Evidence

Luke Havergal • Richard Cory • Lucinda Matlock • Richard Bone

Edgar Lee Masters
Edwin Arlington Robinson

Summaries The two poems by Robinson focus on the pain of loss. In **"Luke Havergal,"** the speaker describes how Luke Havergal is grieving for his beloved. Havergal questions whether he can go on living. In contrast, **"Richard Cory"** describes a whole town in shock and grief over the suicide of wealthy man.

The two poems by Masters describe characters who have the ability to face life in a changing world. From the grave, both characters speak about their lives. **"Lucinda Matlock"** died when she was ninety-six after a hard but fullfilling life. She does not listen to the complaints of young people who she thinks do not embrace life. **"Richard Bone"** tells the story of the man who carves messages on tombstones.

Note-taking Guide

Use this chart to describe the title character in each poem.

	What character does	Key character trait
Luke Havergal		
Richard Cory		prestige and charm
Lucinda Matlock		
Richard Bone	carves tombstones	

Luke Havergal • Richard Cory • Lucinda Matlock • Richard Bone

1. **Interpret:** In "Luke Havergal," the speaker has come from "out of the grave." What is the speaker's message?

_____

2. **Infer:** Lucinda Matlock died at ninety-six. Why might she have thought she "lived enough"?

_____

3. **Literary Analysis:** Masters writes poems in which the **speakers** are dead. Why would a dead speaker feel free to talk about his or her life?

_____

4. **Reading Strategy:** Does the speaker in "Richard Cory" have an attitude about Richard Cory that differs from Cory's attitude toward himself? Explain

_____

_____

5. **Reading Strategy:** Analyze Lucinda Matlock's outlook on life by filling in the chart.

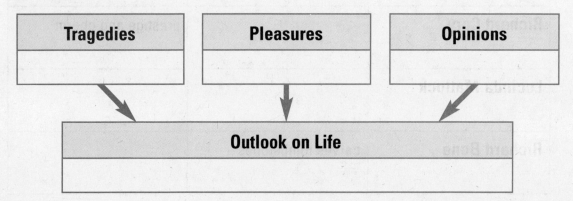

Tragedies	Pleasures	Opinions

Outlook on Life

A Wagner Matinée

LITERARY ANALYSIS

An author shows a character's personality through **characterization.** Characterization is a method of writing that uses the following elements:

- direct statements about the character
- descriptions of the character's appearance
- a character's actions, thoughts, and comments
- comments about the character made by other characters

As you read, pay attention to the ways in which you learn what characters are like.

READING SKILL

"A Wagner Matinée" contains many details about Aunt Georgiana. To understand Aunt Georgiana, you must **clarify** those details. Clarifying details means checking to make sure you know what the details mean. There are many ways to clarify details:

- Read a footnote.
- Look up a word in a dictionary.
- Reread a passage.
- Read ahead for more information.

Use this chart to clarify details in the text.

Difficult passage	Choose a strategy:	Reread	Use a dictionary	Use a footnote
	→			

PREVIEW

A Wagner Matinée

Willa Cather

Summary Aunt Georgiana was a music teacher who lived in Boston. She met her husband and moved to the Nebraska Territory. She returns to Boston many years later. The narrator meets her at the train station. He remembers his early years with her in Nebraska. He wants to share something special with her, so he takes her to hear a performance of an opera by Wagner. The narrator is surprised by the effect the music has on his aunt.

Note-taking Guide

Use this chart to take notes about the two important places in this story.

Details about Boston	Details about Nebraska

A Wagner Matinée

1. **Interpret:** As a boy, Clark played music on the parlor organ in his Aunt's house. Aunt Georgiana told him: "Don't love it so well, Clark, or it may be taken from you." What does she mean?

_____

_____

_____

_____

2. **Literary Analysis:** Cather uses several methods of **characterization** to show what Aunt Georgiana is like. Use the chart to write down examples of each method listed.

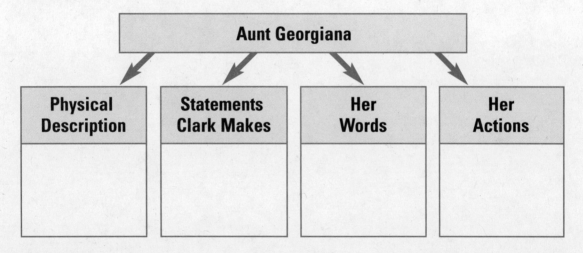

3. **Literary Analysis:** What does Aunt Georgiana's reaction to the opera show about her?

_____

_____

_____

_____

A Wagner Matinée (cont'd)

4. **Reading Strategy:** Clarify your understanding of Aunt Georgiana's life. Find two details that describe the difficulties of her life in Nebraska.

_____

_____

_____

_____

The Love Song of J. Alfred Prufrock

LITERARY ANALYSIS

In this poem, a character named J. Alfred Prufrock shares his thoughts and feelings. This type of poem is called a dramatic monologue. A **dramatic monologue** is a poem or speech in which a character talks to a silent listener. This form of poem lets you learn a great deal about the speaker. Use the chart below to write down what you learn about Prufrock. Write down his thoughts about life and details that show what kind of person he is. Also, write down details that show how he struggles with his own thoughts, desires, and feelings.

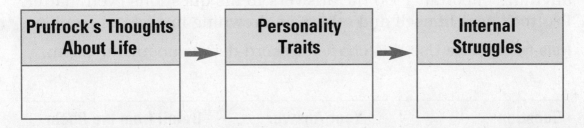

Prufrock's Thoughts About Life		Personality Traits		Internal Struggles
	→		→	

READING STRATEGY

This poem contains many famous lines. One reason for why the lines are famous is that they are musical. Repetition and rhyme create the music, or feeling of a song. You must **listen** to this poem to understand this musical quality.

For example, notice the rhymes and repetition in these lines. The repetitions are in darker type. The rhymes are underlined:

And **would it have been worth** it, **after** all,

After the cups, the marmalade, the <u>tea</u>,

Among the porcelain, **among** some talk of you and <u>me</u>,

Would it have been worth <u>while</u>,

To have bitten off the matter with a <u>smile</u> . . .

Try reading the poem aloud to hear the musical quality.

The Love Song of J. Alfred Prufrock

T. S. Eliot

Summary J. Alfred Prufrock invites someone to go for a walk in a city at evening. The city he describes is gloomy and sad. Then, Prufrock asks some questions about himself: Could he have done more with his life? Can he express love for a woman? Is he able to do anything important? Do the answers to his questions even matter? Prufrock sees himself and others as drowning in a sea of troubles.

Note-taking Guide Use this chart to record details about the poem.

Question	Your Answer	Detail from the Poem that Tells You
Who is speaker?		
At what time of the day does the poem take place?		
Where does the speaker go?		
What question does the speaker ask?		
What does the speaker seem to feel about himself?		

The Love Song of J. Alfred Prufrock

1. **Analyze:** In line 51, Prufrock says he has "measured out" his life with "coffee spoons." What does this say about how he has lived?

   _____

2. **Literary Analysis:** In this **dramatic monologue**, Prufrock does not come right out and say "I wish I were different than I am." How do you know that he feels sad about himself? Explain.

   _____

3. **Literary Analysis:** Prufrock makes many **allusions** to works of art. These allusions show how he sees himself. Use this chart to write down two allusions. Explain their meaning. Then, tell what they say about how Prufrock sees himself. One has been done for you.

Allusion		Meaning	How Prufrock Sees Himself
No! I am not Prince Hamlet . . .	→	Hamlet is the troubled hero in a play.	He does not think he can be a hero.

4. **Reading Strategy:** The speaker repeats the words "there will be time" in lines 23–34 and again in lines 37–48. Why might someone say such a phrase over and over?

   _____

Poems by Ezra Pound, William Carlos Williams, and H.D.

LITEARY ANALYSIS

Imagist poems use **images** to bring out emotions. Images are words or phrases that appeal to sight, sound, taste, touch, or smell. For example, "purple flowers" is an image. You can see a purple flower.

The poem titled "In a Station of the Metro" is an Imagist poem. It has only two lines, and fourteen words. It contains just two images. Yet it is full of meaning.

READING STRATEGY

These poems are filled with strong images. As you read each image, **engage your senses.** This means that you replay in your mind the sights, sounds, smells, tastes, and feel of a poem's image. For example, you can see *and* feel the heaviness in the air as the speaker calls to the wind in "Heat":

Cut the heat— /plow through it, /
Turning it on either side. . .

Engage your senses as you read these poems. Use this chart to record what you see, smell, hear, taste, and feel.

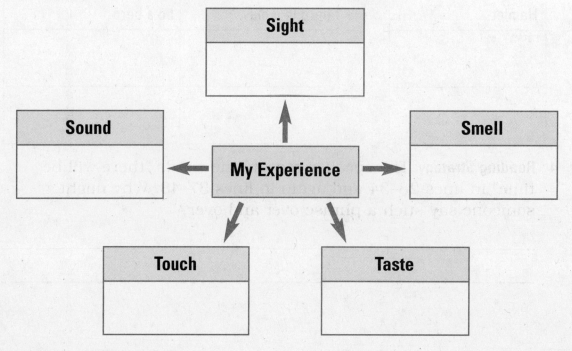

The Imagist Poets

Summaries In the essay "A Few Don'ts by an Imagiste," Ezra Pound talks about rules for writing Imagist poetry. He says it is important to use few words and to make sure they are strong and specific.

In "The River-Merchant's Wife: A Letter," a young Chinese woman writes to her husband, who is away. She longs for his return.

In "In a Station of the Metro," the speaker compares faces in a crowded subway station to flower petals on a tree branch.

In "The Red Wheelbarrow," the speaker describes a wheelbarrow and some chickens.

In "The Great Figure," the speaker describes a moving fire truck.

"This Is Just to Say" is in the style of a personal note. The speaker is sorry for eating plums someone left in the refrigerator.

In "Pear Tree," the speaker describes a tree in bloom.

In "Heat," the speaker talks to the wind. The speaker asks the wind to attack and break up the extreme heat.

Note-taking Guide
Use this chart to record the main image or images in each poem.

Poem	Main Image(s)
"In a Station of the Metro"	
"The Red Wheelbarrow"	
"The Great Figure"	
"This Is Just to Say"	
"Pear Tree"	
"Heat"	

The Imagist Poets

1. **Compare and Contrast:** In "The River-Merchant's Wife," the speaker's feelings for her husband change when she turns fifteen. What is this change?

_____

_____

2. **Evaluate:** Which words in "The Red Wheelbarrow" and "This is Just to Say" show that the poet was interested in everyday life? Explain your answer.

_____

_____

3. **Compare and Contrast:** Color is often an important element in **Imagist poetry.** Use the chart below to explain what the colors in poems by William Carlos Williams and H.D. make you see, think, and feel.

Poem	Main Image(s)	Feeling It Creates
The Red Wheelbarrow	a red wheel barrow	
	white chickens	
The Great Figure	figure 5 / in gold / on a red fire truck	
Pear Tree	Silver dust / lifted from the earth	
	a white leaf	
	purple hearts (of flowers)	

4. **Reading Skill:** You can use the sense of sight to experience this image: "Petals on a wet, black bough." What other **senses** could you **engage** to experience this image? Explain.

_____

_____

Winter Dreams

LITERARY ANALYSIS

Authors use **characterization** to show a character's personality. Characterization can be direct or indirect.

- **Direct characterization:** The author tells what a character is like.

- **Indirect characterization:** The author uses the words, actions, and thoughts of the character, as well as other characters' words, to show what a character is like.

An important part of characterization is a character's **motivations**—the reasons for acting as they do. These may come from their own feelings, or from something outside of them. As you read, identify the characters' motivations for their actions.

READING STRATEGY

Draw conclusions about characters by combining story details with your own experience. Read this example:

> Dexter stood perfectly still ... if he moved forward a step his stare would be in her line of vision—if he moved backward he would lose his full view of her face.

You can tell from this description that Dexter wants to look at Judy but does not want her to catch him staring.

Use this chart to draw conclusions about the characters in "Winter Dreams."

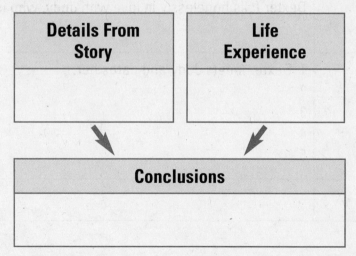

Details From Story	Life Experience

Conclusions

Winter Dreams

Summary Dexter Green is the son of a grocer in a small Minnesota town. He loves Judy Jones, the daughter of a wealthy local family. Dexter and Judy meet at a country club when he is fourteen and she is eleven. He is attracted to her and quits his caddying job to avoid the humiliation of carrying her clubs. After college they meet again and begin a serious romance for one summer. Judy, however, does not want a commitment and dates other men. Dexter decides to marry the more sensible Irene Scheerer. On the eve of the engagement, Judy returns. She renews the relationship with Dexter, which causes Dexter to lose Irene. Judy then leaves Dexter once more. Years later, Dexter learns that Judy is now trapped in an unhappy marriage and has lost her beauty.

Note-taking Guide Use this story map to record the main elements of the story.

Characters	
Setting	
Problem or Conflict	Dexter falls hopelessly in love with Judy, who is a big flirt.
Main Events	1. Dexter meets Judy and dates her. 2. 3. 4. 5.
Ending	

Winter Dreams

1. **Interpret:** Dexter says that he wants the glittering things of wealth. In what way does Judy represent Dexter's dreams?

   _____

   _____

2. **Literary Analysis:** Use this chart to analyze Fitzgerald's **characterization** of Dexter.

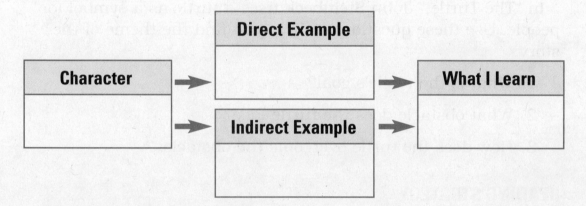

3. **Literary Analysis:** Success was very important to Dexter. What details in the story show Dexter's **motivation** to succeed?

   _____

   _____

4. **Reading Strategy:** Draw conclusions about the **characters** of Dexter and Judy. What does wealth mean to each of them?

   _____

   _____

   _____

The Turtle *from* The Grapes of Wrath

LITERARY ANALYSIS

A story's **theme** is its message about life. Authors reveal themes in these ways:

- Through characters' words and actions

- Through what happens in the plot

- By using **symbols**. A symbol is a person, place, or object that stand for something else.

In "The Turtle," John Steinbeck uses a turtle as a symbol for people. Use these questions to help you find the theme of the story:

1. What is the turtle's goal?

2. What obstacle does the turtle face?

3. How does the turtle overcome the obstacles?

READING STRATEGY

Become a literary detective to understand a story's theme. Look carefully for **clues to the theme** in the writer's use of symbols. Also, look at the writer's choice of details and characters' actions. For example, Steinbeck includes only slight descriptions of how two motorists react when they spot the turtle. These descriptions give you important clues to the theme. When you come across such clues, think about the other meanings that they suggest. Gather clues in the following chart.

Clue +	Clue +	Clue =	Theme

The Turtle *from* The Grapes of Wrath

John Steinbeck

Summary A turtle crawls over some grass toward a highway. As he moves, some wild oat seeds become attached to the turtle's legs. With great effort, the turtle gets onto the highway. One car nearly hits the turtle. Another vehicle does hit the turtle, and it rolls off the highway onto its shell. After some time, the turtle rolls itself over. As it rolls, the wild oat seeds fall onto the ground. As the turtle moves, it drags dirt over the seeds.

Note-taking Guide Complete the following sequence chart.

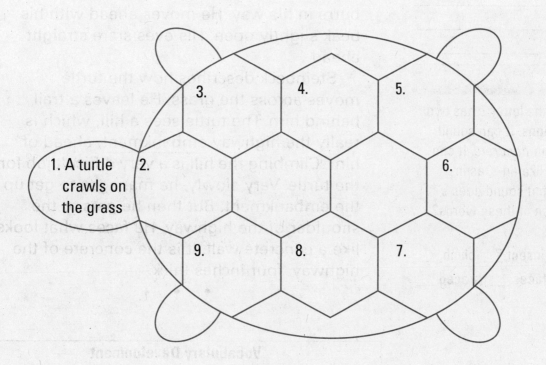

1. A turtle crawls on the grass

2.

3.

4.

5.

6.

7.

8.

9.

The Turtle *from* The Grapes of Wrath
John Steinbeck

Steinbeck opens by describing the land at the edge of a concrete highway. It is covered with a mat of dry grass full of various kinds of seeds. The seeds are waiting to be picked up by passing animals or to be carried by the wind.

Steinbeck continues by saying that the sun warms the grass. In the shade of the grass, many insects live.

◆ ◆ ◆

And over the grass at the roadside a land turtle crawled, <u>turning aside for nothing,</u> <u>dragging his high-domed shell over the grass.</u> <u>His hard legs and yellow-nailed feet</u> <u>threshed</u> <u>slowly through the grass, not really walking,</u> <u>but boosting and dragging his shell along.</u>

◆ ◆ ◆

The turtle does not notice seeds and burrs in his way. He moves ahead with his beak slightly open. His eyes stare straight ahead.

Steinbeck describes how the turtle moves across the grass. He leaves a trail behind him. The turtle sees a hill, which is really the highway <u>embankment</u>, ahead of him. Climbing the hill is a very difficult job for the turtle. Very slowly, he manages to get up the embankment. But then he gets to the shoulder of the highway. He faces what looks like a concrete wall. It is the concrete of the highway, four inches thick.

◆ ◆ ◆

Literary Analysis

Read the underlined sections in this paragraph. Then complete this sentence based on the **theme** of the story.

We can tell that the turtle is determined to get across the road because he does the following things:

he _____,

_____

and he _____

_____.

Vocabulary and Pronunciation

In English, the letter *c* has two pronunciations. It can sound like a *k*, as in *concrete*. It can also sound like an *s*, as in *cement*. What sound does *c* have in each of these words? Write *k* or *s*.

clover____ insect____ climb____

fierce____ faces____ braced____

Vocabulary Development

threshed (THRESHT) *v.* struck over and over again
embankment (em BANK ment) *n.* a long mound of earth or stone that keeps water back or supports a road

As though they worked independently the hind legs pushed the shell against the wall. The head upraised and peered over the wall to the broad smooth plain of cement.

◆   ◆   ◆

After much straining, the turtle lifts itself on the edge of the wall. As the turtle rests, a red ant runs into the turtle's shell. The turtle crushes it between its body and legs.

Steinbeck describes how some wild oat seeds are brought into the shell by the turtle's front leg. The turtle lies still for a moment. Then his head, legs, and tail come out of the shell. The turtle begins straining to reach the top of the cement. The hind legs slowly boost the rest of the turtle's body up. At last he gets to the top. The wild oat seeds are still attached around the turtle's front legs.

Movement is easy for the turtle now. The turtle begins to cross the highway.

◆   ◆   ◆

A sedan driven by a forty-year-old woman approached. She saw the turtle and swung to the right, off the highway, the wheels screamed and a cloud of dust boiled up.

◆   ◆   ◆

The car tips with the sudden swerve. After regaining control, the woman drives on slowly. The turtle had hidden in its shell in fear. But now the turtle hurries across the road.

◆   ◆   ◆

Vocabulary Development

hind (HYND) *adj.* back
sedan (si DAN) *n.* a hard-top car big enough for four to seven people

---

TAKE NOTES

Reading Check

How does the turtle defend himself against the red ant?

_____

_____

Vocabulary and Pronunciation

In English, the past tense is usually shown by adding -d or -ed to a verb. Sometimes this ending sounds like d, as in covered. Sometimes this ending sounds like ed, as in lifted. And sometimes it sounds like t, as in picked. Write d, ed, or t to tell how the ending sounds in each of these words:

pushed _____ upraised _____

peered _____   braced _____

Reading Strategy

To **find clues to the theme,** underline the part that tells how the woman acted when she saw the turtle. Circle the part on the next page that tells how the man acted. Then answer these questions:

1. What do you think the woman symbolizes?

_____

_____

2. What do you think the man symbolizes?

_____

_____

Sometimes a noun is described by two or more words that work together as a single adjective that comes before the noun. When this happens, the words are connected by hyphens. Rewrite these phrases, changing the underlined words to a hyphenated adjective before the noun. Example: a woman who is forty years old = a forty-year-old woman.

concrete that is four inches thick =

_____

a turtle with a hard shell =

_____

Stop to Reflect

More cars are on the road in the United States than in any other country. What forms of transportation are commonly used in your native country?

_____

_____

Stop to Reflect

1. How does the turtle help the wild oat seeds?

_____

2. What do you think Steinbeck is saying about how different forms of life relate to one another?

_____

_____

And now a light truck approached, and as it came near, the driver saw the turtle and swerved to hit it.

◆　◆　◆

The front wheel of the truck hits the turtle. The turtle flips over and rolls off the highway.

Steinbeck describes how the turtle lies on its back. Its body is drawn into its shell. Finally, the legs come out and start waving around in the air. The turtle is looking for something to grab onto. At last its front foot gets hold of a piece of quartz. Very slowly, the turtle manages to pull itself over. At this point, the wild oat seeds fall out and get stuck in the ground.

As the turtle moves along, its shell buries the seeds with dirt.

◆　◆　◆

The turtle entered a dust road and jerked itself along, drawing a wavy shallow trench with its shell. The old humorous eyes looked ahead, and the horny beak opened a little. His yellow toe nails slipped a fraction in the dust.

Vocabulary Development

swerved (SWERVD) *v.* turned aside from a straight course

trench (TRENCH) *n.* a deep ditch dug in the ground

The Turtle *from* The Grapes of Wrath

1. **Make a Judgment:** Name three obstacles the turtle faces.

   _____

   Which is the most dangerous obstacle?

   _____

2. **Literary Analysis:** What do the turtle's experiences have in common with peoples' life experiences?

   _____

3. **Literary Analysis:** Use this chart to examine the turtle's actions and to understand what they **symbolize**.

	Obstacles	Turtle's Reactions	Symbolic Meaning
Climbs Embankment			
Crosses Road			

4. **Reading Strategy:** Find clues to the **theme** by studying the author's word choices. Steinbeck uses words, such as *dragging* and *thrashed slowly*, to describe the turtle's actions. How do you think Steinbeck wants readers to see to the turtle?

   _____

   _____

5. **Reading Strategy:** Which do you think Steinbeck feels is more important—nature or the modern world? Explain your answer.

   _____

   _____

old age sticks • anyone lived in a pretty how town • The Unknown Citizen

LITERARY ANALYSIS

Satire is writing that makes fun of the faults of individuals, groups, organizations, or even people in general. Satire can be funny, but it has another purpose. Satire encourages readers to understand the problems that it points out. Satirists hope to persuade readers to accept their point of view.

As you read, think about the serious point each poet makes by using satire.

Stories or poems that use satire vary in **tone**—a quality that reveals a writer's attitude toward his or her subject, characters, or audience. The tone of a satirical work can be funny, angry, or cruel. The tone of a literary work is shown through the writer's choice of words and details.

READING STRATEGY

You can often connect the ideas of poetry with the form the words take:

- **Structure** is the way a poem is put together in words, lines, and stanzas.

- **Meaning** is the central idea the poet wants to express.

In his poems, Cummings plays games with words and phrases. He breaks rules of grammar and syntax. His poems' structures suit their themes because he is challenging common ideas. Use this chart to link structure to meaning.

anyone lived in a pretty how town		old age sticks		The Unknown Citizen	
Structure	**Meaning**	**Structure**	**Meaning**	**Structure**	**Meaning**

old age sticks • anyone lived in a pretty how town • The Unknown Citizen

E. E. Cummings • W. H. Auden

Summaries In "old age sticks," the speaker says that the young ignore the warnings of the elderly. He suggests that although the young tear down warning "signs," one day they will be posting such "signs" themselves. In **"anyone lived in a pretty how town,"** the speaker tells about an anonymous town in which people live routine and ordinary lives. The main characters, "anyone" and "noone," do nothing special and are basically unnoticed by other people in the town. **"The Unknown Citizen"** honors a model citizen of his society. The speaker calls this man a saint because he served the Greater Community. However, no one knows anything about his true life experiences.

Note-taking Guide As you read each poem, consider who is the subject of each poem and what happens. Use this chart to keep track of your information.

old age sticks
Who is the subject?
What happens?

anyone lived in a pretty how town
Who is the subject?
What happens?

The Unknown Citizen
Who is the subject?
What happens?

old age sticks • anyone lived in a pretty how town • The Unknown Citizen

1. **Interpret:** In the final stanza of "old age sticks," the poem says that youth is "growing old." What is interesting about this final stanza?

_____

_____

2. **Literary Analysis:** What small-town qualities and behaviors does Cummings satirize in "anyone lived in a pretty how town"?

_____

_____

3. **Literary Analysis:** Use this chart to name four groups that report on the unknown citizen's activities in "The Unknown Citizen." Then, tell what the concerns of these groups show about society.

```
┌───────────────────┐              ┌───────────────────┐
│ _____ │              │ _____ │
│ _____ │              │ _____ │
│ _____ │              │ _____ │
└───────────────────┘              └───────────────────┘
           ↖            ┌─────────────┐          ↗
             ↘          │             │        ↙
                        └─────────────┘
           ↙                                    ↘
┌───────────────────┐              ┌───────────────────┐
│ _____ │              │ _____ │
│ _____ │              │ _____ │
│ _____ │              │ _____ │
└───────────────────┘              └───────────────────┘
```

   Society: _____

   _____

4. **Reading Strategy:** Tell how Auden's style of capitalization affects the **meaning** and **tone** of his poem.

_____

_____

The Far and the Near

LITERARY ANALYSIS

Climax and Anticlimax

A **climax** is the high point of a story. Sometimes that point is a letdown. It might be a disappointment to the characters, or even to the reader. When this happens, it is called an **anticlimax**.

To keep readers interested, writers must grab their attention early. Once a story's central conflict is introduced, the events leading up to the climax help build readers' interest. These events make up a story's **rising action**.

READING STRATEGY

Predicting

When you **predict**, you tell what you think will happen next. Your prediction should be based on your knowledge of real life. Use your own experience and knowledge to help you make predictions.

As you read, practice making predictions by filling in this chart.

Story Detail	My Knowledge About This Detail	My Prediction

The Far and the Near

Thomas Wolfe

Summary The main character in this story is a train engineer. Every day for twenty years, he passes by a pleasant little cottage near the tracks. A woman and her daughter come out each time and wave to him as he passes. The woman, her daughter, and the house become symbols of happiness for him. At last, when he retires, he goes to visit the house. He soon discovers that the women are nothing like he expected.

Note-taking Guide Use this chart to keep track of the sequence of events in the story.

Sequence of Events					
1. For twenty years, a train engineer passes a white cottage with green blinds.	2.	3.	4.	5.	6.

The Far and the Near

Thomas Wolfe

The story opens with a description of a tidy little cottage. It is white with green blinds. It has a vegetable garden, a grape arbor, and flower beds. In front of the house are three big oak trees. The house looks neat and comfortable. Every afternoon, just after two o'clock, an express train passes by the house.

◆   ◆   ◆

Every day for more than twenty years, as the train had approached this house, the engineer had blown on the whistle, and every day, as soon as she heard this signal, a woman had appeared on the back porch of the little house and waved to him.

◆   ◆   ◆

The woman brings her young daughter to the porch. The girl also waves to the engineer each day. As the years pass, the girl grows up.

The engineer grows old and gray during these twenty years. His own children have also grown up.

He has seen terrible tragedies on the tracks. One time, his train hit a wagon full of children. Another time a cheap car stalls on the tracks. The people inside are so frightened that they cannot move. Once an old, deaf hobo is walking along the tracks. He does not hear the warning whistle.

◆   ◆   ◆

But no matter what peril or tragedy he had known, the vision of the little house and the women waving to him with a brave free motion of the arm had become fixed in the mind of the engineer as something beautiful and enduring, something beyond all change and ruin, and something that would always be the same, no

TAKE NOTES

Read Fluently

Read the bracketed paragraph aloud. Then underline the part that tells what the engineer did every day.

English Language Development

The word *tragedies* is the plural of *tragedy*. In English, when you add an *s* to a word that ends in *y*, you sometimes have to change the *y* to *i* and add *es* instead. This is true if a consonant comes before the *y*. If a vowel comes before the *y*, you don't change the *y* to *i*. Here are some examples: *story—stories, toy—toys*.

Write the plurals of these words:

day_____

country_____

Culture Note

Hobo is a word that is not used very much anymore. The word refers to a person who wanders from place to place, usually by sneaking rides on freight trains. The words *hobo, tramp*, and *bum* have similar meanings. The only difference is that a hobo will work from time to time, if work is available. What is the word for someone like this in your native language?

How does the engineer feel about the woman and the house? Based on his feelings, **predict** what will happen next.

_____

_____

_____

_____

_____

Vocabulary and Pronunciation

In English, the letter *g* has two sounds. It has its own sound, as in *garden*. It also borrows the sound of *j*, as in *engineer*. For each of the following words, write *g* or *j* to tell how the letter *g* is pronounced.

_____ green _____ grape

_____ signal _____ change

_____ sagged _____ gesture

_____ strange _____ visage

_____ magic _____ imagined

_____ gone _____ again

Vocabulary and Pronunciation

How does the man feel as he walks toward the house?

_____

_____

_____

matter what <u>mishap</u>, grief or error might break the iron schedule of his days.

◆   ◆   ◆

Wolfe goes on to say that the engineer has tender feelings toward the women and their house. He makes up his mind that someday he will go and visit them.

At last that day comes. The engineer is retired. He has no more work to do. He rides the train to the town where the women live. He walks through the station and out into the town. As he does this, he begins to feel strange. It doesn't seem like the same town he saw from the train. He becomes more and more puzzled as he walks on. The engineer walks down the hot and dusty road until he gets to the house. The experience seems more and more like a bad dream. He knocks at the door. Then he hears the steps from inside. Finally, the door opens. The woman stands before him.

◆   ◆   ◆

And instantly, with a sense of bitter loss and grief, he was sorry he had come. He knew at once that the woman who stood there looking at him with a mistrustful eye was the same woman who had waved to him so many thousand times. But her face was harsh and pinched and <u>meager</u>; the flesh sagged wearily in <u>sallow</u> folds, and the small eyes peered at him with timid suspicion and uneasy doubt. All the brave freedom, the warmth and the affection that he had read into her gesture, vanished in the moment that he saw her and heard her unfriendly tongue.

◆   ◆   ◆

Vocabulary Development

mishap (MIS hap) *n.*   accident
meager (MEE ger) *adj.*   having little flesh, thin
sallow (SAL loh) *adj.*   sickly, pale yellow

Wolfe describes how the man explains why he came. The woman finally invites him in, but she seems unwilling to do so. She calls to her daughter in a harsh, shrill voice. They have a short visit in the women's ugly little parlor. As the man tries to talk, the women stare at him in a dull way. They seem hostile and afraid.

The engineer feels disappointed and leaves the cottage. He suddenly feels old and sad. The things that he thought he knew were not the way he expected them to be.

◆ ◆ ◆

And he knew that all the magic of that bright lost way, the vista of that shining line, the imagined corner of that small good universe of hope's desire, was gone forever, could never be got back again.

Literary Analysis

How does the man feel when he meets the woman? Complete these sentences about the moment of **anticlimax**.

The man is disappointed when he meets the woman because she looks at him

_____

Her face is

_____

Her eyes are filled with

_____

He had thought she was warm and friendly, but

_____

Literary Analysis

Imagine that you are the mother or the daughter. Do you think their reaction to the man is normal? Explain why you feel as you do.

_____

Culture Note

The word *parlor* comes from a root word that means "to speak." That was what was done in the old-fashioned parlor. People gathered there for conversation. The room was usually not used for anything but entertaining company. It usually had the best furniture in the house. If you have a room like this in your house, what do you call it?

© Pearson Education, Inc., publishing as Pearson Prentice Hall.

The Far and the Near **235**

The Far and the Near

1. **Interpret:** Everyday for twenty years, the engineer passes a cottage in a small town and a woman and her daughter wave at him. What does this tell you about the engineer's life?

2. **Literary Analysis:** What is the story's **anticlimax**?

   _____

3. **Literary Analysis:** What effect does the anticlimax have on both the engineer and the reader?

   _____

   _____

4. **Literary Analysis:** Use this chart to list three events in the **rising action** that lead to the anticlimax.

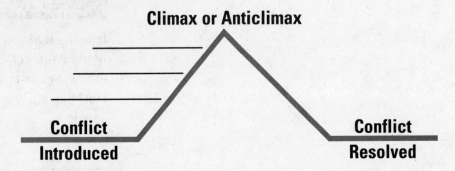

Climax or Anticlimax

Conflict Introduced

Conflict Resolved

5. **Reading Strategy:** When you read about the engineer's decision to visit the two women after retiring, what did you **predict** would happen?

   _____

   _____

6. **Reading Strategy:** Based on your own experience, did you predict that the engineer's view of the world would change when he stepped down from the "high windows of his cab"? Explain.

   _____

Of Modern Poetry • Anecdote of the Jar • Ars Poetica • Poetry

LITERARY ANALYSIS

A **simile** compares two seemingly different things. The connecting words *like* or *as* signal the comparison. The word *like* signals the comparison in this simile:

The sound of the explosion echoed through the air *like thunder.*

This simile compares the sound of an explosion to thunder. The comparison stresses the loudness of the noise.

Similes also help writers to create imagery. **Imagery** is language that uses **images.** These are words or phrases that relate to one or more of the five senses (sight, smell, touch, sound, or taste). As you read, notice the similes and imagery each poet uses.

READING STRATEGY

Writers use words differently in poems than they do in stories or essays. Poems may have surprising words and images. One way to make sure that you understand a poem is to **paraphrase**. This means to notice important ideas and say or write them in your own words. Paraphrasing can make difficult poems easier to understand. Use this chart to list difficult passages in a poem. Then, write the ideas in your own words.

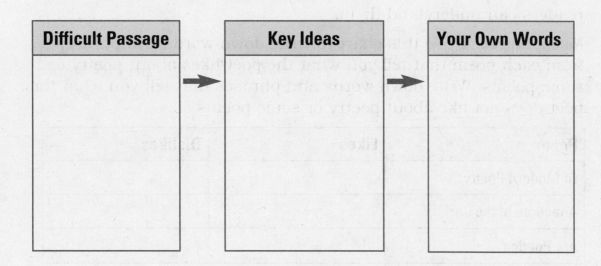

Difficult Passage		Key Ideas		Your Own Words
	→		→	

Of Modern Poetry • Anecdote of the Jar

Wallace Stevens

Ars Poetica

Archibald MacLeish

Poetry

Marianne Moore

Summaries All of these poems are about poems. Each poet says what he or she thinks a poem is or should be. They say what they like or do not like about poems. Sometimes, they say these things directly. Sometimes, they use images to give you a feeling about what they mean. In "Of Modern Poetry," the speaker says that a poem must use the language of its own time. In "Anecdote of the Jar," the presence of a jar on a hill gives order to the wilderness. The jar itself is "gray and bare." In "Ars Poetica," the speaker compares a poem to several other things. He says that the image is the most important part of a poem. The meaning of the poem does not matter as much. In "Poetry," the speaker feels sad for those who do not like poems. She thinks poems should be written so that readers can understand them.

Note-taking Guide Use this chart to write down words and phrases from each poem that tell you what the poet likes about poetry or some poems. Write down words and phrases that tell you what the poet does not like about poetry or some poems.

Poem	Likes	Dislikes
Of Modern Poetry		
Anecdote of the Jar		
Ars Poetica		
Poetry		

Of Modern Poetry • Anecdote of the Jar • Ars Poetica • Poetry

1. **Speculate:** In "Ars Poetica," the speaker talks about **images** that show grief and love. Why do you think the poet chose to write about these feelings?

   _____

2. **Synthesize:** In "Poetry," the speaker says "we do not admire what / we cannot understand." What kinds of poems do you think the speaker does admire?

   _____

3. **Literary Analysis:** A **simile** uses the words *like* or *as* to compare two things. Find two **similes** in "Ars Poetica." Use this chart to explain what each simile means.

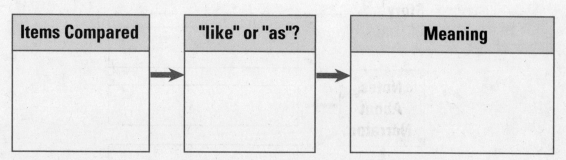

Items Compared	"like" or "as"?	Meaning

4. **Reading Strategy:** These are lines 6-9 from "Of Modern Poetry" with some words and phrases missing. Complete these lines with your own words. Keep the meaning of the original lines.

   It has to be _____, to learn the _____.

   It has to _____ the men _____ and to _____

   The women _____. It has to _____

   And it has to find what will _____...

5. **Reading Strategy:** Write out your **paraphrase** of lines 6-9 from "Of Modern Poetry."

   _____

In Another Country • The Corn Planting • A Worn Path

LITERARY ANALYSIS

Point of view is the perspective from which a story is told.

- In the **first-person point of view**, the person telling the story takes part in the action, uses the pronoun *I*, and shares his or her own thoughts and feelings.

- In the **limited third-person point of view**, the narrator stands outside the action and does not use the pronoun *I*. However, this narrator sees the world through one character's eyes and shows only what that character is thinking and feeling.

As you read, use this chart to analyze the point of view in each story.

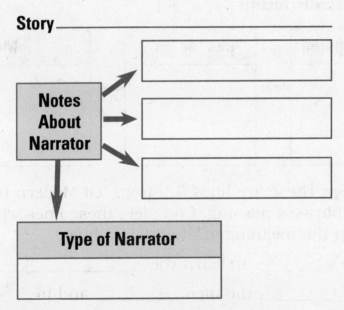

Story _____

Notes About Narrator

Type of Narrator

READING STRATEGY

When you **identify with characters**, you connect characters' thoughts and feelings with your own experiences. As you read, identify with characters by thinking of how you felt in similar situations.

In Another Country

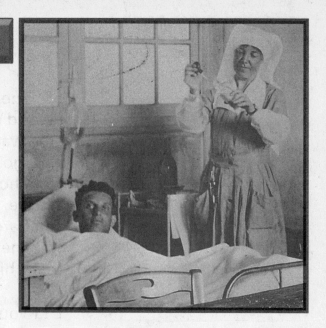

Summary In "In Another Country," an American officer recovering from a war injury meets three young Italian officers and an older major. All of the men are wounded. The major helps the American with his Italian grammar, advises him not to marry, and mourns the death of his own wife.

Note-taking Guide Use this chart to record information about Hemingway's story "In Another Country."

Setting	Characters	Problem	Resolution

In Another Country
Ernest Hemingway

The *ou* in English can sound like the *oo* in food. Or it can sound like *ow* as in *cow*. Write *oo* or *ow* to tell how the *ou* is pronounced in each of these words:

_____ wounded   _____ about

_____ bounce   _____ shouted

Identify with the narrator, or put yourself in his place. How would you feel about what the doctor says in the underlined sentence?

_____

_____

_____

In English, quotation marks are used to show the exact words of a speaker. Circle the quotation marks that are around the major's words in the bracketed paragraph.

The story opens in Milan, Italy, during World War I. The narrator has been injured in the war. He and the other wounded men do not go to the front anymore. Instead, they go to a hospital for treatment every afternoon. There, they are treated with new machines that are supposed to help them heal.

The doctor approaches the narrator and asks him what he did before the war.

♦ ♦ ♦

Did you practice a sport?"

I said: "Yes, football."

"Good," he said. "You will be able to play football again better than ever."

♦ ♦ ♦

The narrator tells about another patient, a major. The major's hand is being treated in a machine. Before the war, the man had been the greatest fencer in Italy. The doctor shows the major a picture of a hand that had been almost as small as the major's. He also shows him a picture of the same hand after treatment. In the second picture, the hand is a little larger.

The major asks if the hand in the picture had been wounded.

♦ ♦ ♦

"An industrial accident," the doctor said.

"Very interesting, very interesting," the major said, and handed it back to the doctor.

"You have confidence?"

"No," said the major.

♦ ♦ ♦

Vocabulary Development

confidence (KAHN fuh duhns) *n.*   being sure, being certain

Other patients include three boys from Milan. Sometimes, when they are done with the machines, they walk to a nearby café. They are sometimes joined by another boy. He wears a black silk handkerchief across his face because he has no nose. He was injured within an hour of going to the front line for the first time.

He doesn't have any medals because he hasn't been in the service long enough. One boy, who was to be a lawyer, has three medals because he had a dangerous job. The rest of the boys and the narrator each have one medal. They are all dealing with death.

◆　◆　◆

We were all a little detached, and there was nothing that held us together except that we met every afternoon at the hospital.

◆　◆　◆

The narrator says that the boys once asked him what he had done to get his medals. He shows them the papers, which were full of pretty words. But all they really say was that he had gotten the medals because he was an American. After that, the boys act differently toward the narrator. He is still their friend, especially against outsiders. But he is never really one of them after that. It was different with the three Italian boys. They had really earned their medals.

Reading Check

Why does the boy wear a black handkerchief across his face?

_____

_____

_____

Vocabulary and Pronunciation

In English, the letter combination *ea* can sound like the *e* in *bed.* Or it can sound like the *ee* in *deep.* For each of these words, write *e* or *ee* to show how the *ea* is pronounced.

_____ instead _____ treatment

_____ leather _____ death

_____ speaks

English Language Development

In English, the ending *n* or *an* added to the name of a country can tell where a person is from. For example, an American is from America, and an Italian is from Italy. Sometimes different endings are used. For example, a Spaniard is from Spain, an Iraqi is from Iraq, and a Chinese person is from China. What is the English word for people from your native country?

_____

Literary Analysis

A story in the first-person **point of view** gives the thoughts of the narrator. What are the narrator's thoughts about death?

_____

_____

_____

_____

Reading Strategy

Circle all the words in the bracketed paragraph that tell you the story is written from the first-person **point of view**.

The narrator had been wounded but agrees that it was an accident.

◆   ◆   ◆

I was never ashamed of the ribbons, though, and sometimes, after the cocktail hour, I would imagine myself having done all the things they had done to get their medals; but walking home at night through the empty streets with the cold wind and all the shops closed, trying to keep near the street lights, I knew that I would never have done such things, and I was very much afraid to die, and often lay in bed at night by myself, afraid to die and wondering how I would be when I went back to the front again.

◆   ◆   ◆

The major, the former fencer, does not believe in bravery. He spends a lot of time correcting the narrator's Italian grammar as they sit in the machines. The narrator had once said that Italian seemed like such an easy language. But then the major starts helping him with the grammar. Soon Italian seems so hard that the narrator is afraid to speak until he has the grammar straight in his mind.

The major comes to the hospital every day. He doesn't believe in the machines but feels that they must be tested.

◆   ◆   ◆

It was an idiotic idea, he said, "a theory, like another." I had not learned my grammar, and he said I was a stupid impossible disgrace, and he was a fool to have bothered with me.

◆   ◆   ◆

The narrator and the major then start talking. The major asks if the narrator is married. The narrator says no, but he hopes to be. The major says that a man must not marry. When asked to explain, he says that a man should not place himself in a position to lose. Instead, he should find things he cannot lose. He speaks with anger and bitterness. The narrator speaks up.

◆ ◆ ◆

"But why should he necessarily lose it?"

"He'll lose it," the major said. He was looking at the wall. Then he looked down at the machine and jerked his little hand out from between the straps and slapped it hard against his thigh. "He'll lose it," he almost shouted. "Don't argue with me!"

◆ ◆ ◆

The major then asks the attendant to turn off the machine. He goes to the other room for more treatment. Then he asks the doctor if he can use the phone. When he returns, he comes toward the narrator and puts his arm on his shoulder.

◆ ◆ ◆

"I am so sorry," he said, and patted me on the shoulder with his good hand. "I would not be rude. My wife has just died. You must forgive me."

"Oh—" I said, feeling sick for him. "I am so sorry."

He stood there biting his lower lip. "It is very difficult," he said. "I cannot <u>resign</u> myself."

Stop to Reflect

Why do you think the major is so upset?

_____

_____

_____

_____

Reading Check

How does the major explain his behavior?

_____

_____

_____

_____

Vocabulary Development

resign (ree ZYN) *v.* to accept one's fate

Read Fluently

Read aloud the bracketed paragraph. Then describe how the major walked out of the hospital.

_____

_____

_____

Culture Note

In the United States, black is traditionally used as a symbol of mourning. In some other countries, white or yellow might be used. What color symbolizes mourning in your native country?

_____

Reading Check

How long had the major's wife been sick?

_____

_____

_____

Reading Strategy

Identify with the character of the major. What do you think he is thinking about as he looks out the window?

1. _____

2. _____

He looked straight past me and out through the window. Then he began to cry. "I am utterly unable to resign myself," he said and choked. And then crying, his head up looking at nothing, carrying himself straight and soldierly, with tears on both his cheeks and biting his lips, he walked past the machines and out the door.

◆　◆　◆

The doctor tells the narrator that the major's young wife had died of pneumonia. She had been sick for only a few days. No one thought she would die. The major stays away from the hospital for three days. When he comes back, he is wearing a black band on his sleeve.[1] Now there are large photographs on the wall of before-and-after pictures of wounds cured by the machines. There are three photographs of hands like the major's, completely cured.

◆　◆　◆

I do not know where the doctor got them. I always understood we were the first to use the machines. The photographs did not make much difference to the major because he only looked out of the window.

Vocabulary Development

utterly (UT er lee) _adv._ completely

---

1. **a black band on his sleeve** a sign of mourning.

The Corn Planting

Summary In "The Corn Planting," an old farmer and his wife have two things they love— their farm and their son. One night, a telegram arrives telling of their son's death in a car accident. They spend the rest of that night planting corn as their way of dealing with grief.

Note-taking Guide Use this diagram to record the message of the story "The Corn Planting." Then write story details that support the message of the story.

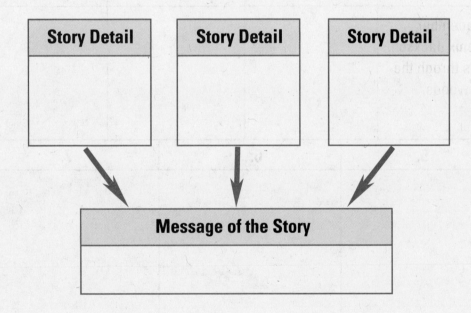

A Worn Path

Summary In "A Worn Path," an old woman makes her way along a country path. Once in town, she goes to a doctor's office to get medicine for her grandson. She has been taking care of him since he swallowed lye some years before.

Note-taking Guide Use this diagram to record information about Phoenix Jackson's journey in "A Worn Path."

Sequence of Events			
1.	**2.**	**3.**	**4.**
In December, Phoenix Jackson walks throgh the pine woods.			
5.	**6.**	**7.**

A Worn Path
Eudora Welty

An old Negro woman named Phoenix Jackson leaves home on a cold December morning. She walks along a country path.

◆ ◆ ◆

She was very old and small and she walked slowly in the dark pine shadows, moving a little from side to side in her steps, with the balanced heaviness and lightness of a <u>pendulum</u> in a grandfather clock.

◆ ◆ ◆

The woman carries a cane that she taps as she walks.

Welty tells us that Phoenix's eyes are blue with age. Her skin is quite wrinkled. Her hair comes down in ringlets from under the red rag.

The woman notices some movement in the bushes.

◆ ◆ ◆

Old Phoenix said, "Out of my way, all you foxes, owls, beetles, jack rabbits, coons and wild animals! . . . Keep out from under these feet, little bobwhites. . . . Keep the big wild hogs out of my path. Don't let none of those come running my direction. I got a long way."

◆ ◆ ◆

Phoenix comes to a hill. She climbs up one side of the hill and down the other. On the way, a bush catches her dress. It takes her a long time to get her dress free. She crosses a creek by walking across a log with her eyes closed.

Vocabulary Development

pendulum (PEN dyoo luhm) *n.*   a weight hanging from a fixed point so as to swing freely under the action of gravity

---

Literary Analysis

How do you know that the **point of view** is **limited third person?**

_____
_____
_____

Vocabulary and Pronunciation

The letter combination *gh* is sometimes silent in English. Other times, it has the same sound as the letter *f*. Write *silent* or *f* to tell how the *gh* is pronounced in each of these words.

_____ bright   _____ through

_____ straight _____ thought

_____ laughter_____ high

_____ laughed_____ enough

_____ lights

English Language Development

English has many **compound words**. These are two words that are put together to make one. *Shoelaces* is an example. It means "laces that tie a shoe." *Pinewoods* is another example. It means "woods with pine trees." What do you think each of these compound words means?

scarecrow

_____

overhead

_____

windmill

_____

Literary Analysis

In the bracketed paragraph, what information about Phoenix does the **limited third-person narrator** suggest?

_____

_____

_____

Background

Barbed-wire fences are common on farms and ranches. They are made of wire that has sharp points sticking out. The sharp points are designed to keep farm animals from getting out and to keep wild animals from getting in.

Reading Check

Phoenix sees something in front of her. What does she think it is?

_____

_____

_____

_____

Phoenix is pleased with herself. She sits down to get comfortable and rest.

♦ ♦ ♦

Up above her was a tree in a pearly cloud of mistletoe. She did not dare to close her eyes, and when a little boy brought her a plate with a slice of marble cake on it she spoke to him. "That would be acceptable," she said. But when she went to take it there was just her own hand in the air.

♦ ♦ ♦

Phoenix keeps on walking. She has to go through a barbed-wire fence. She is very careful. She finally gets through the barbed-wire fence safely. Then she sees a buzzard.[1] She asks him who he's watching. She comes to an old cotton field and then to a field of dead corn. There is no path here. Then she sees something in front of her. It is tall, black, and thin. It is moving.

She sees what she thinks is a man but then is confused by the figure's silence.

♦ ♦ ♦

"Ghost," she said sharply, "who be you the ghost of? For I have heard of nary death close by."

♦ ♦ ♦

The figure moves in the wind but does not answer. She touches its clothes and realizes there is nothing underneath.

♦ ♦ ♦

Vocabulary Development

mistletoe (MIS uhl toh) *n.* a green plant that lives on other plants

nary (NAIR ee) *adj.* not one

---

1. **sees a buzzard** (BUZ erd) A buzzard is a bird that waits for its prey to die, rather than killing it. Buzzards commonly circle dying prey, so they are seen as a sign of death.

"You scarecrow," she said. Her face lighted. "I ought to be shut up for good," she said with laughter. "My senses is gone. I too old. I the oldest people I ever know. Dance, old scarecrow," she said, "while I dancing with you."

❖ ❖ ❖

Phoenix keeps walking through the corn field. She gets to a wagon track. This is the easy part of the walk. She follows the track. She goes past bare fields, past some trees, past some old cabins. The doors and windows are all boarded. They remind Phoenix of old women who are under a spell, just sitting there.

❖ ❖ ❖

In a <u>ravine</u> she went where a spring was silently flowing through a hollow log. Old Phoenix bent and drank. "Sweet gum[2] makes the water sweet," she said, and drank more. "Nobody know who made this well, for it was here when I was born."

❖ ❖ ❖

As she walks along the path near a swamp, Phoenix speaks to the alligators. Then, she crosses a road that is shaded by oak trees.

A black dog comes up to Phoenix. He knocks her down, and she falls into a ditch. She cannot get out of it. A young white hunter comes along. He has a dog with him.

Vocabulary Development

ravine (ruh VEEN) *n.*   a small narrow valley with steep sides

---

2. sweet gum *n.* a tree that has a sweet-smelling juice.

English Language Development

Granny is one English word that is used for a *grandmother*. Other words include *Grandma, Gran,* and *Nana.* What words are used in your native language for *grandmother*?

_____

_____

_____

Literary Analysis

What detail in the bracketed paragraph tells you that the **narrator** is getting into Phoenix's mind? Underline the sentence that gives the answer.

He asks Phoenix what she is doing. She jokes that she is pretending to be an upside-down bug. She needs his help to get up.

◆ ◆ ◆

He lifted her up, gave her a swing in the air, and set her down. "Anything broken, Granny?"

"No sir, them old dead weeds is springy enough," said Phoenix, when she had got her breath. "I thank you for your trouble."

◆ ◆ ◆

The man asks Phoenix where she lives and where she's going. She tells him she's on her way to town. He tells her that's too far. He says she should just go back home.

Phoenix doesn't move.

◆ ◆ ◆

The deep lines in her face went into a fierce and different <u>radiation</u>. Without warning, she had seen with her own eyes a flashing nickel fall out of the man's pocket onto the ground.

◆ ◆ ◆

Phoenix distracts the man. She cries and claps her hands. She tells the black dog to get away. She whispers, "Sic him!"[3] The man tells Phoenix to watch how he gets rid of the dog. He tells his own dog, "Sic him!" The man runs and throws sticks at the black dog. Phoenix uses this time to pick up the nickel. She slowly bends down.

◆ ◆ ◆

Vocabulary Development

radiation (ray dee AY shuhn) *n.*   arrangement from the center to the sides

---

3. **"Sic him!"** a command given to a dog to attack.

Her chin was lowered almost to her knees. The yellow palm of her hand came out from the fold of her apron. Her fingers slid down and along the ground under the piece of money with the grace and care they would have in lifting an egg from under a setting hen. Then she slowly straightened up, she stood erect, and the nickel was in her apron pocket. A bird flew by. Her lips moved. "God watching me the whole time. I come to stealing."

◆ ◆ ◆

The man comes back. He tells Phoenix that he scared the dog off. Then he points the gun at Phoenix. She just stands straight, facing him. He asks her if the gun scares her.

◆ ◆ ◆

"No, sir, I seen plenty go off closer by, in my day, and for less than what I done," she said, holding <u>utterly</u> still.

◆ ◆ ◆

The man admires her bravery. He would give her some money if he had any. He advises her to stay home to be safe. She tells him she has to continue her journey.

The man and Phoenix go in different directions. Phoenix keeps walking. At last she gets to Natchez.[4] The city is decorated for Christmas. Phoenix sees a lady who is carrying an armful of wrapped gifts. Phoenix asks the woman to tie her shoelaces. She says that

Reading Strategy

In the bracketed paragraph, do you think Phoenix did something wrong? Write *yes* or *no*. _____
Identify with Phoenix. What would you have done?

_____

_____

_____

Stop to Reflect

Why does Phoenix think the man is pointing his gun at her?

Vocabulary Development

utterly (UT er lee) *adv.* completely

---

4. **Natchez** (NACH iz): a town in southern Mississippi.

Phoenix is not using Standard English when she says "Here I be." The verb *to be* is one of the most irregular verbs in English as well as in other languages. Complete each sentence with the correct present-tense form of the verb *to be*.

Here I _____.

Here you _____.

Here he _____.

Here we _____.

Here they _____.

Read Fluently

Read the underlined paragraph aloud. Write two words to describe the tone of voice you used.

1. _____

2. _____

Reading Check

What is wrong with Phoenix's grandson? Circle the passages in the bracketed section that answer the question.

untied shoes are fine for the country. But they don't look right in a big building. Phoenix goes into a big building. She says "Here I be" to the woman at the counter. The woman asks Phoenix for her name, but Phoenix does not answer. The woman asks if Phoenix is deaf. Then the nurse comes in.

◆   ◆   ◆

"Oh, that's just old Aunt Phoenix," she said. "She doesn't come for herself—she has a little grandson. She makes these trips just as regular as clockwork. She lives away back off the Old Natchez Trace."[5] She bent down. "Well, Aunt Phoenix, why don't you just take a seat? We won't keep you standing after your long trip."

◆   ◆   ◆

Phoenix sits down. The nurse asks her about her grandson. She wants to know if his throat is any better. At first, Phoenix does not answer. The nurse asks if the boy is dead. At last, Phoenix answers. She tells the nurse that her memory had left her. She had forgotten why she had come. The nurse wonders how she could forget, after coming so far.

◆   ◆   ◆

"Throat never heals, does it?" said the nurse, speaking in a loud, sure voice to old Phoenix. By now she had a card with something written on it, a little list. "Yes. Swallowed lye. When was it?—January—two-three years ago—"

Phoenix spoke unasked now. "No, missy, he not dead, he just the same. Every little while his throat begin to close up again, and he not able

---

Vocabulary Development

lye (LY) *n.* a strong chemical used in making soap

---

5. **the Old Natchez Trace** a trace is an old path or trail left by people, animals, or vehicles.

to swallow. He not get his breath. He not able to help himself. So the time come around, and I go on another trip for the <u>soothing</u> medicine."

"All right. The doctor said as long as you came to get it, you could have it," said the nurse. "But it's an <u>obstinate</u> case."

◆ ◆ ◆

Phoenix talks about her grandson. She says that they are the only two left in the world. The boy suffers, but he is going to last. He is a sweet boy. The nurse then gives Phoenix the medicine. She says "Charity" as she makes a mark in a book. The nurse gives Phoenix a nickel out of her purse for Christmas. Phoenix takes the other nickel out of her pocket and looks at both of them.

She taps her cane to announce her plan. She is going to buy a paper windmill for her grandson. He has never seen one.

◆ ◆ ◆

She lifted her free hand, gave a little nod, turned around, and walked out of the doctor's office. Then her slow step began on the stairs, going down.

© Pearson Education, Inc., publishing as Pearson Prentice Hall.

Stop to Reflect

The narrator has waited until now to tell the reason for Phoenix's journey. Would you rather have known earlier? Write *yes* or *no*, and then explain your opinion.

_____

_____

_____

Stop to Reflect

Identify with the nurse. Why does she give Phoenix a nickel? Give two reasons.

1. _____

2. _____

_____

Reading Check

What does Phoenix plan to buy for her grandson? Circle the answer to the question.

Vocabulary Development

soothing (SOO thing) *adj.* comforting

obstinate (AHB stuh nuht) *adj.* stubborn, not easily changed

A Worn Path **255**

In Another Country • The Corn Planting • A Worn Path

1. **Draw Conclusions:** Choose one of three stories to explain the message about life that it reveals.

   _____

2. **Literary Analysis:** Identify three details that show Hemingway's story was written using a **first-person point of view.**

   _____

3. **Literary Analysis:** How would "A Worn Path" be different if Welty had told the story from Phoenix Jackson's first-person point of view?

   _____

4. **Reading Strategy:** From the three stories, choose the characters with whom you **identify** most and least. Provide reasons for your choices.

   _____

   _____

5. **Reading Strategy:** Using this diagram, list the personality traits, interests, or values that you share with a character in one of the stories. List these in the center. In the two separate circles, list differences.

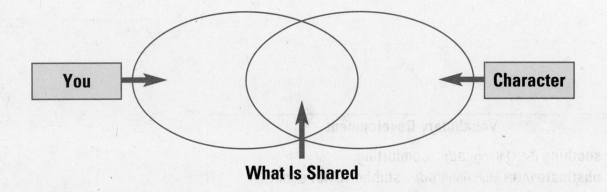

What Is Shared

Chicago • Grass

LITERARY ANALYSIS

Carl Sandburg uses **apostrophe** to tell about Chicago. Apostrophe is a technique in which the speaker talks to a thing, an idea, or a person. In "Chicago," the speaker talks to the city as if it were a person:

> They tell me you are wicked and I believe them . . .

Sandburg uses another technique called **personification**. Poets use personification to give human qualities to a non-human subject. In "Grass," the grass itself speaks:

> I am grass.
> Let me work.

As you read, think about the effect of these two techniques. Use this chart to record the ways in which Sandburg uses personification in each poem.

READING STRATEGY

When you read a poem, you should think about the message the poet is trying to express. **Respond** to the poet's message by deciding how you personally feel about what the poet is saying. When you respond to a poem, think about the following:

- how the poet's message relates to your life

- how the poet's message relates to the world

- how you can use or apply the ideas in the poem

As you read, connect the images and ideas in each poem to your own experiences.

	Detail Expressing Human Trait
Chicago	
Grass	

Chicago • Grass

Carl Sandburg

Summaries: In "Chicago," Sandburg uses simple words to express his love and admiration for the city of Chicago. He challenges the reader to find a city with more life. In "Grass," the grass explains that there is only grass where once important battles between great armies took place. The calmness of nature hides the horror and senselessness of war.

Note-taking Guide: Use the following chart to help you keep track of what each speaker talks about.

Chicago	
To whom is the speaker talking?	
What does the speaker talk about?	
What descriptions does the speaker use?	
Grass	
Who is the speaker	
What does the speaker talk about?	
What does the speaker claim to do?	

Chicago • Grass

1. **Interpret:** In the first stanza of "Chicago," the speaker calls the city by several names. What do these names tell you about the city?

   _____

2. **Draw Conclusions:** In "Grass," what is Sandburg saying about the death and destruction of war?

   _____

3. **Literary Analysis:** In "Chicago," Sandburg uses **apostrophe** to address both the city and another audience. Use this chart to record how Sandburg speaks to the city and how he speaks to others. In the center boxes, record the lines in which he addresses the city and the lines in which he addresses others. In the side boxes, note the imagery Sandburg uses when he addresses each audience.

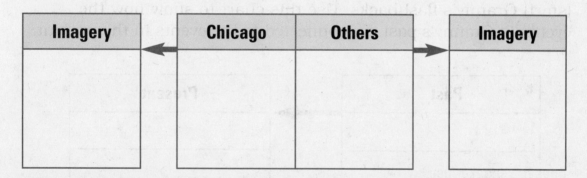

Imagery	Chicago	Others	Imagery

4. **Literary Analysis:** In "Grass," what words does Sandburg use **personification**?

   _____

5. **Reading Strategy:** What is your **response** to the grass's message?

   _____

The Jilting of Granny Weatherall

LITERARY ANALYSIS

Stream of consciousness is a special way of writing. It tries to copy the way people's thoughts flow. These types of stories usually do the following:

- present thoughts as if they are coming directly from a character's mind

- leave out words and phrases that link ideas

- connect details through a character's thoughts and memories

Stream of consciousness stories often use **flashbacks**. These are interruptions that present something that happened earlier. A flashback may be a dream, a daydream, a memory, a story told by a character, or a switch by the narrator to a time in the past.

As you read, notice how Granny Weatherall's thoughts wander from topic to topic. Also, pay attention to the details that trigger (start) Granny's flashbacks. Use this chart to show how the events in Granny's past are connected to the events in the present.

Past	Present

READING STRATEGY

In this story, Granny drifts in and out of reality. She has many flashbacks from her life. To keep track of the story, **clarify the sequence of events**. Watch for jumps in Granny's thinking. Often, these jumps occur when Granny shifts from a conversation to her own thoughts.

The Jilting of Granny Weatherall

Katherine Anne Porter

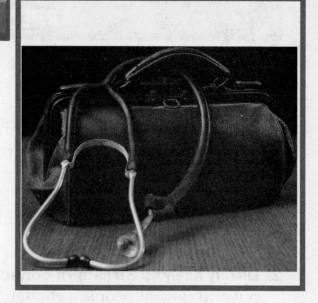

Summary Ellen Weatherall is on her deathbed. Her thoughts drift between moments in the present and memories of the past. She receives visits from her daughter, her doctor, and her priest. She recalls the people and events that filled her life. Her thoughts wander freely among the good and the bad memories.

Note-taking Guide Use this chart to put the events of Granny's life in order.

Event 1	Event 2	Event 3	Event 4	Event 5	Event 6
George leaves Ellen standing at the altar on their wedding day.					

The Jilting of Granny Weatherall

1. **Connect:** George left Granny standing at the altar sixty years ago. How is that experience connected to the last paragraph of the story?

_____

_____

2. **Literary Analysis: Stream-of-consciousness** writing tries to copy the natural flow of people's thoughts. Find two places where Granny's thoughts drift from one topic to another topic that does not seem related. Explain your choices.

_____

_____

3. **Literary Analysis:** Fill in the chart with information about three **flashbacks** in the story.

Form	Trigger	What we learn

4. **Reading Strategy: Clarify the sequence of events** in this story. Write down the events from Granny's life in the order in which they happened.

_____

_____

A Rose for Emily •
Nobel Prize Acceptance Speech

LITERARY ANALYSIS

A **conflict** is a struggle between opposing forces. It is the element that drives most narrative and dramatic works.

- **Internal conflict** happens when a character must deal with competing values or needs.

- **External conflict** occurs when a character struggles with an outside force, such as someone else, society, nature, or fate.

A conflict reaches **resolution** when the struggle ends.

READING STRATEGY

Ambiguity occurs in a literary work when an action, a character, or a statement, can be explained in more than one way. To **clarify ambiguity** in fiction, notice parts of the story that seem unclear. Then, look for clues in the writing that help you clarify what you read. In "A Rose for Emily," Faulkner uses the following to create ambiguity:

- subtle hints or open-ended comments by the narrator

- limited information about the order of events

- vague details about Emily's actions

Use this chart to note details that help you clarify ambiguities.

Ambiguous Event	Details
bad smell from the house	men sniff around cellar, spread lime in cellar, Emily watches, smell goes away
Emily buys poison	
Baptist minister visits Emily	

A Rose for Emily

William Faulkner

Summary Emily Grierson is a woman in a small Southern town. She lives under the watchful eyes of the community. Because she is secretive and private, the townspeople believe that she may be crazy. When Emily shows interest in a man from another town, people wonder whether she will marry him. When the man disappears from town, Emily begins keeping to herself again. After her death, people find something shocking in her bedroom.

Note-taking Guide Faulkner tells this story in five sections. These sections do not occur in time order. To make sense of the story, analyze what happens in each section. Use the following chart to record your observations:

Section I   What happens: Officials confront Emily about taxes.
Section II   What happens:
Section III   What happens:
Section IV   What happens:
Section V   What happens:

Nobel Prize Acceptance Speech

William Faulkner

Summary William Faulkner received the Nobel Prize for literature in 1950. In his acceptance speech, Faulkner presents his opinions about world affairs. He also talks about the role of literature in help-ing people make sense of the world. Faulkner tells young writers to set aside their fear of world destruction and address the basic problems of love, honor, and caring for others. He explains that it is the writer's duty to help people carry on. Writers can do this by reminding people of the glory of their past.

Note-taking Guide In the chart, record the main idea of each para-graph of Faulkner's speech.

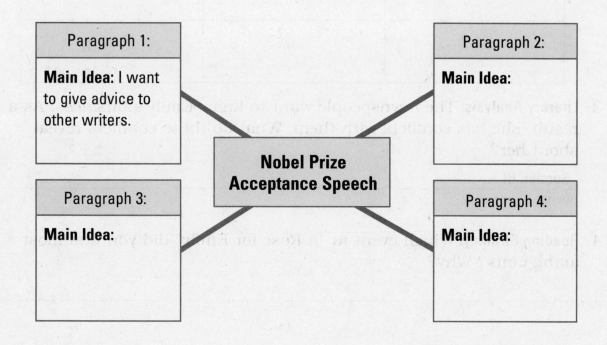

Paragraph 1:

Main Idea: I want to give advice to other writers.

Paragraph 2:

Main Idea:

Nobel Prize Acceptance Speech

Paragraph 3:

Main Idea:

Paragraph 4:

Main Idea:

A Rose for Emily • Nobel Prize Acceptance Speech

1. **Make a Judgment:** In his Nobel Prize acceptance speech, Faulkner claims that the conflicts of the heart make worthy subjects for good writing. How well does "A Rose for Emily" show this quality? Explain.

   _____

2. **Literary Analysis:** Emily has **conflicts** with townspeople and with herself. Use the following chart to list one **external conflict** and one **internal conflict** in Emily's life. Then, tell whether the conflict has been resolved.

Conflict	Who vs. Who/What?	Resolution
nonpayment of taxes	Emily vs. town	

3. **Literary Analysis:** The townspeople want to know Emily's business. As a result, she has conflicts with them. What do these conflicts reveal about her?

   _____

4. **Reading Strategy:** Which event in "A Rose for Emily" did you find most **ambiguous**? Why?

   _____

5. **Reading Strategy:** Do you think "A Rose for Emily" would be a better story if Faulkner had made it less ambiguous? Why or why not?

   _____

Robert Frost's Poetry

LITERARY ANALYSIS

Many of Robert Frost's poems do not have rhyme. However, they have a pattern of stressed and unstressed syllables. This pattern is called **meter**.

- The basic unit of meter is a foot. A *foot* usually has one stressed syllable (´) and one or more unstressed syllables (˘).

- The most common foot is the iamb. An *iamb* is one unstressed syllable followed by a stressed syllable (˘ ´).

- A line that has five iambs is called *iambic pentameter*.

- A poem made up of lines of iambic pentameter that do not rhyme is called **blank verse.**

As you read Frost's poems, use this chart to identify which poems are written in blank verse.

READING STRATEGY

One way to appreciate **blank verse** is to read it aloud in sentences. Use these tips:

- Do not pause at the end of each line.

- Follow the punctuation.

- Pause briefly after commas and longer after periods.

As you read, notice how blank verse has the natural rhythms of speech.

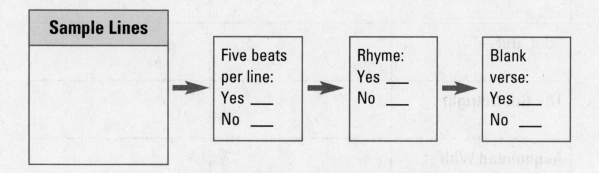

Sample Lines	Five beats per line: Yes ___ No ___	Rhyme: Yes ___ No ___	Blank verse: Yes ___ No ___

Robert Frost's Poetry

Summaries In "**Birches**," the speaker recalls the pleasure of swinging from birch trees as a child. "**Stopping by Woods on a Snowy Evening**" describes a man tempted to linger in the peaceful woods. In "**Mending Wall**," the speaker and his neighbor meet to repair breaks in the wall that separates their fields. The speaker wonders about the purpose of the wall and the forces of nature that continually pull it down. "**Out, Out—**" tells the harsh story of a young farm boy who loses control of his power saw while cutting wood. "**The Gift Outright**" examines the colonial spirit that struggled to tame a new land and form a nation. In "**Acquainted With the Night**," the speaker admits to moments of loneliness in his life.

Note-taking Guide Use this chart to record the main idea and an important detail from each of Frost's poems.

Poem	Main Idea	Important Detail
Birches		
Stopping by Woods on a Snowy Evening		
Mending Wall		
"Out, Out—"		
The Gift Outright		
Acquainted With the Night		

Robert Frost's Poetry

1. **Interpret:** The neighbor in "Mending Wall" repeats the statement, "Good fences make good neighbors." What does this saying mean?

   _____

   _____

2. **Generalize:** "The Gift Outright" tells a story about early American history. What picture of American history does Frost create?

   _____

   _____

3. **Literary Analysis:** A poem made up of lines of iambic pentameter that do not rhyme is called **blank verse**. Name one of Frost's poems that is not written in blank verse?

   _____

   _____

4. **Literary Analysis:** In "Birches," the speaker expresses conflicting feelings about life. Yet he adds "Earth's the right place for love." Use this chart to analyze his feelings.

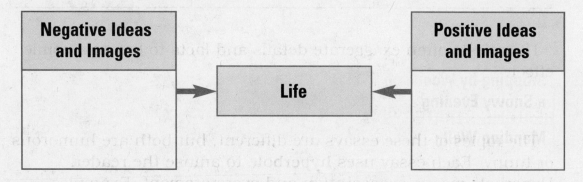

5. **Reading Strategy:** Rewrite the blank verse of "The Gift Outright" as five sentences. Then **read them aloud.**

   _____

   _____

The Night the Ghost Got In • *from* Here Is New York

LITERARY ANALYSIS

"The Night the Ghost Got In" and "Here Is New York" are both **informal essays**, or brief pieces of nonfiction. Often, they include the following: relaxed, conversational style and structure; narrow subject; loose organization; wanderings from the main point; and clues about the writer's personality.

As you read, think about what each piece suggests about its author. Use this chart to record your findings.

Informal Essays	Thurber	White
Writer's Style		
Writer's Purpose		
Writer's Personality		

Humorists often exaggerate details and facts to create a comic effect.

READING STRATEGY

The topics of these essays are different, but both are humorous or funny. Each essay uses **hyperbole** to amuse the reader. Hyperbole means exaggeration and overstatement. Examples include the strange events in Thurber's essay and the many possible disasters in White's essay. To **recognize hyperbole**, look for details that seem too unlikely to be true.

The Night the Ghost Got In

James Thurber

Summary One night, the narrator hears footsteps. He wakes up his family. All of the confusion makes the narrator's crazy grandfather angry.

Note-taking Guide:

As you read use the chart to identify the topic, or the main idea, of each paragraph. An example is provided below.

Paragraph	Topic/main Idea of the Paragraph
1	A ghost got into the house on November 17, 1915, and caused a great deal of confusion.
2	
3	
4	
5	
6	
7	
8	
9	
10	
11	
12	
13	
14	

from Here Is New York

E. B. White

Summary New York City has a little bit of everything. This excerpt from **"Here Is New York"** tells why New York is such a special city. Outsiders are often uncomfortable in the city because it seems so big. People who live there know that the city has thousands of tiny neighborhoods, where everybody knows everybody else.

Note-taking Guide

White's essay shows that different people view the world in different ways. People who live in New York may appreciate different traits of the city than tourists and visitors. As you read, record the positive and negative traits as White presents them.

Positive Traits	Negative Traits

The Night the Ghost Got In • *from* Here Is New York

1. **Distinguish:** In "The Night the Ghost Got In," how does Thurber portray himself differently than he portrays the other characters?

_____

_____

2. **Compare and Contrast:** White describes New York's neighborhoods as small towns. In what way does he say the neighborhoods compare to small towns?

_____

_____

3. **Literary Analysis:** Quote a passage from "The Night the Ghost Got In" that shows the conversational style of an **informal essay**.

_____

_____

4. **Literary Analysis:** White uses humor to show the city's many unique qualities. Write two funny passages from the essay in this chart. Explain what each passage reveals about the city.

Humorous Passage	What It Reveals

5. **Reading Strategy:** Cite an example of **hyperbole** from each essay. Remember to look for details that seem unlikely to be true.

_____

_____

from Dust Tracks on the Road

LITERARY ANALYSIS

- **Autobiography** is nonfiction written by an author about his or her life. An author writes an autobiography to tell about the events, people, thoughts, and feelings from his or her life.

- **Social context** means the attitudes and culture of the time and place in which the author lived. Culture is the way of life of a group of people. Culture includes language, laws, beliefs, and traditions.

The experiences from an author's life include details about the author's community and culture. This information provides social context.

This excerpt from Hurston's autobiography gives the reader information about Hurston and about her African American community in the South in the early 1900s.

READING STRATEGY

Hurston had two **purposes** for writing. First, she wanted to tell about her life. Second, she wanted to show the experiences of the African American community at that time. These two purposes helped her choose the words, details, characters, and events to use in her writing.

As you read, use this chart to note important details, characters, and events from the excerpt.

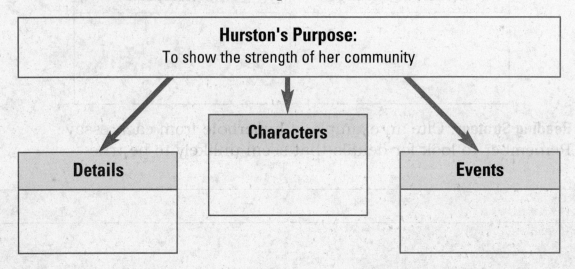

from Dust Tracks on a Road

Zora Neale Hurston

Summary This is a section from a longer work. The author describes events from her childhood in a small Florida town. She used to wait at the side of the road for white travelers to pass by. She would ask to go with them for a short distance. Hurston also talks about an experience that changed her life. Her school had visitors one day. These were two white women. Hurston read aloud and the women were impressed. They invited Hurston to visit them at their hotel. They gave her gifts. The gifts of books pleased Hurston more than the candy or pennies.

Note-taking Guide

As you read this selection, write down details about the characters in the chart below.

Character	What the Character Wants	What the Character Does
Zora		
Grandmother		
Mrs. Calhoun		
Mrs. Johnstone and Miss Hurd		

from Dust Tracks on a Road

1. **Support:** Two white women visit Zora's school. How can you tell that these women affect Zora strongly? List two details from the story.

   _____

   _____

2. **Literary Analysis:** What do you learn about the **social context** of Hurston's story from each of these details: (a) the schoolroom being cleaned for visitors, (b) Zora going to school barefoot?

   _____

   _____

3. **Literary Analysis:** Hurston's **autobiography** contains many details. These details provide clues about the culture in the South in the early 1900s. In the first column of this chart, record two details about customs or behaviors in this excerpt. In the second column, explain the attitude that each detail reveals.

Detail of Social Context		Attitude It Reveals

4. **Reading Strategy:** For what **purpose** do you think Hurston told this story about meeting the women from Minnesota?

   _____

   _____

The Negro Speaks of Rivers • I, Too • Dream Variations • Refugee in America • The Tropics in New York

LITERARY ANALYSIS

The **speaker** is the voice that "says" a poem. Often, the speaker is the poet. However, a speaker may also be an imaginary person, a group of people, an animal, or an object. In "The Tropics in New York," Claude McKay's speaker is a homesick adult who is probably the poet himself:

> A wave of longing through my body swept,
> And, hungry for the old, familiar ways
> I turned aside and bowed my head and wept.

As you read each poem, look for clues that reveal the identity of the speaker. Use this chart to record your observations.

	Clues in Poem	Identity of Speaker
The Negro Speaks of Rivers		
I, Too		
Dream Variations		
Refugee in America		
The Tropics in New York		

READING STRATEGY

Writers do not always directly reveal who the speaker is. Instead, the reader must **draw inferences**. Drawing inferences means using details from the poem to reach conclusions about the speaker's attitudes, feelings, and experiences.

As you read each poem, look for clues about the speaker. Draw inferences about each speaker's personal qualities, feelings, and opinions.

PREVIEW

The Negro Speaks of Rivers • I, Too • Dream Variations • Refugee in America

Langston Hughes

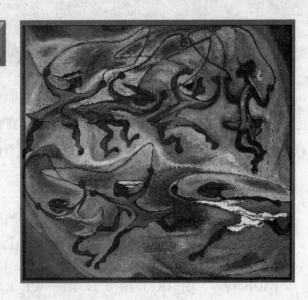

"The Tropics in New York"

Claude McKay

Summaries In "**The Negro Speaks of Rivers**," the speaker recalls the experience of his people along ancient rivers of the world. "**I, Too**" is Langston Hughes's response to a poem by Walt Whitman. Whitman's poem describes the variety that exists in America. The speaker in "**Dream Variations**" imagines a world in which he can play and rest freely and in which the blackness of his skin is accepted. "**Refugee in America**" challenges the reader to think more carefully about words such as *freedom* and *liberty*. In "**The Tropics in New York**," a window fruit display in New York takes the speaker back home to the tropics.

Note-taking Guide

As you read each poem, enter an example of what each speaker says and then explain what he means in the chart.

	What Does the Speaker Say?	What Does the Speaker Mean?
The Negro Speaks of Rivers		
I, Too		
Dream Variations		
Refugee in America		
The Tropics in New York		

The Negro Speaks of Rivers • I, Too • Dream Variations • Refugee in America • The Tropics in New York

1. **Interpret:** The theme of a poem is its main message. Reread lines 3 and 10 in "I, Too." What do these lines say about the theme of the poem?

   _____

   _____

2. **Literary Analysis:** Who is the speaker in "The Negro Speaks of Rivers"?

   _____

3. **Literary Analysis:** What do the speakers in "Dream Variations" and "Refugee in America" both want?

   _____

   _____

4. **Reading Strategy:** An **inference** is something you believe to be true based on information you have. To **draw inferences** about the speaker in a poem, look closely at the speaker's choice of words. In three of these poems, find a line that tells you something about the speaker. Use this chart to record the inferences you make.

Poem	Line	What It Reveals About the Speaker

From the Dark Tower • A Black Man Talks of Reaping • Storm Ending

LITERARY ANALYSIS

A **metaphor** is a comparison that compares two very different things. It does not use the words *like* or *as* to compare things. A metaphor may be directly stated or only suggested. It is usually brief.

An **extended metaphor** is a longer comparison. It is often very detailed. An extended metaphor is developed throughout several lines or an entire poem.

Metaphors use **imagery**. This is descriptive language that appeals to the senses. These three poets use imagery to express their feelings about the African American experience. Use this chart to analyze each poem's imagery as you read. Think about the emotions and ideas it describes.

Poems	Metaphor	Image	Emotion/Ideas
From the Dark Tower	African Americans compared to farm workers	Silently working hard in fields of gold; weeping	Sorrow; anger
A Black Man Talks of Reaping			
Storm Ending			

READING STRATEGY

Historical context is the time and place in which a work of literature is written. **Connecting to historical context** can help readers better understand literature. These three poems were written during the Harlem Renaissance in the 1920s. Reread the information about this cultural movement on pages 910–911 of your textbook to better appreciate the poems.

From the Dark Tower • A Black Man Talks of Reaping • Storm Ending

Summaries In "From the Dark Tower," the speaker seems to say that better times are coming for those who plant "while others reap." He says the night is no less lovely because it is dark. He closes by referring to waiting in the dark, tending "our agonizing seeds." In **"A Black Man Talks of Reaping,"** the speaker describes his careful planting of a large crop from which he reaped only a small harvest. While his brother's sons gather the crops, his own children eat bitter fruit gathered from fields they have not sown. In **"Storm Ending,"** thunder and the storm are compared with huge, hollow flowers blossoming overhead. As the flowers bleed rain and drip like honey, the sweet earth flies from the storm.

Note-taking Guide Use this diagram to record details from the three poems and the shared message the details suggest.

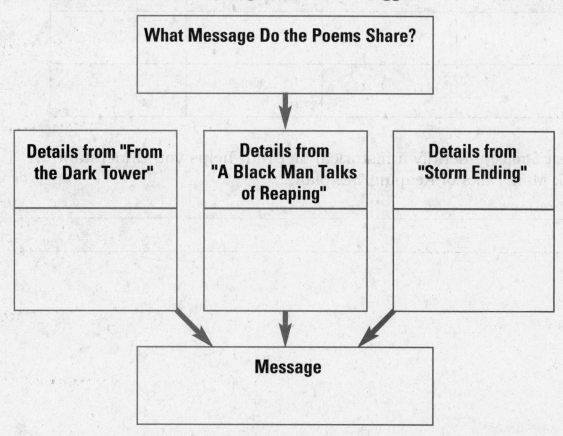

What Message Do the Poems Share?

Details from "From the Dark Tower"	Details from "A Black Man Talks of Reaping"	Details from "Storm Ending"

Message

From the Dark Tower • A Black Man Talks of Reaping • Storm Ending

1. **Infer**: In "A Black Man Talks of Reaping," who reaps what the speaker has sown?

   _____

2. **Literary Analysis**: A **metaphor** compares two different things. Identify one metaphor that Countee Cullen uses in "From the Dark Tower."

   _____

   _____

3. **Literary Analysis**: Use this chart to identify and analyze the main **image** in two of the poems.

Poem	Image	Interpretation	Emotion

4. **Reading Strategy**: Identify a historical fact that helps you understand "A Black Man Talks of Reaping." Explain.

   _____

   _____

ABOUT PUBLIC RELATIONS DOCUMENTS

A **public relations document** shows the public face of a company or organization. Some familiar public relations documents are advertisements and press releases. Equally important are mission statements. These statements tell the mission, or purpose, of a business or organization by presenting three kinds of information:

1. "Who We Are"—a description of the purpose of the organization or business
2. "What We Do"—details that describe services or products
3. "Why We Do It"—a summary of an organization's goals and way of thinking

Read the mission statement and calendar of events from the Museum of Afro-American History. As you read, think about how the museum's mission is carried out through the events it holds.

READING STRATEGY

Inferences are assumptions or information that is not directly stated in a text. Good readers use their previous knowledge to fill in these gaps. As you read, make inferences and constantly test them by reading further. If reading further makes you doubt your inferences, change them or form new ones.

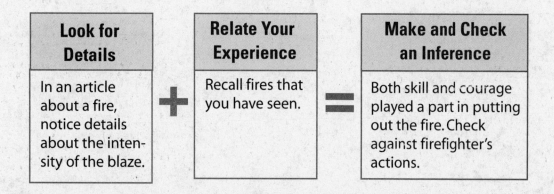

Look for Details		Relate Your Experience		Make and Check an Inference
In an article about a fire, notice details about the intensity of the blaze.	+	Recall fires that you have seen.	=	Both skill and courage played a part in putting out the fire. Check against firefighter's actions.

Build Understanding

Knowing this term will help you understand the information on this Web site.

artifacts (ART uh FAKTS) *n.* man-made objects that survive from earlier times.

A **mission statement** defines the limits of an organization. Based on the first paragraph, would the museum display the pen President Lincoln used to sign the Emancipation Proclamation (p. 223)? Why or why not?

_____

_____

Read aloud the philosophy and goals of the museum contained in the bulleted list. In what way does the museum provide "A Foundation for the Future"?

_____

_____

_____

_____

MUSEUM OF AFRO-AMERICAN HISTORY

Boston and Nantucket

Mission Statement
A Foundation for the Future

The mission of the Museum of Afro-American History is to preserve, conserve and interpret the contributions of people of African descent and those who have found common cause with them in the struggle for liberty, dignity, and justice for all Americans. Therefore, we:

- collect and exhibit artifacts of distinction in this field and acquire and maintain physical structures and sites through the end of the 19th century;
- educate the public about the importance of the Afro-American historical legacy in general, its Boston and New England heritages, in particular;
- celebrate the enduring vitality[1] of African American culture;
- and advance on our own and in collaboration with others an appreciation of the past for the benefit of the custodians of the future.

---

1. **vitality** (vy TAL uh tee) *n.* power and endurance.

MUSEUM OF AFRO-AMERICAN HISTORY BOSTON
Calendar of Events

Events take place at 8 Smith Court, Beacon Hill, unless otherwise noted.

SATURDAY, FEB. 3, 7:30 P.M.

READING AND BOOK SIGNING

**On Her Own Ground: The Life and Times
of Madam C.J. Walker**[2]

A'Lelia Bundles, former deputy bureau chief of ABC News in Washington and great-great grand-daughter of Madam C.J. Walker, will discuss the writing of *On Her Own Ground,* the first historically accurate account of this legendary entrepreneur and social activist.

Sponsored by the Collection of African American Literature, a partnership between the Museum of Afro-American History, Suffolk University, and Boston African American Historic Site.

Refreshments and book sales following. FREE

TUESDAYS, 10:30–11:30 A.M.

Stories from African American Literature and Lore
Vibrant stories and activities presenting history for preschool aged children and parents. FREE

---

2. Madame C.J. Walker (1867–1919) an African American woman who started her own beauty products company geared to the needs of African Americans. Praised as "the first black woman millionaire," Walker donated freely to charities and social causes.

Read the description of the first event. Do you think Ms. Bundles's portrayal of C.J. Walker would be positive?

_____

What clues from the text and from previous experience allow you to make that **inference**?

_____

_____

_____

_____

How could you check your inference?

_____

_____

Jazz is a style of music that began in southern cities like New Orleans, then spread northward in the 1920s. Jazz rhythms have roots in West African music, and many famous jazz musicians have been African American. Early New Orleans jazz groups played at a variety of places, from house parties to funeral processions.

A **calendar of events** provides the public with basic information about upcoming events. Circle the dates, times, and admission fees for the Underground Railroad and jazz concert events.

FRIDAY, FEB. 16, 6 P.M.–9 A.M.

Museum Overnight: Underground Railroad[3]

Spend the night at the Museum exploring the Underground Railroad through the escape routes on Beacon Hill. Design and build your own safe house. Includes dinner, storytelling, activities, breakfast and a special "bundle" to take home.

GRADE 5-6. $30 NON-MEMBER $25 MEMBERS.

SUNDAY, MARCH 18, 3 P.M.

Marian Anderson/Roland Hayes Concert Series: A New Beginning

Makanda Ken McIntyre Jazz Quartet. Original jazz selections and standard favorites from this world-class composer and improviser.[4] McIntyre, a Boston native and NY resident, is a master of the alto sax, bass clarinet, oboe, flute, and bassoon. Reception immediately following.

Sponsored in part by the Office of Community Collaborations and Program Development at the New England Conservatory.

$10 NON-MEMBER; FREE MEMBER; GROUP RATES AVAILABLE.

---

3. Underground Railroad a system of safe houses set up by opponents of slavery before the Civil War. The "railroad" was established to help escaped slaves reach the Free States and Canada.
4. improviser (IM pruh VYZ er) *n.* a musician who composes music on the spot as he or she plays.

THINKING ABOUT A PUBLIC RELATIONS DOCUMENT

1. What is the main goal of the museum?

_____

_____

_____

2. How does the museum work to achieve its mission and goals?

_____

_____

_____

_____

READING STRATEGY

3. Name one **inference** that you can make from reading the mission statement and the calendar of events.

_____

_____

_____

_____

4. The program for preschool-aged children is free. What can you infer the museum wishes to encourage from this fact? Explain.

_____

_____

_____

_____

TIMED WRITING: EVALUATION (25 minutes)

To help you write your mission statement, focus on writing for one of the following organizations:

• a museum devoted to a scientific or an artistic subject

• a magazine devoted to a sport or hobby

Before you write, consider what the organization does. Then, list the goals that the organization would have. Use these ideas to write your mission statement.

The Life You Save May Be Your Own

LITERARY ANALYSIS

The word *grotesque* in literature does not mean ugly or disgusting. A **grotesque character** is one who is strange, often because of an obsession. A **character** may express grotesque qualities through physical appearance, actions, or emotions.

O'Connor reveals the personality of the characters through **characterization**. With **direct characterization**, a writer simply tells the reader what a character is like. With **indirect characterization**, a writer reveals each character's personality through

- the character's words, thoughts, and actions.

- descriptions of the character's appearance or background.

- what other characters say about him or her.

- the ways in which other characters react or respond.

Use this chart to examine O'Connor's use of indirect characterization.

Shiftlet
Physical Appearance One-armed
Words
Thoughts
Actions
What others say

READING STRATEGY

When you wonder what will happen next in a story, stop and **make predictions**, or guess what will happen. To predict, first look back and think about what you have read. Then, pay attention to hints in the story.

The Life You Save May Be Your Own

Flannery O'Connor

Summary A one-armed man, Mr. Shiftlet, approaches a woman and her mentally challenged daughter, Lucynell. He agrees to fix up the old woman's property in exchange for food and a place to sleep. The woman wants him to marry her daughter. Eventually, he agrees. The woman gives him money to take a wedding trip. When Mr. Shiftlet and his new wife stop for food, he leaves her at the counter. He heads toward Mobile in the car. On the way, he picks up a hitch-hiker. They argue and the boy jumps out of the car. Mr. Shiflet drives toward Mobile alone.

Note-taking Guide

Use the chart shown to record what each character does in the story.

Character	Actions
Lucynell (daughter)	Learned the word *bird* Fell asleep in the restaurant
Mrs. Crater	
Mr. Shiftlet	

The Life You Save May Be Your Own

1. **Make a Judgment:** Is Mrs. Crater's decision to marry Lucynell to Mr. Shiftlet a good decision? Explain.

_____

_____

_____

2. **Literary Analysis:** Write one example of physical description that makes Mrs. Crater a **grotesque**.

_____

_____

3. **Literary Analysis:** Use this chart to examine Mr. Shiftlet. Identify his primary goal or obsession. Write the goal or obsession in the "Controlling Goal" column. Then, tell what actions he undertakes as a result of the obsession. Write these actions in the "Actions Undertaken" column.

Character	Controlling Goal	Actions Undertaken

4. **Reading Strategy:** Think about the point in the story when Mr. Shiftlet first appeared. What **predictions** did you make about the way he would treat Mrs. Crater and her daughter?

_____

_____

The First Seven Years

LITERARY ANALYSIS

Usually, the plot of a short story moves toward a resolution. This is the point at which a conflict is settled. **Conflict** is a struggle between two forces. There are two main types of conflict:

- An **internal conflict** takes place within a character. It involves a person's struggle with his or her own ideas, beliefs, or feelings.

- An **external conflict** takes place between a character and an outside force. The outside force can be society, nature, or an enemy.

Some modern writers stopped writing stories with resolutions. Instead, they wrote stories in which a character suddenly understands something. This moment of understanding is called an **epiphany** (uh PIF uh nee). The epiphany changes the way the character sees the conflict. It does not really make the conflict end. In this story, the main character has an epiphany. This epiphany makes him re-think his hopes for his daughter.

As you read, think about the conflicts each character experiences. Use this chart to examine the conflicts of the main character, Feld.

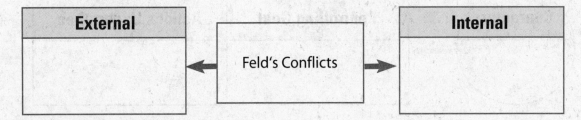

External		Internal
	Feld's Conflicts →	

READING STRATEGY

To understand stories better, try to **identify with characters.** Identifying with a character means finding ways in which their thoughts, feelings, actions, and circumstances are similar to yours. Think about things that you and the character have in common.

The First Seven Years

Bernard Malamud

Summary This story is about a shoemaker named Feld who runs a shop. He has an assistant named Sobel. He also has a daughter named Miriam. Feld wants his daughter to have a better life than he and his wife have had. He asks a college student named Max to call on her. He hopes the two will get married. Sobel hears the conversation Feld has with Max and runs out of the shop. He does not come back. Feld struggles to manage the shop and find a new assistant. When Feld meets Sobel again, Feld learns something about love and happiness.

Note-taking Guide

This story is about differences between people in what they value or desire. As you read, write down details that show the things each character finds important (values) and the things each character wants (desires).

Character	Values	Desires
Field		
Miriam		
Max		
Sobel		

This story takes place in the 1950s in the United States. It was a time of peace and prosperity. Many parents had worked hard so that their children would have easier lives. Look at a library book, a social studies textbook, or the Internet —or talk to your grand- parents or an older person you know—to find out more about the 1950s in the United States.

• What key events hurt the economy in the years before the 1950s?

_____

_____

_____

• What common values did many Americans hold in the 1950s?

_____

_____

_____

• What advances in technology, business, or popular culture took place?

_____

_____

_____

The First Seven Years
Bernard Malamud

Feld is a shoemaker who came to America from Poland. He has a helper named Sobel. Feld wishes that his daughter, Miriam, would go to college. Miriam enjoys reading books that Sobel lends her, but she would rather work than go to school. Feld admires a college student named Max because he has worked hard to get an education.

◆ ◆ ◆

A figure emerged from the snow and the door opened. At the counter the man withdrew from a wet paper bag a pair of battered shoes for repair. Who he was the shoemaker for a moment had no idea, then his heart trembled as he realized, before he had thoroughly discerned the face, that Max himself was standing there, embarrassedly explaining what he wanted done to his old shoes. Though Feld listened eagerly, he couldn't hear a word, for the opportunity that had burst upon him was deafening.

◆ ◆ ◆

Feld would like Max to date his daughter. He is afraid to suggest the idea. He does not know whether Max would agree or whether Miriam would be angry with him. Feld decides that there is no harm in bringing the idea up. If his daughter will not think about going to college herself, Feld wants her to marry an educated man. He wants her to have a better life.

Vocabulary Development

discerned (di SERND) *v.* perceived or recognized; made out clearly

---

Max describes to Feld what he wants done to his shoes. Then he asks about the price. Before answering, Feld asks Max to step into the hall for a conversation.

◆ ◆ ◆

"Ever since you went to high school," he said, in the dimly-lit hallway, "I watched you in the morning go to the subway to school, and I said always to myself, this is a fine boy that he wants so much an education."

"Thanks," Max said, nervously alert. He was tall and <u>grotesquely</u> thin, with sharply cut features, particularly a beak-like nose. He was wearing a loose, long <u>slushy</u> overcoat that hung down to his ankles, looking like a rug draped over his bony shoulders, and a soggy, old brown hat, as battered as the shoes he had brought in.

"I am a business man," the shoemaker abruptly said to conceal his embarrassment, "so I will explain you right away why I talk to you. I have a girl, my daughter Miriam—she is nineteen—a very nice girl and also so pretty that everybody looks on her when she passes by in the street. She is smart, always with a book, and I thought to myself that a boy like you, an educated boy—I thought maybe you will be interested sometime to meet a girl like this." He laughed a bit when he had finished and was tempted to say more but had the good sense not to.

Vocabulary Development

grotesquely (groh TESK lee) *adv.* absurdly; strikingly

slushy (SLUHSH ee) *adj.* covered with partly melted snow or ice

TAKE NOTES

Reading Strategy

Identify with Max, or put yourself in his place. Circle one word or phrase in this paragraph that shows how Max feels during his conversation with Feld.

Reading Check

What hope does Feld hold for Miriam and the college boy Max?

_____

_____

_____

Identify with Max. Why does he ask Feld for a picture of Miriam?

_____

_____

_____

_____

Read this paragraph aloud. Circle three words that reveal how Sobel feels.

Max stared down like a hawk. For an uncomfortable second he was silent, then he asked, "Did you say nineteen?"

"Yes."

"Would it be all right to inquire if you have a picture of her?"

"Just a minute." The shoemaker went into the store and hastily returned with a snapshot that Max held up to the light.

"She's all right," he said.

Feld waited.

"And is she sensible—not the flighty kind?"

"She is very sensible."

After another short pause, Max said it was okay with him if he met her.

◆   ◆   ◆

Feld gives Max his telephone number. Max puts it away and asks again about the price of the shoes. Feld gives him a price of "a dollar fifty," which is less than he usually charges. Then Feld goes back into the store.

◆   ◆   ◆

Later, as he entered the store, he was startled by a violent clanging and looked up to see Sobel pounding with all his might upon the naked last.[1] It broke, the iron striking the floor and jumping with a thump against the wall, but before the enraged shoemaker could cry out, the assistant had torn his hat and coat from the hook and rushed out into the snow.

◆   ◆   ◆

Feld is upset that Sobel has left. He depends on Sobel because he has a heart condition. Sobel, a thirty-year-old Polish refugee, had come looking for work five years before. Now Feld trusts Sobel to run his business but feels guilty because he pays him so poorly. While Sobel does not seem to care about money, he is interested in books.

---

1. **last** _n._ a block shaped like a person's foot, on which shoes are made or repaired.

He has loaned books to Miriam and shared his written comments about them with her.

After working alone for a week, Feld goes to Sobel's rooming house to ask him to return. Sobel's landlady tells him that Sobel is not there. Feld is forced to hire a new assistant who is neither as trustworthy nor as skilled as Sobel is. Feld keeps his mind off his problems by thinking about Max and Miriam's first date. He hopes they will like each other.

◆ ◆ ◆

At last Friday came. Feld was not feeling particularly well so he stayed in bed, and Mrs. Feld thought it better to remain in the bedroom with him when Max called. Miriam <u>received</u> the boy, and her parents could hear their voices, his throaty one, as they talked. Just before leaving, Miriam brought Max to the bedroom door and he stood there a minute, a tall, slightly <u>hunched</u> figure wearing a thick, droopy suit, and apparently at ease as he greeted the shoemaker and his wife, which was surely a good sign. And Miriam, although she had worked all day, looked fresh and pretty. She was a large-framed girl with a well-shaped body, and she had a fine open face and soft hair. They made, Feld thought, a first-class couple.

Miriam returned after 11:30. Her mother was already asleep, but the shoemaker got out of bed and after locating his bathrobe went into the kitchen, where Miriam, to his surprise, sat at the table, reading.

"So where did you go?" Feld asked pleasantly.

"For a walk," she said, not looking up.

"I advised him," Feld said, clearing his throat, "he shouldn't spend so much money."

"I didn't care."

TAKE NOTES

Reading Check

How does Feld run his business when Sobel refuses to return to work?

_____

_____

_____

_____

_____

Vocabulary and Pronunciation

The word *received* has several different meanings. For example, it can mean "gotten," "contained," "caught a kicked football," "welcomed," or "supported." Which meaning of *received* does Malamud use in this paragraph?

_____

_____

_____

Vocabulary Development

hunched (HUNCHT) *adj.* humped over

Underline two sentences in the bracketed paragraphs that reveal Miriam's reaction to her first date with Max.

Identify with Miriam, or put yourself in her position. Why do you think she delays before answering her father's question about a second date with Max?

_____

_____

_____

_____

How does Miriam feel about Max after their second date?

_____

_____

_____

_____

The shoemaker boiled up some water for tea and sat down at the table with a cupful and a thick slice of lemon.

"So how," he sighed after a sip, "did you enjoy?"

"It was all right."

He was silent. She must have sensed his disappointment, for she added, "You can't really tell much the first time."

"You will see him again?"

Turning a page, she said that Max had asked for another date.

"For when?"

"Saturday."

"So what did you say?"

"What did I say?" she asked, delaying for a moment—"I said yes."

◆   ◆   ◆

Miriam asks her father about Sobel. Feld tells her Sobel has another job. Throughout the week, Feld asks Miriam about Max. He is disappointed when he finds out that Max is taking business classes to become an accountant. Max and Miriam have a second date on Saturday. When Miriam comes home, she tells her father that Max bores her because he is only interested in things. Miriam says Max did not ask her on another date, but she has no interest in going out with him anyway. Feld still hopes that Max will call his daughter again. Instead, Max avoids the shoemaker's shop on his way to school.

One afternoon Max comes to the shop. He pays for his shoes and leaves without saying a word about Miriam. Later that night, Feld has a heart attack after finding out that his new assistant has been stealing from him. Feld stays in bed for three weeks. When Miriam offers to get Sobel, Feld reacts angrily. Once he returns to work, he feels tired. He realizes he needs Sobel's help. Feld visits Sobel at his rooming house. He notices stacks of books and wonders why Sobel reads so much.

◆ ◆ ◆

"So when you will come back to work?" Feld asked him.

To his surprise, Sobel burst out, "Never."

Jumping up, he strode over to the window that looked out upon the miserable street. "Why should I come back?" he cried.

"I will raise your wages."

"Who cares for your wages!"

The shoemaker, knowing he didn't care, was at a loss what else to say.

"What do you want from me, Sobel?"

"Nothing."

"I always treated you like you was my son."

Sobel <u>vehemently</u> denied it. "So why you look for strange boys in the street they should go out with Miriam? Why you don't think of me?"

The shoemaker's hands and feet turned freezing cold. His voice became so hoarse he couldn't speak. At last he cleared his throat and croaked, "So what has my daughter got to do with a shoemaker thirty-five years old who works for me?"

"Why do you think I worked so long for you?" Sobel cried out. "For the stingy wages I sacrificed five years of my life so you could have to eat and drink and where to sleep?"

"Then for what?" shouted the shoemaker.

"For Miriam," he blurted—"for her."

The shoemaker, after a time, managed to say, "I pay wages in cash, Sobel," and <u>lapsed</u> into silence. Though he was <u>seething</u> with

---

English Language Development

In a question in English, the subject follows the verb or comes in the middle of a verb phrase. For example, the subject *I* comes in the middle of the verb phrase *should come* in this question from the story: Why *should I come* back? Which question in the bracketed passage does not have correct subject-verb order?

_____
_____
_____

Reading Strategy

Put yourself in Sobel's position, or **identify with** him. Why is he so angry with Feld?

_____
_____
_____

Vocabulary Development

vehemently (VEE huh ment lee) *adv.* forcefully; intensely
lapsed (LAPST) *v.* passed gradually
seething (SEETH ing) *adj.* boiling

How does Sobel feel about Miriam?

_____

_____

Underline a sentence in this paragraph that tells you Feld is having an **epiphany**.

How does Feld's **epiphany** change his plans for Miriam?

_____

_____

_____

excitement, his mind was coldly clear, and he had to admit to himself he had sensed all along that Sobel felt this way. He had never so much as thought it consciously, but he had felt it and was afraid.

"Miriam knows?" he muttered hoarsely.

"She knows."

"You told her?"

"No."

"Then how does she know?"

"How does she know?" Sobel said, "because she knows. She knows who I am and what is in my heart."

Feld had a sudden insight. In some devious way, with his books and commentary, Sobel had given Miriam to understand that he loved her. The shoemaker felt a terrible anger at him for his <u>deceit</u>.

"Sobel, you are crazy," he said bitterly.

"She will never marry a man so old and ugly like you."

♦ ♦ ♦

Sobel becomes very angry and then begins to cry. Feld feels sorry for Sobel. He realizes that Sobel barely escaped being killed by the Nazis during World War II and has patiently waited for five years for the girl he loves to grow up. Feld apologizes for calling Sobel ugly. He feels sad when he thinks about the kind of life his daughter will have if she marries Sobel. Feld believes his dreams for a better life for Miriam are dead.

♦ ♦ ♦

"She is only nineteen," Feld said <u>brokenly</u>. "This is too young yet to get married. Don't ask her for two years more, till she is twenty-one, then you can talk to her."

Vocabulary Development

deceit (duh SEET) *n.* deception; misrepresentation

brokenly (BROH kuhn lee) *adv.* as if crushed by grief

Sobel didn't answer. Feld rose and left. He went slowly down the stairs but once outside, though it was an icy night and the crisp falling snow whitened the street, he walked with a stronger stride.

But the next morning, when the shoemaker arrived, heavy-hearted, to open the store, he saw he needn't have come, for his assistant was already seated at the last, pounding leather for his love.

Stop to Reflect

Identify the ambitions that Feld, Miriam, and Sobel have for Miriam's future.

1._____

_____

_____

2._____

_____

_____

3._____

_____

_____

The First Seven Years

1. **Interpret:** Max is a college student Feld sees as he walks to school. Why does Feld like Max?

   _____

   _____

2. **Literary Analysis:** An **epiphany** is a moment when a character has a flash of understanding. One epiphany in this story happens when Feld visits Sobel. Use this chart to write down your ideas about this epiphany.

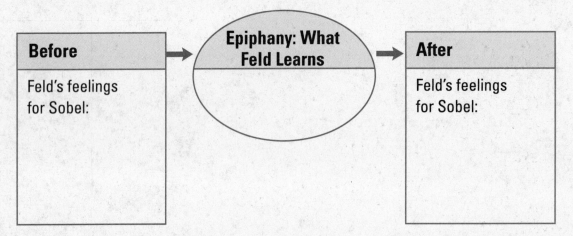

Before	**Epiphany: What Feld Learns**	**After**
Feld's feelings for Sobel:		Feld's feelings for Sobel:

3. **Literary Analysis:** What **external** and **internal conflicts** does Sobel have?

   _____

   _____

4. **Reading Strategy: Identify with a character** in this story. Choose a character and list ways in which his or her life reminds you of your own. Consider the thoughts, feelings, actions, and situations that you and the character have in common.

   _____

   _____

Aliceville

LITERARY ANALYSIS

The **tone** of a literary work is the writer's attitude toward his or her subject and audience. Here are some examples of tone:

- serious or humorous

- objective or emotional

- angry or joyous

Tone comes mainly from a writer's word choice. As you read "Aliceville," listen for the tone that Earley's narrator uses as the story progresses.

READING STRATEGY

You **visualize** when you form a mental image of what you are reading. Visualizing helps you enter the world of the story so that you can "see" the action.

The narrator of "Aliceville" uses visual details to make word pictures of what he sees around him. Read this description of a flock of geese:

> The geese flew across the field and turned in a climbing curve against the wooded ridge on the other side of the creek . . . .

You may be able to visualize this scene by seeing the "climbing curve" of the geese flying out one way and then turning back. As you read, use this chart to record other details that help you visualize.

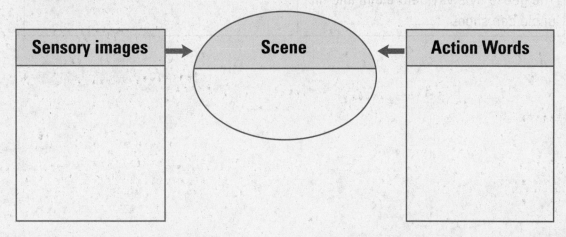

Sensory images	Scene	Action Words

Aliceville

Tony Earley

Summary The narrator, Jim Glass, is a boy living with his mother and his uncle. One evening, Jim and his uncle are driving home. They see a flock of geese settling down for the night. Jim and his uncle form a plan to sneak out to hunt the geese. Jim is very excited. The next morning, Jim and his uncle sneak up on the geese. Something goes wrong, and the geese fly away.

Note-taking Guide

Using the chart, track Jim's emotions by recording his feelings after various events in the story.

Event	Jim's Emotions
Jim and his uncle see the geese for the first time.	He is amazed and a little frightened.
Jim keeps the secret of the hunt from his family.	
The geese fly away before Jim and his uncle can shoot.	

Aliceville

1. **Generalize:** What does Uncle Zeno's behavior during the expedition tell you about him as a person?

_____

_____

2. **Literary Analysis:** Choose one passage from the story. Analyze the **tone** of the passage. Use the chart to identify the passage, list the details that create the tone, and decide the tone of the passage.

Passage	Words/Details Creating Tone		Tone
		→	

3. **Literary Analysis:** Select one passage from the story in which the tone clearly sounds like that of an adult. Write the passage on the lines.

_____

_____

_____

4. **Reading Strategy:** Identify an action, a description, or a scene in the story that you can **visualize**. Tell how the passage helps you form a mental image.

_____

_____

_____

Gold Glade • The Light Becomes Brighter • Traveling Through the Dark

LITERARY ANALYSIS

A writer's **style** is the manner in which he or she puts ideas into words. In poetry, a poet uses these elements to create style:

- Tone

- Sounds (such as alliteration)

- Symbolism

- Rhythm

- Figurative language (such as metaphors)

- Punctuation and capitalization

Another element of style is **diction**, or word choice. A poet uses diction to create a unique voice—a way of "speaking" on the page.

READING STRATEGY

Some poems are hard to understand because they have new vocabulary or complex sentences. To find meaning in difficult lines, **paraphrase** any difficult passages. To paraphrase means to restate in your own words. As you read these poems, use this chart to paraphrase difficult lines.

Lines from poem	Paraphrase

Gold Glade • The Light Becomes Brighter • Traveling Through the Dark

Robert Penn Warren, Theodore Roethke, William Stafford

Summaries In "Gold Glade," the speaker recalls an autumn walk through the woods. He remembers finding a beautiful hickory tree in the woods. He no longer remembers its location, but he knows that it still stands. In **"The Light Comes Brighter,"** the speaker describes the arrival of spring. In **"Traveling Through the Dark,"** the speaker finds a dead doe on the edge of the road. He hesitates before he pushes the animal into a river.

Note-taking Guide

Each of the speakers in these three poems sees something. What he sees has a powerful effect on him. Use this chart to record words from the poems that describe these experiences.

	What did the speaker see?	What words did the speaker use to describe what he saw?
"Gold Glade"	a glowing tree in a glade	"geometric," "circular," "gold"
"The Light Comes Brighter"		
"Traveling Through the Dark"		

Gold Glade • The Light Becomes Brighter • Traveling Through the Dark

1. **Evaluate:** Which of these three poems made the strongest impression on you? Why?

_____

_____

_____

2. **Literary Analysis:** Use this chart to analyze each poet's **diction**. Decide whether the language in each poem is formal or informal, plain or ornate, or abstract or concrete. Then, in the last column, identify the effect of this language.

Poet	Formal or Informal	Plain or Ornate	Abstract or Concrete	Effect
Warren				
Roethke				
Stafford				

3. **Reading Strategy:** To **paraphrase** means to restate something in your own words. Reread lines 16–20 from "Gold Glade," and think about what the speaker wants you to know or see. Then, write a paraphrase of these lines

_____

_____

_____

Average Waves in Unprotected Waters

LITERARY ANALYSIS

Foreshadowing is the use of clues that hint at what will happen later in a story. Foreshadowing builds suspense because it makes the reader wonder what will happen next. **Suspense** is a feeling of uncertainty about how a story will end. Because you are curious, you want to keep reading to find out what will happen next.

As you read, notice how foreshadowing and suspense keep you guessing about the story's outcome.

READING STRATEGY

Many writers tell about events in a story in the order in which they happen. Sometimes, writers place a flashback into the order of events. A flashback is a scene or an event from an earlier time. As you read Tyler's story, **put the events in order**. Note the order in which they actually happen. Use this chart to record the events in order, from the earliest to the latest.

Order of Events

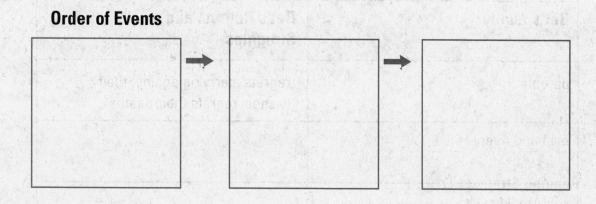

Average Waves in Unprotected Waters

Anne Tyler

Summary Bet feels that she can no longer care for her mentally challenged nine-year-old son, Arnold. She takes him to the state hospital. There, a nurse takes Arnold to a hallway lined with cots. The nurse tells Bet to wait six months before visiting Arnold. Bet's train home is late, but she distracts herself by listening to a speech by the Mayor.

Note-taking Guide

Use this chart to record Bet's regrets and struggles as they relate to members of her family.

Bet's family	Bet's Regrets and Struggles
parents	regrets marrying against their wishes; regrets their deaths
husband Avery	
son Arnold	

Average Waves in Unprotected Waters

1. **Infer:** Why does Bet tell the cab driver to wait for her outside the hospital?

_____

_____

2. **Literary Analysis:** Arnold's actions early in the story are clues to later events. For example, Arnold does not want to eat at the beginning of the story. In what way does his behavior **foreshadow** the story's main event?

_____

_____

3. **Literary Analysis:** Use this chart to list another example of foreshadowing from the story. Then, tell its effect on the reader.

Foreshadowing	Effect on Reader

4. **Reading Strategy:** State the main events of the story in chronological order.

_____

_____

_____

_____

from The Names • Mint Snowball • Suspended

LITERARY ANALYSIS

An **anecdote** is a little story about a funny or interesting event. People tell anecdotes all the time, mostly for entertainment. Writers include anecdotes to make a point or generalization. A generalization is a larger truth you learn from a specific experience.

Identify the anecdotes in these essays. Decide why the writer included each one. This is the same thing as saying what its purpose is. Then, write down the generalizations each one inspires. Use a chart like the one shown to help you.

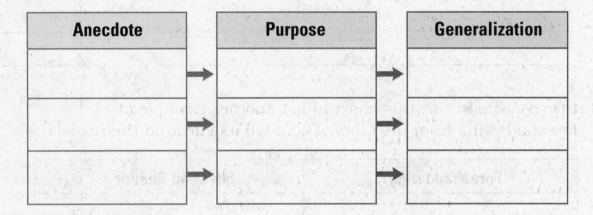

Anecdote		Purpose		Generalization
	→		→	
	→		→	
	→		→	

READING STRATEGY

You have probably taken a long trip, longed for the past, or realized something important. If so, you can find a connection between yourself and the authors of these essays. **Relating to your own experiences** will increase your understanding and enjoyment as you read.

from The Names • Mint Snowball • Suspended

N. Scott Momaday • Naomi Shihab Nye • Narjo

Summaries *The Names* is from a longer work. In this section, the author tells about the horse his parents gave him as a child. The horse's name was Pecos. The author still thinks about Pecos. In "Mint Snowball," the author recalls the drugstore that her great-grandfather used to own. She remembers an ice cream treat that he invented. After he died, nobody could ever make the treat the same way. In "Suspended," the author remembers a moment in her life before she could talk. She listened to jazz on the radio and realized music gave people a way to communicate.

Note-taking Guide

Each of these authors writes about something that affected his or her life. Use the chart below to collect important details about the subjects of each essay.

Essay	Subject	Details
from *The Names*		
Mint Snowball		
Suspended		

from The Names • Mint Snowball • Suspended

1. **Draw Conclusions:** Horses are important to the Kiowa Indians. Why do you think Momaday's journey on horseback meant so much to him?

_____

_____

2. **Interpret:** Nye says she longs for "something she has never seen or tasted." What connections does she make between the lost recipe and her own life?

_____

_____

3. **Analyze:** How does Harjo feel about her father? Use one detail from the essay in your answer

_____

_____

_____

4. **Literary Analysis:** Identify one **anecdote** from Momaday's essay. Explain the idea it helps the author to share.

_____

_____

_____

5. **Reading Strategy: Relate your own experiences** to those of the writers. Use this chart to write down similarities you see between the experiences these writers describe and your own experiences. Consider your personal situations, feelings, and actions.

Writer's Experience	My Experience	How They Relate

Everyday Use

LITERARY ANALYSIS

Motivation is the reason or reasons behind a character's thoughts, actions, and speech. Understanding a character's motivation will help you understand the character and the story. As you read, look for clues to a character's motivation by looking for details about the character's:

- values
- needs
- experiences
- dreams

Ask yourself these questions:

- Why is the character doing or saying this?
- What need or goal does the character hope to satisfy?

READING STRATEGY

In this story, you will meet two sisters who have had very different experiences. The author builds the conflict of the story around these differences. **Contrasting characters** will help you understand the conflict. Contrasting characters means identifying the ways in which they differ. Use this Venn diagram to note the differences between Dee and Maggie. Consider details such as behavior, speech, appearance, and history.

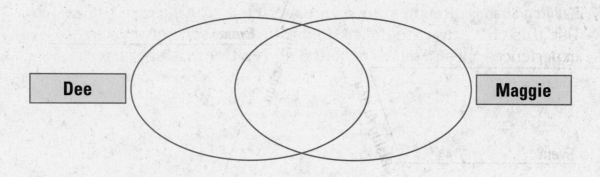

Dee — Maggie

Everyday Use

Alice Walker

Summary The narrator and her daughter Maggie wait in the yard for the narrator's other daughter, Dee. The narrator is a hard-working woman from the Georgia countryside. Maggie is a shy young woman who was badly scarred during a house fire. Dee is an educated, confident woman. As a teenager, Dee abandoned her childhood home and culture. When Dee returns, she tries to take pieces of her heritage. Dee's visit helps Magggie and her mother discover their own pride.

Note-taking Guide

Use this plot diagram to keep track of the events in the story.

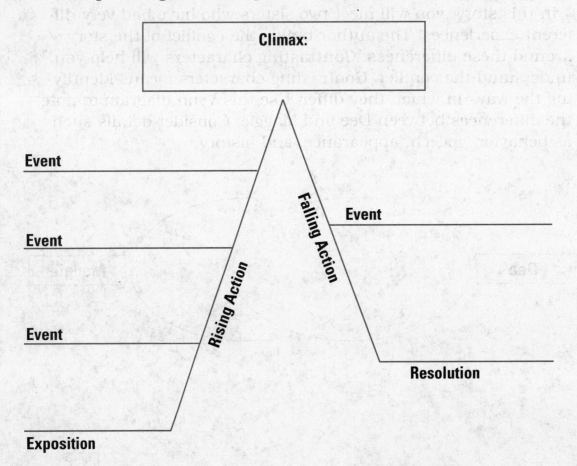

Climax:

Event _____

Event _____

Event _____

Rising Action

Falling Action

Event _____

Resolution

Exposition

Everyday Use
Alice Walker

How is Maggie related to Dee?

_____

_____

The narrator, or storyteller, waits anxiously for her daughter, Dee, to arrive. She knows that her other daughter, Maggie, will be nervous during Dee's visit. Maggie is embarrassed about the burn scars she has on her arms and legs. As she waits, the narrator dreams what it would be like if she and Dee were brought together for a surprise reunion on television. She imagines that Dee hugs her tearfully and pins a beautiful flower on her dress. In this dream, the narrator sees herself as elegant and witty. In reality, she is big, heavy, and strong with rough hands from hard work. She believes Dee would rather have a mother who is thin and has nice skin and hair.

◆ ◆ ◆

"How do I look, Mama?" Maggie says, showing just enough of her thin body <u>enveloped</u> in pink skirt and red blouse for me to know she's there, almost hidden by the door.

"Come out into the yard," I say.

Have you ever seen a lame animal, perhaps a dog run over by some careless person rich enough to own a car, <u>sidle</u> up to someone who is ignorant enough to be kind to him? That is the way my Maggie walks. She has been like this, chin on chest, eyes on ground, feet in shuffle, ever since the fire that burned the other house to the ground.

Circle words and phrases in the bracketed paragraph that tell how Maggie feels about herself. Then underline words and phrases that reveal what **motivates** her to feel this way.

Vocabulary Development

enveloped (en VEL ohpt) *v.* surrounded
sidle (SYD ul) *v.* to move sideways in a shy way

Contrast two **characters** by underlining one sentence that shows how Maggie and Dee are different.

How is Dee's life different from Maggie's?

_____

_____

_____

The word *bright* has several meanings. For example, it can mean "shining" or "intelligent." Which meaning of *bright* is used in this paragraph?

_____

Dee is lighter than Maggie, with nicer hair and a fuller figure. She's a woman now, though sometimes I forget. How long ago was it that the other house burned? Ten, twelve years?

◆ ◆ ◆

The narrator can still remember the horror of the fire. Maggie was burned terribly.

◆ ◆ ◆

And Dee. I see her standing off under the sweet gum tree she used to dig gum out of; a look of <u>concentration</u> on her face as she watched the last dingy gray board of the house fall in toward the red-hot brick chimney.

◆ ◆ ◆

The narrator knows that Dee had hated the house. She wonders why Dee doesn't celebrate as the house burns down.

The narrator remembers how the church helped her raise enough money to send Dee to school in Augusta. The narrator says that Dee always got what she wanted. For example, she got a nice graduation dress and a pair of black shoes to match a suit. In the narrator's opinion, Dee was a stubborn teenager with a mind of her own.

The narrator was not educated. Her school was closed after second grade, but she doesn't know why. Maggie reads to her, although she struggles because she can't see well.

◆ ◆ ◆

She knows she is not <u>bright</u>. Like good looks and money, quickness passed her by. She will marry John Thomas (who has mossy teeth in an earnest face) and then I'll be free to sit here and I guess just sing church songs to myself.

◆ ◆ ◆

Vocabulary Development

concentration (kahn sen TRAY shun) *n.* close, undivided attention

The narrator describes her house. It has three rooms, a tin roof, and holes for windows. The narrator believes Dee will hate this house. She says Dee never brought friends to visit. Maggie asks her mother if Dee ever had friends. The narrator remembers a few boys and girls who liked Dee because she was smart.

◆ ◆ ◆

When she comes I will meet—but there they are!

◆ ◆ ◆

Dee and a male friend arrive. Dee wears a flowing yellow and orange dress, long gold earrings, and bracelets. Her friend is short with long hair and a beard. Dee's friend tries to hug Maggie, but she nervously falls back against her mother's chair. While Dee snaps photographs, her mother sits with Maggie behind her. Finally, Dee puts the camera away and kisses her mother on the forehead. Dee's friend tries to shake Maggie's hand, but she doesn't want to.

Dee explains to her mother that her name is now Wangero Leewanika Kemanjo. Her mother wonders what happened to her real name, Dee.

◆ ◆ ◆

"She's dead," Wangero said. "I couldn't bear it any longer, being named after the people who oppress me."

"You know as well as me you was named after your aunt Dicie," I said. Dicie is my sister. She named Dee. We called her "Big Dee" after Dee was born.

"But who was *she* named after?" asked Wangero.

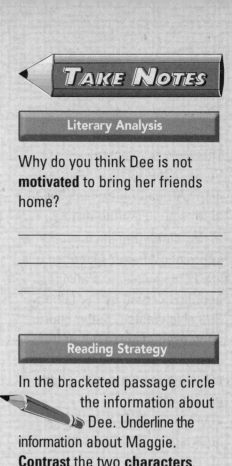

Literary Analysis

Why do you think Dee is not **motivated** to bring her friends home?

_____

_____

_____

Reading Strategy

In the bracketed passage circle the information about Dee. Underline the information about Maggie. **Contrast** the two **characters**. How do they seem different?

_____

_____

_____

Reading Check

Why has Dee changed her name?

_____

_____

_____

Vocabulary Development

oppress (oh PRES) *v.* keep down by cruel or unjust use of power or authority

This story takes place in the South in the 1960s. At this time, many African Americans began to take pride in their history.

In this story, Dee shows her interest in African American folk art. For example, she admires benches carved by her father. She also wants a butter churn once used to make butter from milk. In addition she wants two quilts made by her mother and grandmother.

• Why do you think Dee is so interested in folk art?

_____

_____

_____

_____

Vocabulary and Pronunciation

Over dinner, Dee "talked a blue streak over the sweet pota-toes." The expression "blue streak" means "a fast stream of words." This expression proba-bly comes from the way a bolt of lightning looks when it strikes. Lightning strikes quickly and creates a blue streak in the sky. How do you picture Dee as she talks?

_____

_____

_____

_____

"I guess after Grandma Dee," I said.

"And who was she named after?" asked Wangero.

"Her mother," I said, and saw Wangero was getting tired.

♦   ♦   ♦

To prevent further discussion, the narrator tells Dee (Wangero) that she doesn't know any more history. She actually does.

The narrator talks more about her daughter's new name. Dee (Wangero) tells her mother she does not have to use this name, but the narrator tries to learn how to say it. The narrator also tries to say the name of Dee's friend. She has trouble, so he tells her to call him Hakim-a-barber.

♦   ♦   ♦

We sat down to eat and right away he said he didn't eat collards¹ and pork was unclean. Wangero, though, went on through the chitlins² and corn bread, the greens and everything else.

♦   ♦   ♦

Dee (Wangero) loves everything on the table. She even loves the handmade benches they are sitting on. Her daddy had made them because they didn't have money to buy chairs.

Dee (Wangero) tells Hakim-a-barber that she hadn't appreciated the benches until now. She carefully feels the wood.

♦   ♦   ♦

Then she gave a sigh and her hand closed over Grandma Dee's butter dish. "That's it!" she said. "I knew there was something I wanted to ask you if I could have."

♦   ♦   ♦

_____

1. **collards** (KAHL erdz) *n.* leaves of the collard plant, often referred to as "collard greens".
2. **chitlins** (CHIT linz) *n.* chitterlings, a pork dish popular among southern African Americans.

Dee (Wangero) asks her mother if she can have the top and handle to an old butter churn. She wants to use the top as a centerpiece. Dee (Wangero) asks who made it. Maggie says that their aunt's first husband, Stash, made it. Dee (Wangero) wraps up the pieces to the churn. After dinner, Maggie washes the dishes. Dee (Wangero) looks through a trunk in her mother's room and finds two quilts. Dee's grandmother, mother, and aunt made the quilts from scraps of old dresses and shirts. One quilt pattern is Lone Star. The other is Walk Around the Mountain.

◆ ◆ ◆

"Mama," Wangero said sweet as a bird. "Can I have these old quilts?"

<u>I heard something fall in the kitchen, and a minute later the kitchen door slammed.</u>

◆ ◆ ◆

The narrator offers some other quilts instead. She explains that she made them but that Grandma had started them.

◆ ◆ ◆

"No," said Wangero. "I don't want those. They are stitched around the borders by machine."

"That'll make them last better," I said.

"That's not the point," said Wangero. "These are all pieces of dresses Grandma used to wear. She did all this stitching by hand. Imagine!" She held the quilts securely in her arms, stroking them.

◆ ◆ ◆

Dee (Wangero) is still admiring the quilts, but the narrator explains that she has promised them to Maggie as a wedding present.

◆ ◆ ◆

Short Story

Why do you think Dee wants the pieces to the churn?

_____

_____

Read Fluently

Read the underlined sentence aloud. How does Maggie feel about Dee's asking for the quilts?

_____

_____

English Language Development

In English, verbs must agree in number with their subject. A singular subject names one thing. A plural subject names more than one thing. List a singular subject and verb and a plural subject and verb in the bracketed passage.

_____

_____

Literary Analysis

Underline two reasons that show why Dee values the quilts and is motivated to ask for them.

Reading Check

Circle two words or phrases that show how Dee feels about Maggie having the quilts.

Stop to Reflect

Dee seems to think that using the quilts for "everyday use" is the wrong way to use them. Do you agree? Why or why not?

_____

_____

_____

Reading Strategy

Contrast the two **characters** of Maggie and Dee. How do they differ in their views of the quilts?

_____

_____

_____

Stop to Reflect

Do you think Maggie or Dee would better appreciate the quilts? Circle your answer.

Maggie   Dee

Explain your answer.

_____

_____

_____

She gasped like a bee had stung her. "Maggie can't appreciate these quilts!" she said. "She'd probably be backward enough to put them to everyday use."

◆ ◆ ◆

The narrator exclaims that she hopes Maggie will use the quilts. No one has used them all this time that she has saved them. She also remembers that Dee (Wangero) had once told her that the quilts were old-fashioned and that she didn't want to take one to college with her.

◆ ◆ ◆

"But they're <u>priceless</u>!" she was saying now, furiously; for she has a temper. "Maggie would put them on the bed and in five years they'd be in rags. Less than that!"

◆ ◆ ◆

Dee (Wangero) becomes angry at the thought of Maggie having the quilts. The narrator asks Dee (Wangero) what she would do with them. Dee (Wangero) replies that she would hang them on the wall. Maggie listens nearby.

◆ ◆ ◆

"She can have them, Mama," she said, like somebody used to never winning anything, or having anything <u>reserved</u> for her. "I can 'member Grandma Dee without the quilts."

◆ ◆ ◆

The narrator looks at Maggie. She remembers that Maggie learned how to quilt from her grandmother and aunt. She sees that Maggie is slightly afraid of Dee (Wangero) but is not angry.

◆ ◆ ◆

Vocabulary Development

reserved (ree ZERVD) *v.* kept back or set apart for later use

When I looked at her like that something hit me in the top of my head and ran down to the soles of my feet. Just like when I'm in church and the spirit of God touches me and I get happy and shout. I did something I never had done before: hugged Maggie to me, then dragged her on into the room, snatched the quilts out of Miss Wangero's hands and dumped them into Maggie's lap. Maggie just sat there on my bed with her mouth open.

◆　◆　◆

The narrator tells Dee (Wangero) to choose other quilts, but Dee (Wangero) leaves and joins her friend, who is waiting in the car. Dee (Wangero) tells the narrator and Maggie that they do not understand their heritage. She also says they are living in the past. She puts on large, modern sunglasses.

◆　◆　◆

She put on some sunglasses that hid everything above the tip of her nose and her chin.

Maggie smiled; maybe at the sunglasses. But a real smile, not scared. After we watched the car dust settle I asked Maggie to bring me a dip of snuff.[3] And then the two of us sat there just enjoying, until it was time to go in the house and go to bed.

3. **snuff** (SNUHF) *n.* powdered tobacco.

TAKE NOTES

Literary Analysis

What do you think **motivates** Mama to give Maggie the quilts?

_____

_____

English Language Development

The past tense of a regular English-language verb ends in *-ed*. For example, *snatched* is the past tense of *snatch*. Many common verbs are irregular, however. For example, *said* is the past tense of *say*. Find and circle the irregular past tense of *sit* in the bracketed passage.

_____

_____

Stop to Reflect

How does Maggie feel after her sister's visit?

_____

_____

_____

Everyday Use

1. **Take a Position:** Should Dee's mother have given the quilts to Dee? Why or why not?

_____

_____

2. **Literary Analysis:** What seems to motivate Dee's interest in her heritage?

_____

_____

3. **Literary Analysis:** Use this chart to analyze the narrator's feelings.

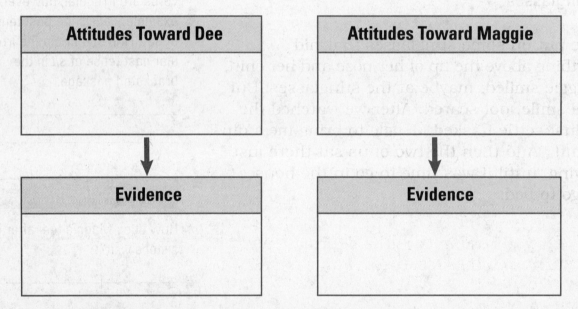

Attitudes Toward Dee	Attitudes Toward Maggie

Evidence	Evidence

4. **Reading Strategy:** Contrast the two sisters. How has each learned about her heritage?

_____

_____

The Woman Warrior

Most **memoirs**

- are nonfiction narratives.
- are written in the first-person point of view.
- tell about historical or personal events of importance to the writer.

This memoir is unusual because it is told from the **limited third-person point of view**. It is told by a narrator who uses the pronoun *she* to describe herself.

Kingston's memoir tells about a special day in her life. It also includes details about culture and history.

You can find background information on a book jacket, in an introduction, or in a footnote. Background information can help you better understand a literary work. In this textbook you will find background information in these places:

- author biography
- Build Skills pages
- Background

As you read, record the information you learn from these features in this chart.

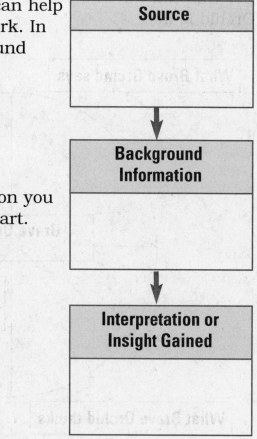

Source

↓

Background Information

↓

Interpretation or Insight Gained

The Woman Warrior

Maxine Hong Kingston

Summary Brave Orchid goes to the San Francisco airport. She waits for her sister to arrive from Hong Kong. The sisters have not seen each other in thirty years. Brave Orchid has brought her niece and two of her children. They wait at the airport for more than nine hours. Finally, the plane lands. Then, they must wait another four hours. Finally, the sisters greet each other. Neither can believe how old the other looks.

Note-taking Guide

Use this chart to find details in the memoir that show what Brave Orchid is like.

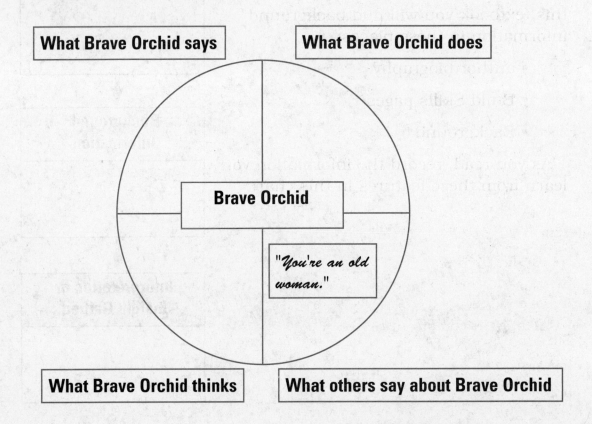

What Brave Orchid says

What Brave Orchid does

Brave Orchid

"You're an old woman."

What Brave Orchid thinks

What others say about Brave Orchid

The Woman Warrior

1. **Infer:** What does Brave Orchid's attitude toward America and American culture seem to be? Give an example to support your answer.

   _____

   _____

   _____

2. **Draw Conclusions:** Why do the two sister call each other old and speak to each other as they do?

   _____

   _____

   _____

3. **Literary Analysis:** List two historical details and two personal details from the **memoir.** Write your information in this chart.

Historical Details	Personal Details

4. **Literary Analysis:** Whose impressions provide the **limited third-person point of view** of this excerpt?

   _____

   _____

5. **Reading Strategy:** The Build Skills page in the Student Edition of the textbook gives information about the author. Apply **background information** to explain where the family might go after they leave the airport.

   _____

   _____

Antojos

LITERARY ANALYSIS

Plot is the pattern of events in a literary work. In most stories or novels, the plot involves characters and a conflict, or problem. Most plots follow a specific order:

- **Exposition:** introduces the basic situation of the story.

- **Inciting incident:** reveals the central conflict or struggle

- **Development:** The conflict becomes more serious.

- **Climax:** The conflict reaches its most intense point.

- **Resolution, or Denouement:** The conflict is solved, and the main character reveals something he or she has learned as a result.

Plot events that lead to the climax make up the **rising action**. The events that follow the climax are called the **falling action**.

READING STRATEGY

You can get more out of reading if you **identify with a character.** Think about what you and the character have in common. For example, as you read "Antojos," note personality traits you share with the main character, Yolanda. List them in a chart like the one shown.

	Yolanda	Me
Background		
Personality		
Attitudes		
Behavior		
Reasons for Behavior		

Antojos

Julia Alvarez

Summary Yolanda's aunts warn her not to take a trip north by herself. She goes anyway. Yolanda stops to ask some boys to help her pick guavas. Yolanda finishes picking. By this time all the boys except Jose have left. She and Jose find that she has a flat tire. Jose goes for help. Yolanda stays alone with the car. Suddenly two men with machetes appear. Yolanda is frightened, but the men change her tire. They refuse any payment. Yolanda finds Jose walking on the road. He says that no one would help him because they did not believe his story.

Note-taking Guide

Use this chart to record key story events in the order in which they occur.

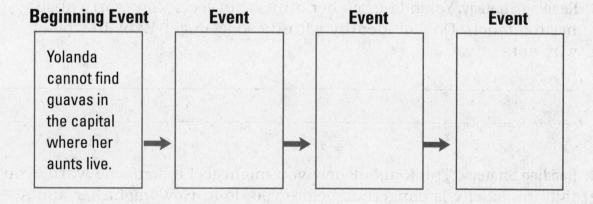

Beginning Event	Event	Event	Event
Yolanda cannot find guavas in the capital where her aunts live.			

Antojos

1. **Analyze:** Why does Yolanda pretend not to speak Spanish?

_____

_____

2. **Literary Analysis:** Use this chart to list events that are part of the **plot**.

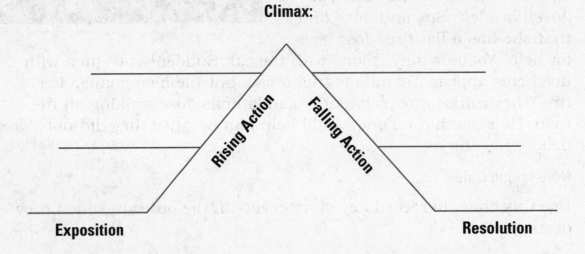

Climax:

Rising Action

Falling Action

Exposition

Resolution

3. **Reading Strategy:** Yolanda loves her aunts, but feels they worry about her too much. Do you **identify** with these feelings? Explain why or why not.

_____

_____

4. **Reading Strategy:** Think about how you might feel if someone warns you that an activity is dangerous before you do it. How might her aunts' fears about traveling alone affect Yolanda's feelings?

_____

_____

Who Burns for the Perfection of Paper • Most Satisfied by Snow • Hunger in New York City • What For

LITERARY ANALYSIS

Each person has his or her own way of speaking. The same is true for poets. Every poet has a unique **voice,** or literary personality. A poet's voice is based on these elements: word choice; pace; tone; attitude; sound devices; patterns of vowels and consonants; rhyme (or its absence).

As you read these poems, note each poet's distinctive voice.

READING STRATEGY

Sometimes, you can understand the meaning of a poem better if you **summarize** it. A summary should:

- tell about the beginning, middle, and end of the poem

- be short, usually one sentence, and give the poem's message

Use this chart to create summaries for each poem.

Poem	Main Points (Beginning)	Main Points (Middle)	Main Points (End)	Summary
"Perfection of Paper"				→
"Most Satisfied by Snow"				→
"Hunger in New York City"				→
"What For"				→

PREVIEW

Who Burns for the Perfection of Paper • Most Satisfied by Snow • Hunger in New York City • What For

Martín Espada, Diana Chang, Simon J. Ortiz, Garrett Hongo

Summaries In "Who Burns for the Perfection of Paper," the speaker describes the physical labor of an after-school job. In "Most Satisfied by Snow," the poet contrasts the empty spaces of fog with the physical presence of snow. In "Hunger in New York City," the speaker thinks about home, which is far from the city. In "What For," the speaker recalls his childhood in Hawaii and the power of his heritage.

Note-taking Guide

Use this chart to identify the subject and important details in each poem.

Poem	Subject of the Poem	Important details
"Who Burns for the Perfection of Paper"		
"Most Satisfied by Snow"		
"Hunger in New York City"		
"What For"		

Who Burns for the Perfection of Paper • Most Satisfied by Snow • Hunger in New York City • What For

1. **Interpret:** What key words in "Hunger in New York City" does the speaker use to describe New York City as a difficult place?

   _____

2. **Literary Analysis:** Use the following chart to select the adjectives that best describe each poet's **voice**.

   > **Adjectives:** angry, thoughtful, regretful, yearning, respectful

Poet	Voice	Evidence
Espada		
Chang		
Ortiz		
Hongo		

3. **Literary Analysis:** A poet's voice may reflect his cultural background. In what way does the voice of Ortiz reflect his cultural background?

   _____

   _____

4. **Reading Strategy:** Write a **summary** of "Who Burns for the Perfection of Paper."

   _____

   _____

   _____

5. **Reading Strategy:** What poetic effects and meanings are lost in the summary you wrote?

   _____

   _____

   _____

Onomatopoeia • Coyote v. Acme • Loneliness . . . An American Malady • One Day, Now Broken in Two

LITERARY ANALYSIS

An **essay** is nonfiction writing in which a writer gives a personal view on a topic. The many types of essays include

- the **analytical essay.** This essay breaks down and interprets a topic.

- the **expository essay.** This essay explains a topic.

- the **satirical essay.** This essay uses irony, ridicule, parody, or sarcasm to make a point.

- the **reflective essay.** This essay looks at a personal experience or important event.

The greatest difference in the essays you are going to read is in their tone. **Tone** is the author's attitude toward the subject or audience. You can hear that tone—humorous, critical, or serious—in each writer's choice of words and details.

READING STRATEGY

A person who writes an essay offers a **line of reasoning** to convince readers that his or her ideas are sound. Follow these steps to identify a line of reasoning.

- Identify the key points of each essay.

- Note the reasons, facts, and examples that support them.

Use this chart to record the line of reasoning and its evidence from one of the essays.

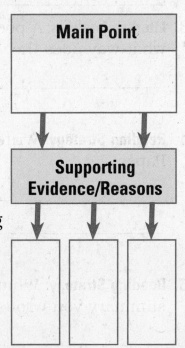

Onomatopoeia

William Safire

Summary "Onomatopoeia" is a humorous essay. In it, William Safire explains the meaning and history of the term *onomatopoeia*. Onomatopoeia refers to words that sound like the action they describe, such as *buzz* or *hiss*. He then talks about the word *zap*, which takes the concept one step further. It imitates an imaginary noise—the sound of a paralyzing ray gun.

Note-taking Guide

Use this word map to explore the meaning of *onomatopoeia*.

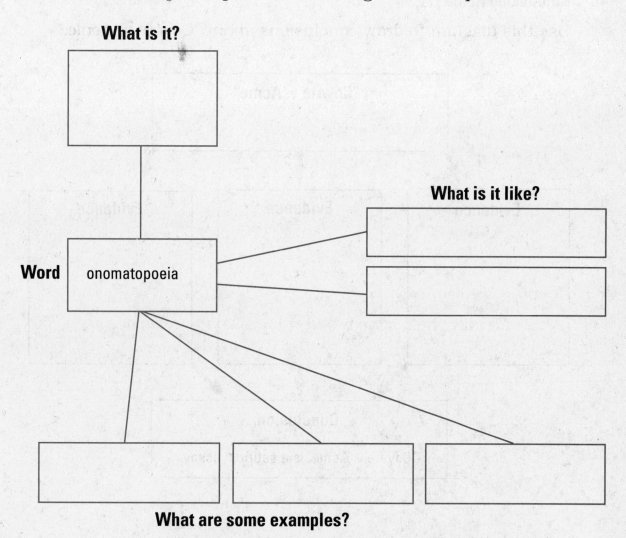

What is it?

What is it like?

Word   onomatopoeia

What are some examples?

PREVIEW

Coyote v. Acme

Ian Frazier

Summary "Coyote v. Acme" is the opening statement of a fictional lawsuit by Wile E. Coyote against the Acme Company. The lawsuit charges that Acme's faulty equipment caused Coyote to injure himself while chasing the Road Runner. These characters come from the Warner Brothers cartoon "Road Runner and Coyote," which made its debut in 1949.

Note-taking Guide

Use this diagram to draw conclusions about "Coyote v. Acme."

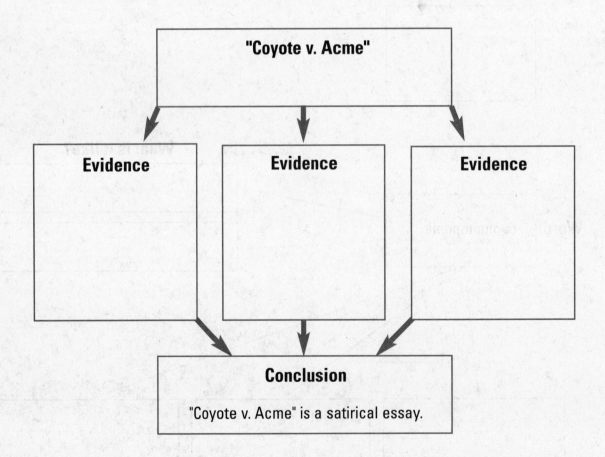

Loneliness . . . An American Malady

Carson McCullers

Summary In this essay, McCullers talks about what loneliness is. She says that human beings need to fit in, but that Americans are lonely because they need to be individuals, too.

Note-taking Guide Use this web to identify the nature of loneliness.

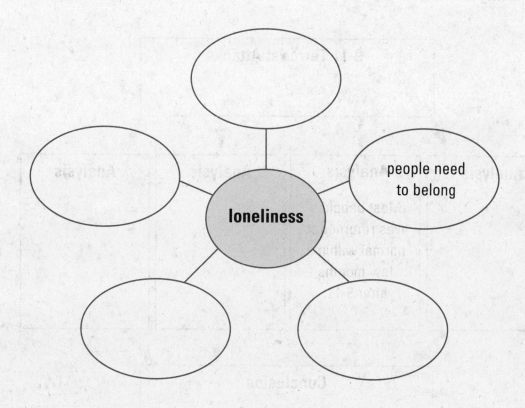

people need to belong

loneliness

One Day, Now Broken in Two

Anna Quindlen

Summary In this essay, Anna Quindlen looks at the impact of the events of 9-11 on Americans. She thinks that Americans have become better people as a result of having to face this tragedy.

Note-taking Guide Use this chart to analyze the effects of 9-11.

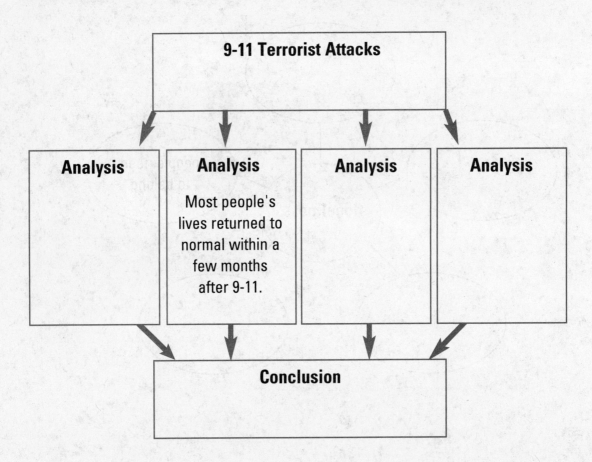

9-11 Terrorist Attacks

Analysis	Analysis	Analysis	Analysis
	Most people's lives returned to normal within a few months after 9-11.		

Conclusion

Onomatopoeia • Coyote v. Acme • Loneliness. . . An American Malady • One Day, Now Broken in Two

1. **Support:** Why does Wile E. Coyote continues to buy products from the Acme company despite some bad outcomes? Support your answer.

_____

_____

2. **Literary Analysis:** What type of essay you think "Onomatopoeia" is? Give examples from the essay to support your answer.

_____

_____

3. **Literary Analysis: Tone** is the author's attitude toward his or her subject. Use this chart to gather information about the author's tone. Choose one of the essays. Explain what attitude the author's tone reveals about his or her subject.

Summary of first paragraph	Words/details that indicate tone	Tone

4. **Reading Strategy:** "In Loneliness . . . An American Malady," what supporting information does McCullers give to show that love is a means of overcoming loneliness?

_____

_____

Straw Into Gold: The Metamorphosis of Everyday Things • For the Love of Books • Mother Tongue

LITERARY ANALYSIS

A **reflective essay** has the following characteristics:

- It is a short work of nonfiction.

- It tells a writer's personal view of a topic.

- The topic of the essay might be a personal experience or an important event.

- The writer sometimes explores an experience or event to find a deeper meaning.

An essay writer usually looks closely at an experience in order to understand its importance. To help you keep track of each writer's reflections, complete the chart below as you read.

Essay	Straw Into Gold	For the Love of Books	Mother Tongue
Experiences			
Feelings/ Significance			
Understanding			

READING STRATEGY

In a reflective essay, a writer often explores the meaning of his or her personal experiences. When you read a reflective essay, first identify the message, or main point, the writer is trying to make about these experiences. Then **evaluate a writer's message** by judging whether you do or do not agree with it.

Straw Into Gold: The Metamorphosis of the Everyday

Sandra Cisneros

Summary In this essay, Cisneros shares anecdotes about her childhood in a Mexican American family. The excerpt opens with a humorous story about the first time she tried to make tortillas. She compares this to spinning a roomful of straw into gold. She lists other things she has done that she didn't think she could. She describes her travels through Europe trying to be a writer. While telling her stories, Cisneros discusses her strengths that she did not even know she had.

Note-taking Guide

Use the web below to list experiences that shaped Sandra Cisneros's life and career.

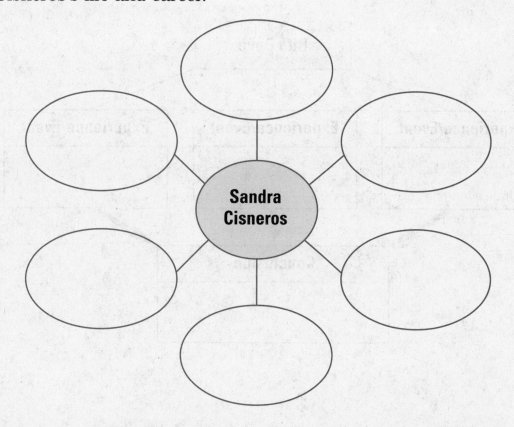

For the Love of Books

Rita Dove

Summary In "For the Love of Books," Rita Dove says her career as a writer came from her love of books. Since childhood, Dove loved to read books. She not only loved to read them, she loved holding them, smelling them, and turning their pages. She read everything from Shakespeare to science fiction. When her eleventh-grade English teacher took her to a book-signing, she realized writers were real people.

Note-taking Guide

Use the chart below to list experiences that influenced Rita Dove's life and career.

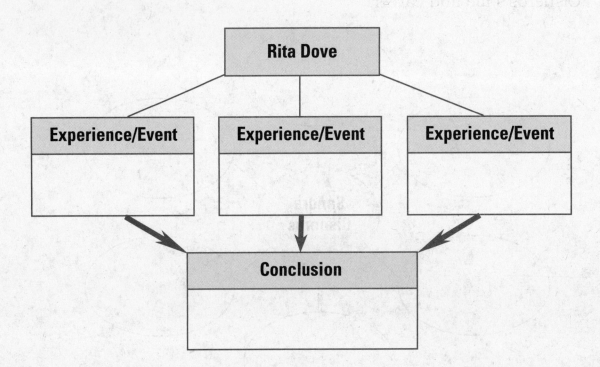

Mother Tongue

Amy Tan

Summary In "Mother Tongue," Amy Tan describes her mother as an intelligent and perceptive woman. However, her mother is regularly confronted by problems because of her non-standard English. Tan writes about the differences between the lessons she has learned from her mother with the English-speaking world's view of her mother. Tan explains that when she began to think of her mother as her reader, she found her voice as a writer.

Note-taking Guide

Use the following cluster diagram to take notes about Amy Tan's mother.

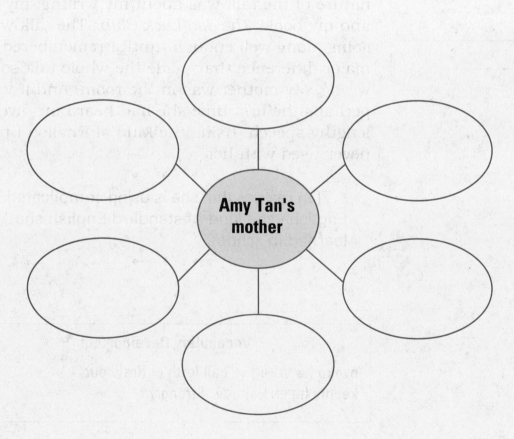

Underline three words, phrases, or sentences in the bracketed paragraphs that let you know this will be a **reflective essay**.

What makes Tan aware of the "different Englishes" she uses?

_____

_____

_____

_____

Mother Tongue
Amy Tan

I am not a scholar of English or literature. I cannot give you much more than personal opinions on the English language and its variations in this country or others.

I am a writer. And by that definition, I am someone who has always loved language. I am fascinated by language in daily life. I spend a great deal of my time thinking about the power of language—the way it can <u>evoke</u> an emotion, a visual image, a complex idea, or a simple truth. Language is the tool of my trade. And I use them all—all the Englishes I grew up with.

Recently, I was made <u>keenly</u> aware of the different Englishes I do use. I was giving a talk to a large group of people, the same talk I had already given to half a dozen other groups. The nature of the talk was about my writing, my life, and my book, *The Joy Luck Club.*[1] The talk was going along well enough, until I remembered one major difference that made the whole talk sound wrong. My mother was in the room. And it was perhaps the first time she had heard me give a lengthy speech, using the kind of English I have never used with her.

◆ ◆ ◆

Tan realizes that she is using complicated English—the kind of standard English she learned in school.

◆ ◆ ◆

Vocabulary Development

evoke (ee VOHK) *v.* call forth or draw out
keenly (KEEN lee) *adv.* Strongly

---

1. *The Joy Luck Club* Amy Tan's highly praised 1989 novel about four Chinese American women and their mothers.

Just last week, I was walking down the street with my mother, and I again found myself conscious of the English I was using, the English I do use with her. We were talking about the price of new and used furniture and I heard myself saying this: "Not waste money that way." My husband was with us as well, and he didn't notice any switch in my English. And then I realized why. It's because over the twenty years we've been together I've often used the same kind of English with him, and sometimes he even uses it with me. It has become our language of intimacy, a different sort of English that relates to family talk, the language I grew up with.

◆ ◆ ◆

Tan shares a conversation she had with her mother, demonstrating what her "family talk" sounds like. When Tan's mother speaks, she does not use Standard English. However, Tan's mother understands more than her limited use of English suggests. For example, Tan's mother follows complicated business and finance news. While Tan's friends do not always completely understand her mother, Tan understands her mother's English because it is what she grew up with. Tan explains that the way her mother speaks English influences the way she views the world.

◆ ◆ ◆

Lately, I've been giving more thought to the kind of English my mother speaks. Like others, I have described it to people as "broken," or "fractured" English. But I <u>wince</u> when I say that. It has always bothered me

---

Vocabulary Development

wince (WINS) *v.* draw back slightly as if in pain

Reading Check

How does Tan's language change when she speaks with her mother?

_____

_____

_____

English Language Development

A **sentence** is a group of words that expresses a complete thought. A sentence has two basic parts: a **subject** that answers the question Who? or What? and a **verb** that tells what the subject does, what is done to the subject, or what the condition of the subject is. A group of words expresses a complete thought if it can stand by itself and still make sense. Which group of words in the bracketed paragraph does not express a complete thought?

_____

_____

_____

Literary Analysis

Underline one sentence in this paragraph that points to the fact that this essay is **reflective**.

Circle one word or phrase in this paragraph that reveals how Tan used to feel about her mother's use of the English language.

As she was growing up, Tan thought her mother's English reflected the quality of her thoughts. What evidence seemed to support Tan's thoughts?

_____

_____

_____

_____

that I can think of no way to describe it other than "broken," as if it were damaged and needed to be fixed, as if it lacked a certain wholeness and soundness. I've heard other terms used, "limited English," for example. But they seem just as bad, as if everything is limited, including people's perceptions of the limited English speaker.

I know this for a fact, because when I was growing up, my mother's "limited" English limited my perception of her. I was ashamed of her English. I believed that her English reflected the quality of what she had to say. That is, because she expressed them imperfectly her thoughts were imperfect. And I had plenty of <u>empirical</u> evidence to support me: the fact that people in department stores, at banks, and at restaurants did not take her seriously, did not give her good service, pretended not to understand her, or even acted as if they did not hear her.

◆   ◆   ◆

Tan explains that her mother herself also realized how her limited use of English created problems. When Tan was fifteen, she was asked to call people to get information for her mother. For example, Tan once called a stockbroker to find out about a missing check. More recently, Tan's mother went to the hospital to learn the results of a brain scan. After the hospital claimed to have lost the scan, Mrs. Tan refused to leave until the doctor called her daughter. Tan arranged to get the information her mother wanted. She also received an apology for the hospital's mistake.

◆   ◆   ◆

Vocabulary Development

empirical (em PEER i kuhl) *adj.* obtained from observation or experiment

I think my mother's English almost had an effect on limiting my possibilities in life as well. Sociologists[2] and linguists[3] probably will tell you that a person's developing language skills are more influenced by peers. But I do think that the language spoken in the family, especially in immigrant families which are more <u>insular</u>, plays a large role in shaping the language of the child. And I believe that it affected my results on achievement tests, IQ tests, and the SAT.[4] While my English skills were never judged as poor, compared to math, English could not be considered my strong suit.

◆ ◆ ◆

Tan did fairly well in English in school. However, she always had higher scores in math and science achievement tests. Tan believes she did well on math tests because there was only one right answer. On the other hand, she had problems with English tests because she felt that the answers depended on personal experience and opinions. Tan could not sort through all the vivid images that came to mind when she tried to answer fill-in-the-blank sentence completions or word analogies.

◆ ◆ ◆

I have been thinking about all this lately, about my mother's English, about achievement tests. Because lately I've been asked, as a

---

Vocabulary Development

insular (IN syoo lahr) *adj.* suggestive of the isolated life of an island

---

2. **sociologists** (SOH see AHL uh jists) *n.* people who study human social behavior.
3. **linguists** (LING gwists) *n.* people who study human speech.
4. **SAT** Scholastic Aptitude Test; national college entrance exam.

TAKE NOTES

Reading Strategy

What point about developing language skills is Tan making in the bracketed paragraph? What evidence does Tan give to support her point? To **evaluate the message**, tell whether you agree or disagree with her. Why?

_____

_____

_____

_____

Culture Note

Tan believes that her performance on tests reflects the fact that she grew up listening to her mother's "broken" English. With a group, discuss the kinds of standardized tests with which you are familiar.

What is the overall purpose of standardized tests?

_____

_____

_____

_____

Vocabulary and Pronunciation

Tan says, "English could not be considered my strong suit." The compound noun *strong suit* means "a quality, an activity, or a skill at which a person excels." Write a sentence about Tan or her mother in which you use the noun *strong suit.*

_____

_____

_____

Culture Note

Tan wonders why so few Asian-Americans appear in literature. With a group of classmates, share what you know about Asian-American writers. Look at a library book, a literature textbook, or the Internet to find out more about Asian-American authors.

• List the names of two Chinese American writers.

_____

_____

• List one title by each author.

_____

_____

• List the names of two Japanese American writers.

_____

_____

• List one title by each author.

_____

_____

Read Fluently

Read the bracketed paragraph here and on the next page aloud. What four kinds of "Englishes" does Tan use in her writing?

1. _____

2. _____

3. _____

4. _____

asked, as a writer, why there are not more Asian Americans represented in American literature. Why are there few Asian Americans enrolled in creative writing programs? Why do so many Chinese students go into engineering? Well, these are broad sociological questions I can't begin to answer. But I have noticed in surveys—in fact, just last week—that Asian students, as a whole, always do significantly better on math achievement tests than in English. And this makes me think that there are other Asian-American students whose English spoken in the home might also be described as "broken" or "limited." And perhaps they also have teachers who are <u>steering</u> them away from writing and into math and science, which is what happened to me.

♦ ♦ ♦

Tan describes how she rebelled against Asian-American stereotypes to become a writer. First, she chose to study English rather than science in college. Then she became a freelance writer after an employer told her that she could not write. In 1985 Tan started writing fiction. At first, she wrote difficult sentences to prove she could use English well.

♦ ♦ ♦

Fortunately, for reasons I won't get into today, I later decided I should <u>envision</u> a reader for the stories I would write. And the reader I decided upon was my mother, because these were stories about mothers. So with this reader in mind—and in fact she did read my early drafts—I began to write stories using all the Englishes I grew up with: the English I spoke

Vocabulary Development

steering (STEER ing) *v.* guiding; directing
envision (en VIZH uhn) *v.* picture in the mind; imagine

to my mother, which for lack of a better term might be described as "simple"; the English she used with me, which for lack of a better term might be described as "broken"; my translation of her Chinese, which could certainly be described as "watered down"; and what I imagined to be her translation of her Chinese if she could speak in perfect English, her internal language, and for that I sought to preserve the essence, but neither an English nor a Chinese structure. I wanted to capture what language ability tests can never reveal: her intent, her passion, her imagery, the rhythms of her speech and the nature of her thoughts.

Apart from what any critic had to say about my writing, I knew I had succeeded where it counted when my mother finished reading my book and gave me her verdict: "So easy to read."

Straw Into Gold: The Metamorphosis of the Everyday • For the Love of Books • Mother Tongue

1. **Analyze:** When Cisneros left home for a reason other than getting married, she broke an important taboo. Who was the enemy in the "quiet war" that she had begun? Explain.

   _____

   _____

2. **Infer:** When Tan gives a speech to a crowd that includes her mother, she realizes that she is using a kind of complex standard English that she would never use at home with her mother. What circumstances account for Tan's having developed more than one "English."

   _____

   _____

3. **Literary Analysis:** Based on her **reflective essay**, how do you think Rita Dove feels about her childhood?

   _____

   _____

4. **Reading Strategy:** Use the chart below to **evaluate each author's message.** For each, list their message, their supporting reasons, and then tell whether you agree with their message.

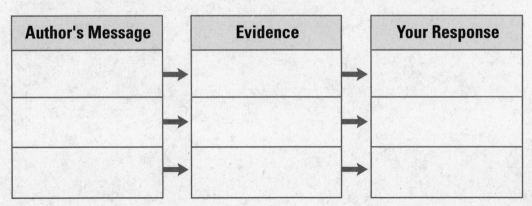

Author's Message		Evidence		Your Response
	→		→	
	→		→	
	→		→	

The Rockpile

LITERARY ANALYSIS

The **setting** is the time and place in which events happen. The setting may include details about weather, location, and elements of a place and time. The setting of "The Rockpile" is Harlem in New York City during the 1930s. Life in Harlem at that time was difficult for many people. As you read, think about how the setting affects the characters' personalities and actions.

READING STRATEGY

In this story, a child disobeys his mother. His disobedience causes a troublesome family situation. You will understand the characters in the story better if you **identify cause-and-effect** relationships among them. Use this chart to list why the characters act as they do. Then list how their actions affect others.

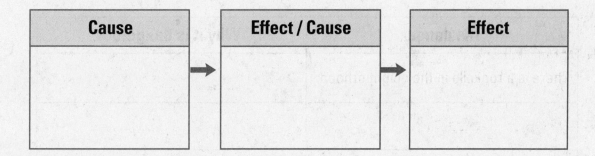

Cause	Effect / Cause	Effect

The Rockpile

James Baldwin

Summary This story is about a boy who disobeys his mother. When he is hurt, his father, a pastor, blames his older stepbrother for not watching him. His mother does not blame the older boy. The conflict between the parents shows that each parent has different expectations for each of the boys.

Note-taking Guide

Use this chart to record the reasons why the neighborhood is dangerous.

The danger	Why it is dangerous
There is a rockpile in the neighborhood.	

The Rockpile

1. **Deduce:** Why is the street "forbidden"?

   _____

   _____

2. **Literary Analysis:** Name three details that describe the **setting** of the neighborhood.

   _____

   _____

   _____

3. **Literary Analysis:** Use the chart below to analyze the rockpile and to tell what it symbolizes, or represents.

The Rockpile				What It Means
What people say about it	Events linked with it	Details used to describe it	→ →	

4. **Reading Strategy:** What **causes** John to avoid telling his mother that Roy went to the rockpile?

   _____

   _____

from Hiroshima • Losses •
The Death of the Ball Turret Gunner

LITERARY ANALYSIS

The **theme** is the main idea that a writer wants to express in a work of literature. Usually, the theme is **implied**. Implied means that it is revealed indirectly. The author reveals the theme through the details and the descriptions of characters and events. These three selections all have implied themes about war.

READING STRATEGY

When the theme of a work of literature is implied, the reader must **draw inferences** to figure out the theme. Inferences are conclusions. You can draw inferences by paying attention to a writer's choice of details, events, and characters. As you read, use this chart to write down important details that help you figure out the implied theme.

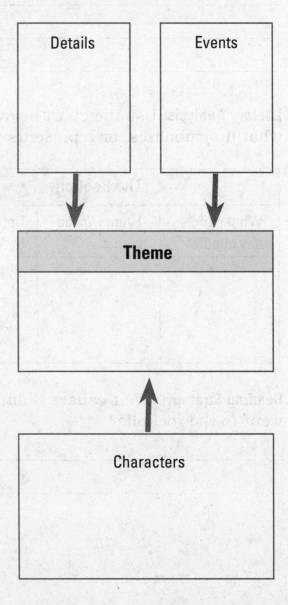

from Hiroshima

John Hersey

Summary On August 6, 1945, at 8:15 in the morning, the United States dropped an atomic bomb on Hiroshima, Japan. More than 100,000 people died as a result of the bombing. Miss Toshiko Sasaki, Dr. Masakazu Fujii, Mrs. Hatsuyo Nakamura, and Mr. Kiyoshi Tanimoto survived. This excerpt tells part of their story.

Note-taking Guide

Use this chart to record what each person was doing when the bomb exploded.

	What were they doing?	How did they experience the blast?
Mr. Kiyoshi Tanimoto		
Mrs. Hatsuyo Nakamura		
Dr. Masakazu Fujii		
Miss Toshiko Sasaki		

Losses • The Death of the Ball Turret Gunner

Randall Jarrell

Summaries: In "Losses," the speaker talks about the sacrifice of human life in war. According to the speaker, death is almost casual and routine.

In **"The Death of the Ball Turret Gunner,"** the speaker uses images to show how deadly war is. The powerful final line shows the violence and finality of death in war

Note-taking Guide:

As you read, use this chart to list striking words and phrases from the two poems.

Poem	Striking words	Striking phrases
"Losses"		
"The Death of the Ball Turret Gunner"		

from Hiroshima • Losses • The Death of the Ball Turret Gunner

1. **Analyze:** Hersey spends a lot of time describing the city of Hiroshima before the atomic blast. Why do you think Hersey does this?

_____

_____

2. **Literary Analysis:** The **implied theme** in _Hiroshima_ is the destructive power of the atomic bomb. List two details from the text that give clues to this implied theme.

_____

_____

3. **Literary Analysis:** Hersey and Jarrell both describe victims of war. Use the Venn diagram below to show similarities and differences in how Hersey and Jarrell show those killed during war.

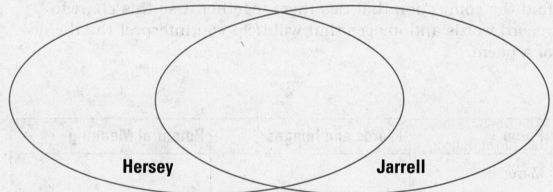

Hersey   **Jarrell**

4. **Reading Strategy:** In "Losses," the speaker says, "We died like aunts or pets or foreigners." **Draw inferences** from this line. What does it suggest about the theme?

_____

_____

Mirror • In a Classroom • The Explorer • Frederick Douglass • Runagate Runagate

LITERARY ANALYSIS

A poem's **theme** is its central idea. Poets hint at themes through the use of certain words or images that trigger strong feelings. These feelings are known as **connotations** of words. For example, in these lines about aging by Sylvia Plath, the words *drowned* and *terrible* have bad connotations.

> In me she has drowned a young girl, and in me an old woman
>
> Rises toward her day after day, like a terrible fish.

From the meaning and connotations of these words, a reader could figure out that the theme is connected with the fear of growing old. As you read these poems, find clues to themes in words and images that trigger negative or positive responses.

READING STRATEGY

In most poems, the central message is not directly stated. It is up to you to **interpret** it by looking for meaning in the words and images. Think about the connotations of the words, and then find the connection that ties them together. Use this chart to record words and images that will help you interpret the theme of a poem.

Poem	Words and Images	Potential Meaning
Mirror		
In a Classroom		
The Explorer		
Frederick Douglass		
Runagate Runagate		

Mirror • In a Classroom • The Explorer • Frederick Douglass • Runagate Runagate

Sylvia Plath, Adrienne Rich, Gwendolyn Brooks, Robert Hayden

Summaries "Mirror" shows a woman's feelings about growing older, as reflected by a mirror. In **"In a Classroom,"** the speaker describes the reaction of her students to a poetry lesson. The speaker in **"The Explorer"** searches for peace in a noisy apartment building. In **"Frederick Douglass,"** the speaker longs for true freedom that will honor Douglass, one of the leading voices opposing slavery. **"Runagate Runagate"** uses rhythm and detail to bring the voices, feelings, risks, and rewards of the Underground Railroad to the reader. The Underground Railroad was a route of safe houses operated by people opposed to slavery who helped slaves escape to the North before the Civil War.

Note-taking Guide

Sometimes rewriting a line of poetry will help you to understand its meaning. Use this chart to rewrite one line from each poem in your own words.

Poem	Line	Rewritten Line
Mirror		
In a Classroom		
The Explorer		
Frederick Douglass		
Runagate Runagate		

Mirror • In a Classroom • The Explorer • Frederick Douglass • Runagate Runagate

1. **Infer:** In "Mirror," who is the speaker? How do you know?

   _____

   _____

2. **Literary Analysis:** In "Runagate Runagate," the speaker uses sensory images to express the **theme** that a journey on the Underground Railroad was full of risk, danger, reward, and emotion. Use this chart to list images that support this theme by appealing to the five senses.

Sight	Hearing	Smell	Touch	Taste

3. **Literary Analysis:** In "Frederick Douglass," Hayden describes Frederick Douglass as "visioning a world where none is lonely, none hunted." Based on the **connotations** of these words, what would you say is the theme of the poem?

   _____

   _____

4. **Reading Strategy:** Interpret the meaning of the word *swallow* in the poem, "Mirror." How does this word contribute to the poem's message?

   _____

   _____

Inaugural Address • *from* Letter from Birmingham City Jail

LITERARY ANALYSIS

Parallelism is repeated words, phrases, clauses, or sentences with the same structure or meaning. It is also called **parallel structure**. It is found in poetry, speeches, and other writing. It is used to

- balance similar ideas
- stress contrasting ideas
- create a pleasing rhythm

READING STRATEGY

Main ideas are key points that a writer wants to get across. **Supporting details** are facts, examples, or reasons that support the main ideas. Use this chart to identify main ideas and supporting details as you read the selections.

	Main Idea	Facts, Examples, and Reasons
Inaugural Address		
Letter from Birmingham City Jail		

Inaugural Address

John F. Kennedy

Summary An inaugural address is the speech a president gives when he takes office. John F. Kennedy delivered his inaugural address in 1961. Tensions were high between the United States and the Soviet Union. The possibility of a nuclear war was real. In his speech, Kennedy spoke to the fears of both the nation and the world. He reminded Americans that they had inherited a responsibility to defend freedom. The new President urged Americans to serve their country with the famous words, "Ask not what your country can do for you—ask what you can do for your country." Then, he called on the citizens of the world to work together for the freedom of people everywhere.

Note-taking Guide

In his speech, Kennedy calls on many groups of people to take action. In the chart, write what he asks each group to do.

	Actions Kennedy Requests
Enemies of the U.S.	
American Citizens	
People of Other Nations	

Letter from Birmingham City Jail

Martin Luther King, Jr.

Summary Martin Luther King, Jr., was a civil rights leader. In April 1963, he was arrested for protesting segregation in Birmingham, Alabama. While in jail, King read a newspaper article that was critical of the civil rights movement. He responded to the article in this letter. In it, King criticized the police for their actions against protestors. He celebrated the real heroes who had the courage to take a stand against segregation. He also expressed confidence that the struggle for freedom would have a positive outcome.

Note-taking Guide

Answer the questions in the chart to keep track of the ideas King expresses in his letter.

Question	Answer from King's Letter
Why will African Americans win freedom?	
Why doesn't King agree that the police deserve praise?	
How does King feel about the "sit-inners" and demonstrators?	

APPLY THE SKILLS

Inaugural Address • Letter from Birmingham City Jail

1. **Respond:** If you had heard Kennedy's speech, which of his ideas would have sparked the strongest response in you? Explain.

_____

_____

2. **Evaluate:** Do you think the last paragraph of King's letter is an effective ending? Why or why not?

_____

_____

3. **Literary Analysis:** Reread the nineteenth paragraph in Kennedy's inaugural. It begins "And if a beachhead of cooperation. . . ." Write **parallel** words and phrases from the paragraph in this chart.

Parallel Words	Parallel Phrases

4. **Reading Strategy:** Kennedy expresses the **main idea** that people should welcome the job of defending freedom. Name one **detail** that supports this idea.

_____

_____

For My Children • Bidwell Ghost • Camouflaging the Chimera

LITERARY ANALYSIS

Lyric poetry was originally written to be sung. Lyric poems express the ideas and feelings of one speaker. They also produce a single effect instead of telling a story.

The speaker in "Bidwell Ghost," for example, gives a vivid picture of a fiery tragedy.

> It has been twenty years
> since her house surged and burst in the dark trees

As you read each poem, use this chart to record the words and phrases that contribute to a single unifying effect.

Detail	Detail	Detail

Single Effect:

READING STRATEGY

Many poems are written in sentences, like prose. Many poems are also written in lines. Sentences in a poem do not always end at the end of lines. Instead, a sentence may extend for several lines. Then, it may end in the middle of a line. This allows the poet to create a certain rhythm and rhyme.

To understand the meaning of a poem, **read in sentences.** Use these tips.

- Pay close attention to the punctuation.

- Stop at the end of a line only for a period, colon, semicolon, or dash.

For My Children •
Bidwell Ghost •
Camouflaging the Chimera

Colleen McElroy, Louise Erdrich, Yusef Komunyakaa

Summaries In "For My Children," the speaker tells of her memories of the stories of her ancestors. She looks for connections between these stories and the realities of present-day life. In "**Bidwell Ghost**," the speaker describes a ghost that "waits by the road." In "**Camouflaging the Chimera**," the poet describes his experiences during the Vietnam War. He tells how soldiers used branches, mud, and grass to camouflage themselves. He relates his memories of being in combat.

Note-taking Guide

Use this chart to record information about the memory of the past in each poem.

	Memory of the Past	**Explanation**
"For My Children"		
"Bidwell Ghost"		
"Camouflaging the Chimera"		

For My Children • Bidwell Ghost •
Camouflaging the Chimera

1. **Infer:** In "For My Children," the speaker is speaking to her children. What is the speaker's reason for addressing the poem to them?

_____

_____

2. **Contrast:** In what way are the ghosts in Komunyakaa's poem different from the ghost in Erdrich's poem?

_____

_____

3. **Literary Analysis:** Describe in your own words the thoughts that the speaker shares in the opening stanza of "For My Children."

_____

_____

4. **Reading Strategy:** Why do you think Erdrich chose to punctuate her poem as she did?

_____

_____

5. **Reading Strategy:** Using this chart, identify the figurative language in the last stanza of "For My Children."

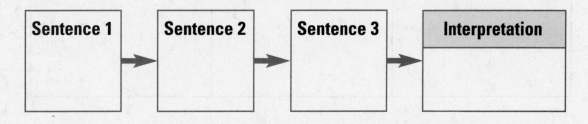

The Crucible, Act I

LITERARY ANALYSIS

The written script of a drama is made up of dialogue and stage directions:

- **Dialogue** is the words a character speaks. Dialogue helps the plot move forward. It also tells about a character's personality and background.

- **Stage directions** usually tell where a scene takes place and what it should look like. They also tell how each character should move and speak. Stage directions usually appear in italic type. This shows they are not dialogue.

As you read Act I of *The Crucible*, look for information about characters and events in the stage directions and the dialogue.

READING STRATEGY

Like people in real life, characters in plays are not always what they seem. Often, we must **question the characters' motives**. A motive is a reason for behaving in a certain way. Fear, greed, guilt, love, loyalty, and revenge are some reasons for human behavior. Use this chart to examine the motives of at least two characters in Act I.

Character	Words and Actions	Motive

The Crucible, Act I

Arthur Miller

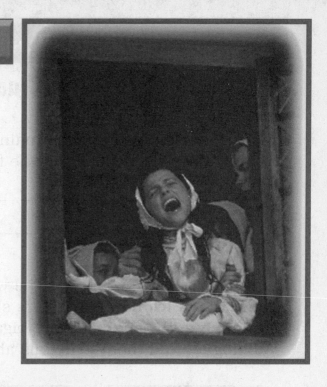

Summary It is 1692 in Salem, Massachusetts. The Reverend Parris is praying for his daughter Betty, who is ill. He says he saw his niece Abigail and Betty dancing in the woods. He asks Abigail why no one will hire her as a mother's helper since Mrs. Proctor fired her. Mary Warren comes in and says the village is accusing the girls of witchcraft. John Proctor comes for Mary and sends her back to his farm, where she works. Parris and all the girls but Abigail leave. Betty begins to wail. Others rush in, including kindly Rebecca Nurse, who calms Betty. Reverend Hale, an expert in witchcraft, enters. He questions Abigail, and she shifts the blame to Tituba, Reverend Parris's slave. Frightened, Tituba says that she saw Sarah Good and Goody Osburn with the Devil. Abby cries out other names, and soon all the girls are crying out names.

Note-taking Guide

Use this chart to record information about the setting, characters, and social or historical background of the play.

Setting	Characters	Background

The Crucible, Act I

1. **Infer:** What seems to be the main motive for Reverend Parris's concern about the girls' behavior in the forest?

   _____

   _____

2. **Literary Analysis:** **Dialogue** is the words characters speak. **Stage directions** tell how characters should move and speak. Use this chart to analyze the character of Abigail Williams. Gather details from her **dialogue**. Add them to details about her in the stage directions.

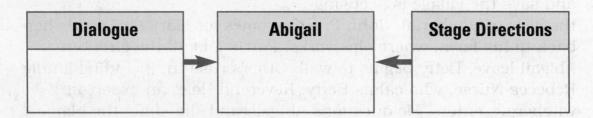

3. **Reading Strategy:** A **motive** is a reason for behaving in a certain way. What do Reverend Parris's words and actions show about his **motives**?

   _____

   _____

   _____

4. **Reading Strategy:** What do Abigail's actions in the forest and her threat to the girls show about her motives?

   _____

   _____

   _____

The Crucible, Act II

LITERARY ANALYSIS

An **allusion** is a brief reference within a work to something outside the work. An allusion usually refers to one of the following:

- Another work of literature
- A well-known person
- A place
- A historical event

The Crucible makes many allusions to the Bible. Act I, for example, includes a reference to the New Jerusalem, a term for the holy city of heaven. Use this chart to record biblical allusions in Act II.

READING STRATEGY

When you **read a drama** instead of watching it, you read the stage directions. Stage directions often break up the dialogue, but they provide important information. Pay close attention to the stage directions as you read. They will help you understand the thoughts, attitudes, and behavior of the characters.

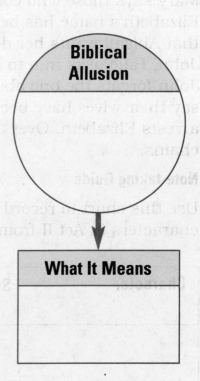

The Crucible, Act II

Summary Act II opens in the Proctor home, eight days later. Elizabeth Proctor says fourteen people have been arrested for witchcraft, based on what Abigail and the other girls said. She urges John to testify that the girls are frauds. They quarrel over his previous affair with Abigail. Mary, back from court, gives Elizabeth a small doll. Mary says those who confess will not be hanged. She says that Elizabeth's name has been mentioned. Elizabeth says she is sure that Abigail wants her dead. Hale appears at the door. To test John, Hale asks him to list the Ten Commandments. Ironically, John forgets the one about adultery. Then two men burst in. They say their wives have been arrested. The marshal arrives and arrests Elizabeth. Over John's protests, she is taken away in chains.

Note-taking Guide

Use this chart to record information that you learn about characters in Act II from stage directions.

Character	Stage Direction	What It Says About the Character

The Crucible, Act II

1. **Interpret:** What is the significance of Mary Warren's gift to Elizabeth Proctor?

   _____

   _____

2. **Literary Analysis:** A footnote explains the biblical **allusion** to Moses and the parting of the Red Sea on page 1293. What does the allusion suggest about how the crowd looks at Abigail?

   _____

   _____

3. **Literary Analysis:** Pontius Pilate was the Roman leader who condemned Jesus to death. What does John Proctor's allusion to Pontius Pilate on page 1309 suggest about the witchcraft trial in Salem?

   _____

   _____

4. **Reading Strategy:** Stage directions help you understand characters' thoughts, attitudes, and behavior. Use the chart to give two examples of dialogue in which a character's attitudes would have been unclear to you if you had not **read** the stage directions.

Dialogue	Attitude Revealed in Stage Direction

The Crucible, Act III

LITERARY ANALYSIS

Irony involves a contrast between what is expected and what really happens. It can also involve a contrast between what someone says and what he or she really means. Look for these two types of irony as you read Act III:

- **Dramatic irony:** a contrast between what a character thinks and what the audience knows to be true

- **Verbal irony:** a character says one thing but means something different

READING STRATEGY

A drama with many characters can become confusing. It may be helpful to **categorize the characters**. One way you can categorize, or classify, characters in *The Crucible* is by their roles in the community. Use this chart to identify the characters and their positions in Salem Village.

Category	Names of Characters in Category
Court Supporters	
Court Officers	
Ministers and Judges	
The Accused	
Court Witness	
Court Opponents	

The Crucible, Act III

Arthur Miller

Summary Act III opens with Giles Corey pleading for his wife's life. Then, Francis Nurse says the girls are lying. Proctor leads in a terrified Mary. Mary admits that she never saw any spirits. Danforth tells John that Elizabeth is pregnant. He says that she will not be executed until after the baby is born. Abigail swears that Mary is lying. To stop Abigail, John admits his infidelity. Elizabeth is brought in to back up John's claim. To protect John, she lies, so John is not believed. Abigail begins pretending that Mary's spirit is bewitching her. Mary hysterically takes back her confession. John is arrested. Hale condemns the court and leaves.

Note-taking Guide

As you read, use this diagram to track the events in Act III.

Beginning Event	Event	Event	Event	Event	Final Outcome
Mary Warren confesses to lying					

The Crucible, Act III

1. **Apply:** Imagine that Elizabeth Proctor had told Danforth the truth. In what way might the outcome of the trials have been different?

_____

_____

_____

2. **Literary Analysis: Dramatic irony** results from a contrast between what a character thinks and what the audience knows. **Verbal irony** is the result of the contrast between what a character says and what he or she means. Use this chart to list one example of dramatic irony and one example of verbal irony from Act III. Identify the type of irony. Also explain what each speaker really means.

Passage	Type of Irony	Analysis

3. **Reading Strategy:** Which characters would you **categorize**, or classify, as static (unchanging)? Explain.

_____

_____

4. **Reading Strategy:** Which characters would you categorize, or classify, as dynamic (changing or growing)? Explain.

_____

_____

The Crucible, Act IV

LITERARY ANALYSIS

A **theme** is the central idea of a work of literature. Like many longer works, *The Crucible* has several themes. They include the following:

- Fear and suspicion can become mass hysteria.

- Guilt and revenge can be very destructive.

- A court system based on beliefs instead of justice will fail.

As you read Act IV, use this chart to consider these and other themes of the play.

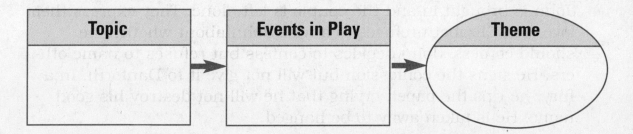

An **extended metaphor** is a comparison that develops throughout a literary work. Miller's imagery of the seventeenth-century witch hunt in Salem builds a comparison to the McCarthy hearings in the 1950s in America. Notice Miller's ability to explore the events of the 1950s as he writes about the Salem witchcraft trials.

READING STRATEGY

There are clear parallels between the events in Miller's play and the McCarthy hearings. As you read Act IV, think about the themes of the play that relate to events during the time when the play was written.

The Crucible, Act IV

Arthur Miller

Summary Act IV opens in the Salem jail. Danforth and Hathorne enter. Parris enters and tells the judges that Abigail and Mercy Lewis have stolen his money and run away. Parris, hoping that John or Rebecca will confess, asks for a postponement of their hangings. Danforth refuses. Hale enters to ask Danforth to pardon the condemned. Elizabeth is brought in. Hale asks her to urge John to confess. John is brought in and the couple is left alone. They express their love, but Elizabeth refuses to advise John about whether he should confess. John decides to confess but refuses to name others. He signs the confession but will not give it to Danforth. In a fury, he rips the paper, crying that he will not destroy his good name. He is taken away to be hanged.

Note-taking Guide

Use this diagram to record themes, or central ideas, of *The Crucible*.

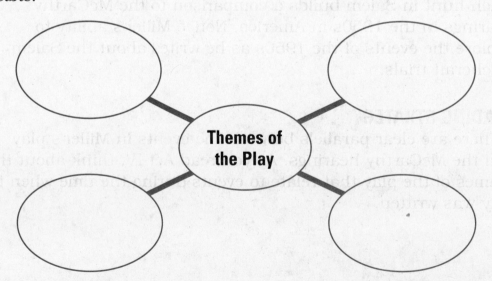

Themes of the Play

The Crucible, Act IV

1. **Interpret:** Why does Elizabeth say that her husband has "his goodness" as he is about to be hanged?

   _____

   _____

2. **Literary Analysis:** One **theme** of *The Crucible* is that fear and suspicion can produce hysteria. Hysteria can destroy public order and reason. Use details from the play to show how Miller expresses this theme.

   _____

   _____

3. **Literary Analysis:** Ideas such as witchcraft and "the work of the Devil" are used in *The Crucible* as **extended metaphors**, or comparisons, for Communism. In this chart, give examples from the text that show how these ideas are used to create extended metaphors.

Passage from the Text	How It Relates to Communism

4. **Reading Strategy:** Miller draws parallels between events in Salem and events in Congress during his own time. What details in the play tell what Miller thinks about the way McCarthy's Senate committee handled people?

   _____

   _____

CRITICAL REVIEWS

About Critical Reviews

A **critical review** is a piece of writing that analyzes and evaluates a work of literature, art, or culture. Critical reviews usually include:

- a brief summary of the work
- strong opinions
- evidence and reasons that support the opinions

The purpose of a critical review is to persuade readers to accept the reviewer's opinions. Effective critical reviews have strong arguments and powerful, persuasive language.

READING STRATEGY

Comparing and Contrasting Critical Reviews Reviewers often have different opinions about the same work. If possible, read several critical reviews on the same subject. Look for points of agreement and disagreement. **Comparing and contrasting critical reviews** can help you make your own decisions. Both Brooks Atkinson and Howard Kissel reviewed *The Crucible*. To compare and contrast their reviews, complete the chart below.

Critical Reviews		
Critic	Brooks Atkinson	Howard Kissel
Script		
Leading Actors/ Actresses		
Director, Sets, Costumes, Lighting		
Overall Evaluation (+ or −)		

The New York Times

January 23, 1953

The Crucible

By Brooks Atkinson

Arthur Miller has written another powerful play. *The Crucible*, it is called, and it opened at the Martin Beck last evening in an equally powerful performance. Riffling back the pages of American history, he has written the drama of the witch trials and hangings in Salem in 1692. Neither Mr. Miller nor his audiences are unaware of certain similarities between the perversions of justice then and today.

But Mr. Miller is not pleading a cause in dramatic form. For *The Crucible*, despite its current implications, is a self-contained play about a terrible period in American history. Silly accusations of witchcraft by some mischievous girls in Puritan dress gradually take possession of Salem. Before the play is over good people of pious nature and responsible temper are condemning other good people to the gallows.

Having a sure instinct for dramatic form, Mr. Miller goes bluntly to essential situations. John Proctor and his wife, farm people, are the central characters of the play. At first the idea that Goodie Proctor is a witch is only an absurd rumor. But *The Crucible* carries the Proctors through the whole ordeal—first vague suspicion, then the arrest, the implacable, highly wrought trial in the church vestry, the final opportunity for John Proctor to save his neck by confessing to something he knows is a lie, and finally the baleful roll of the drums at the foot of the gallows.

Although *The Crucible* is a powerful drama, it stands second to *Death of a Salesman* as a work of art. Mr. Miller has had more trouble with this one, perhaps because he is too conscious of its implications. The literary style is cruder. . . .

It may be that Mr. Miller . . . has permitted himself to be concerned more with the technique of the witch hunt than with its humanity. For all its power generated on the surface, *The Crucible* is most moving in the simple, quiet scenes between John Proctor and his wife. By the standards of *Death of a Salesman*, there is too much excitement and not enough emotion in *The Crucible*.

As the director, Jed Harris has given it a driving performance in which the clashes are fierce and clamorous. Inside Boris Aronson's gaunt, pitiless sets of rude buildings, the acting is at a high pitch of bitterness, anger and fear. As the patriarchal deputy Governor, Walter Hampden gives one of his most vivid performances in which righteousness and ferocity are unctuously mated. Fred Stewart as a vindictive parson, E. G. Marshall as a parson who finally rebels at the indiscriminate ruthlessness of the trial, Jean Adair as an aging woman of God . . . all give able performances.

As John Proctor and his wife, Arthur Kennedy and Beatrice Straight have the most attractive roles in the drama. . . . They are superb—Mr. Kennedy clear and resolute, full of fire, searching his own mind; Miss Straight, reserved, detached, above and beyond the contention. Like all the members of the cast, they are dressed in the chaste and lovely costumes Edith Lutyens has designed from old prints of early Massachusetts.

After the experience of *Death of a Salesman* we probably expect Mr. Miller to write a masterpiece every time. *The Crucible* is not of that stature and it lacks that universality. On a lower level of dramatic history with considerable pertinence for today, it is a powerful play and a genuine contribution to the season.

Atkinson begins by presenting his overall opinion of both the play and the performance. He then provides historical content about the play's subject matter.

This paragraph provides a brief plot summary.

Atkinson argues that The Crucible is not as good as one of Miller's previous plays.

This evaluation of the leading actor and the leading actress is extremely positive.

The reviewer concludes by stating his mixed evaluation of the play.

March 8, 2002

NEW YORK'S HOMETOWN CONNECTION   WWW.NYDAILYNEWS.COM

DAILY ◉ NEWS

NEESON & CO. CAST A POWERFUL SPELL

By Howard Kissel

Four years after Arthur Miller wrote a play about a louse—a man who was a failure as a husband, a father and a salesman—he wrote a play about a hero.

The hero was a man in Puritan Massachusetts who redeemed his failures as a husband by his courageous, self-sacrificial commitment to honesty in a world gone berserk.

The louse, of course, was Willy Loman, whose name has become a by word for the failure of the American dream in the mid-20th century.

John Proctor, the hero of Miller's 1953 *The Crucible*, should be every bit as emblematic as Loman. If he isn't, it may be because he is rarely played as powerfully as he is by Liam Neeson in the current revival, which also stars Laura Linney.

Miller's play about the witch hunts in 17th-century Salem draws much of its power from its subtext. It was written when the country was in the grip of another witch hunt: Congress' attempt to find American Communists in the early years of the Cold War.

This has given the play a longer life than it might have had on its own.

The Crucible is, after all, a melodrama.

An Honest Family Before the play begins, Proctor had been an upstanding citizen. His one failing was a brief fling with a servant girl, Abigail Williams, whom his wife dismissed when she learned of the affair.

Shortly afterward, Mary Warren, a servant who replaced Abigail, joined a band of girls accusing townspeople of witchcraft, often as a way of settling old scores.

The pivot point of the play comes when Proctor's longsuffering wife is called on to denounce him for adultery. Not knowing that he has already confessed, she refuses to condemn him. She thus unwittingly seals his fate, implying to the court that he has lied. Such plotting would normally be dismissed as quaint and old-fashioned, but here the subtext makes it acceptable.

Neeson's haunted, brooding look is perfect for Proctor. Moreover, his easy sensuality brings his difficult past effortlessly onto the stage, making his transformation into a man of unassailable character all the more dramatic and thrilling.

Linney gives a performance of disarming simplicity. She is a woman wronged not only by her husband but by his villainous accusers. But she responds to a mountain of cruel torments with a dignity that is profoundly moving. . . .

Jennifer Carpenter gives a wrenching performance as the ultimately disloyal Mary, and Angela Bettis is wonderfully ruthless as Abigail, the leader of the accusing girls. As the judge who brings about the deaths of innocent people, Brian Murray falls into the trap of signaling us that he knows his character is evil, making the melodramatic aspects of the writing too apparent.

Tim Hatley's costumes and sets, beautifully lit by Paul Gallo, have muted colors that suggest a world desperately trying to keep sensuality at bay. Under Richard Eyre's direction, the large cast handles Miller's artful creation of 17th-century language and inflections with great ease.

The Crucible is one of Miller's most-revived plays, but it is seldom as impressive as this.

Kissel contrasts Miller's play with one of his previous plays.

The reviewer is referring to Miller's *Death of a Salesman*.

Kissel praises the play and the leading actor.

Kissel is more specific than Atkinson in stating the play's political context.

This paragraph identifies the turning point in the plot and provides a positive opinion of its effectiveness.

Kissel praises the leading actress.

Kissel ends with a strongly positive evaluation.

THINKING ABOUT THE CRITICAL REVIEWS

1. Which play does Atkinson prefer, *Death of a Salesman* or *The Crucible*? Explain your answer.

_____

_____

_____

Write words from the review that support your answer.

_____

_____

_____

READING STRATEGY: COMPARING AND CONTRASTING CRITICAL REVIEWS

2. What does each reviewer think is most powerful about *The Crucible?*

_____

_____

_____

3. Which reviewer liked the play more? Explain.

_____

_____

_____

TIMED WRITING: EVALUATION (30 minutes)

Write a critical review of a movie, television show, or other performance. Support your opinion with evidence and reasons. The chart below will help you organize your writing.

Element	Opinion	Evidence/Reasons
script		
acting		
direction		
costumes		
music		

PART 2: TURBO VOCABULARY

The exercises and tools presented here are designed to help you increase your vocabulary. Review the instruction and complete the exercises to build your vocabulary knowledge. Throughout the year, you can apply these skills and strategies to improve your reading, writing, speaking, and listening vocabulary.

Prefixes V2

Word Roots V3

Suffixes V6

Learning About Etymologies V8

How to Use a Dictionary...................................... V12

Academic Words.. V14

Word Attack Skills V16

Vocabulary and the SAT® V18

Communication Guide: Diction and Etiquette V22

Words in Other Subjects V26

Vocabulary Flash Cards V27

Vocabulary Fold-a-List V33

Commonly Misspelled Words V39

The following list contains common prefixes with meanings and examples. On the blank lines, write other words you know that begin with the same prefixes. Write the meanings of the new words.

Prefix	Meaning	Example and Meaning	Your Words	Meanings
Anglo-Saxon *fore-*	before	*foretell:* to tell beforehand; predict		
Greek *auto-*	self	*autobiography:* the story of one's own life written by oneself		
Greek *di-*	away; apart	*digress:* to move away from a subject		
Greek *dys-*	difficult; bad	*dystopia:* a place with dreadful conditions		
Greek *mono-*	alone; one; single	*monologue:* a long speech by one speaker		
Latin *con-*	with; together	*conference:* a meeting for discussion		
Latin *dis-*	apart; not	*dishonest:* not honest		
Latin *ex-*	out	*extort:* to squeeze out		

Prefix	Meaning	Example and Meaning	Your Words	Meanings
Latin *in-*	in; into; not; without	*inescapable:* that cannot be escaped		
Latin *mal-*	bad	*malice:* desire to harm another		
Latin *multi-*	many; much	*multiply:* to increase in number		
Latin *ob-*	against	*object:* showing disapproval		
Latin *omni-*	all; every	*omnipotent:* all-powerful		
Latin *pro-*	forward	*protruded:* thrust forward		
Latin *re-*	again; back	*revolve:* to move in a circle around a point		
Latin *trans-*	across; through	*transportation:* means of moving passengers or goods		

WORD ROOTS

The following list contains common word roots with meanings and examples. On the blank lines, write other words you know that have the same roots. Write the meanings of the new words.

Root	Meaning	Example and Meaning	Your Words	Meanings
Greek *-archy-*	to rule	*anarchy:* without government; without rule		
Greek *-psych-*	soul; mind	*psychology:* the science that deals with the mind		
Latin *-aud-*	hearing, sound	*auditorium:* a room for gathering an audience to hear concerts or speeches		
Latin *-bene-*	good	*benefit:* to do good for		
Latin *-equi-*	equal	*equivalent:* equal in quantity, value, or meaning		
Latin *-fid-*	faith; trust	*confident:* full of certainty or trust		
Latin *-grat-*	pleasing	*grateful:* expressing thankfulness		
Latin *-ject-*	to throw	*eject:* to throw out		

Root	Meaning	Example and Meaning	Your Words	Meanings
Latin -lib-	free	*liberty:* freedom		
Latin -mort-	death	*mortuary:* a place where dead bodies are kept		
Latin -patr-	father	*paternal:* fatherly		
Latin -press-	push	*compress:* to squeeze or push together; make compact		
Latin -scrib-	write	*transcribe:* to write out or type out in full		
Latin -sol-	alone	*solitary:* being alone; without others		
Latin -terr-	earth; land	*terrarium:* a glass container holding small plants or small land animals		
Latin -vid-	to see	*video:* the process of recording and showing television programs, movies, and real events		

SUFFIXES

The following list contains common suffixes with meanings and examples. On the blank lines, write other words you know that have the same suffixes. Write the meanings of the new words.

Suffix	Meaning	Example and Meaning	Your Words	Meanings
Anglo-Saxon -fold	a specific number of times or ways	tenfold: ten times		
Anglo-Saxon -ful	full of	joyful: happy; full of joy		
Anglo-Saxon -hood	state or quality of	parenthood: the state of being a parent		
Anglo-Saxon -less	without	helpless: not able to help oneself		
Anglo-Saxon -ness	the state of being	handedness: the quality of using one hand more skillfully than the other		
Anglo-Saxon -some	tending toward being	awesome: impressive; inspiring awe		
Greek -ate	forms verbs	evaporate: to change into a vapor		
Greek -ic	forms adjectives	hypnotic: causing sleep		

Suffix	Meaning	Example and Meaning	Your Words	Meanings
Greek -itis	disease; inflammation	*bronchitis:* inflammation of the bronchial tubes		
Greek -logy	the science or study of	*biology:* the study of living organisms		
Latin -able/-ible	capable of being	*lovable:* able to be loved		
Latin -al	of, like, suitable for	*theatrical:* having to do with the theater		
Latin -ance/ -ence	quality of; state of being	*permanence:* the state of being permanent; remaining		
Latin -er	one who	*geographer:* one whose profession deals with the study of geography		
Latin -ity	turns adjectives into nouns	*complexity:* the state of being complex or difficult		
Latin -tion	turns a noun into a verb	*deliberation:* the act of deliberating or thinking about very carefully		

Etymology is the history of a word. It shows where the word came from, or its origin. It also shows how it got its present meaning and spelling. Understanding word origins, or etymology, can help you understand and remember the meanings of words you add to your vocabulary.

A good dictionary will tell you the etymology of a word. The word's etymology usually appears in brackets, parentheses, or slashes near the beginning or the end of the dictionary entry. Part of the etymology is the language from which the word comes.

Abbreviations for Languages	
Abbreviation	**Language**
OE	Old English
ME	Middle English
F	French
Gr	Greek
L	Latin

You can find these abbreviations and more in a dictionary's key to abbreviations.

Words from other languages

The English that you speak today began in about the year 500. Tribes from Europe settled in Britain. These tribes, called the Angles, the Saxons, and the Jutes, spoke a Germanic language. Later, when the Vikings attacked Britain, their language added words from Danish and Norse. Then, when Christian missionaries came to Britain, they added words from Latin. The resulting language is called Old English, and it looks very different from modern English.

For example, to say "Listen!" in Old English, you would have said "Hwaet!"

The Normans conquered Britain in 1066. They spoke Old French, and the addition of this language changed Old English dramatically. The resulting language, called Middle English, looks much more like modern English, but the spellings of words are very different.

For example, the word *knight* in Middle English was spelled *knyght*, and the word *time* was spelled *tyme*.

During the Renaissance, interest in classical cultures added Greek and Latin words to English. At this time, English started to look more like the English you know. This language, called Modern English, is the language we still speak.

Modern English continues to add words from other languages. As immigrants have moved to the United States, they have added new words to the language.

For example, the word *boycott* comes from Ireland and the word *burrito* comes from Mexico.

Note-taking Using a dictionary, identify the language from which each of nthe following words came into English. Also identify the word's original and current meaning.

Word	Original language	Original meaning	Current meaning
comb			
costume			
guess			
mile			
panther			

Words that change meaning over time

English is a living language. It grows by giving new meanings to existing words and by incorporating words that have changed their meaning over time and through usage.

For example, the word *dear* used to mean "expensive."

Note-taking Using a dictionary, identify the original meaning and the current meaning of each of the following words.

	original meaning	current meaning
1. havoc	_____	_____
2. magazine	_____	_____

Words that have been invented, or *coined*, to serve new purposes.

New products or discoveries need new words.

For example, the words *paperback* and *quiz* are coined words.

Note-taking Identify one word that has been coined in each of the following categories.

Category	Coined word
sports	
technology	
transportation	
space travel	
medicine	

Words that are combinations of words or shortened versions of longer words

New words can be added to the language by combining words or by shortening words.

For example, the word *greenback* is a combination of the words *green* and *back*, and the word *flu* is a shortened version of the word *influenza*.

Note-taking Generate a word to fill in the blanks in each of the following sentences correctly. Your word should be a combination of two words or a shortened version of a longer word.

Jerome served one of our favorite dinners, spaghetti and _____.

Many years ago, people might take an omnibus to work, but today they would call that vehicle a _____.

We took the most direct route to Aunt Anna's house, which meant driving forty miles on the _____.

We thought we could get to shelter before the storm started, but we did not quite make it. A few _____ dampened our jackets.

HOW TO USE A DICTIONARY

A dictionary lists words in alphabetical order. Look at this sample dictionary entry. Notice the types of information about a word it gives.

Example of a Dictionary Entry

dictionary (dik´ shə ner´ ē) n., pl. –aries
[ML *dictionarium* < LL *dictio*) 1 a book of
alphabetically listed words in a language,
with definitions, etymologies, pronunciations,
and other information 2 a book of alphabetically
listed words in a language with their equivalents
in another language [a Spanish-English
dictionary]

Answer the questions based on the dictionary entry.

1. What is the correct spelling?_____

2. How do you form the plural? _____

3. What language does the word come from? _____

4. How many definitions are there? _____

5. What example is given? _____

Here are some abbreviations you will find in dictionary entries.

Pronunciation Symbols	Parts of Speech	Origins of Words
´ means emphasize this syllable as you say the word	adj. = adjective	Fr = French
¯ means pronounce vowel with a long sound, such as -*ay*- for a and -*ee*- for e	adv. = adverb	Ger = German
ə means a sound like -*uh*-	n. = noun	L = classical Latin
o͞o means the sound of *u* in *cute*	v. = verb	ME = Middle English OE = Old English

As you read, look up new words in a dictionary. Enter information about the words on this chart.

My Words

New Word	Pronunciation	Part of Speech	Origin	Meanings and Sample Sentence

ACADEMIC WORDS

Academic (A kuh DEM ik) words are words you use often in your schoolwork. Knowing what these words mean will help you think and write better.

On the next two pages, you will find a list of these words. You will also see how to pronounce each word and what it means. On the lines below each word, write sentences from your reading in which the word appears. Then, using your own words, explain what the sentence means.

apply (uh PLY) tell how you use information in a specific situation

_____

_____

_____

_____

clarify (KLA´ri FY) make something more understandable

_____

_____

_____

_____

conclude (KUHN klood) use reasoning to reach a decision or opinion

_____

_____

_____

_____

define (dee FYN) tell the qualities that make something what it is

_____

_____

_____

demonstrate (DEM uhn STRAYT) use examples to prove a point

_____

_____

evaluate (ee VAL yoo AYT) determine the value or importance of something

identify (y DEN ti FY) name or show you recognize something

label (LAY bel) attach the correct name to something

predict (pree DIKT) tell what will happen based on details you know

recall (ri KAWL) tell details that you remember

WORD ATTACK SKILLS

When you are reading, you will find many unfamiliar words. Here are some tools that you can use to help you read unfamiliar words.

PHONICS

Phonics is the science or study of sound. When you learn to read, you learn to associate certain sounds with certain letters or letter combinations. You know most of the sounds that letters can represent in English. When letters are combined, however, it is not always so easy to know what sound is represented. In English, there are some rules and patterns that will help you determine how to pronounce a word. This chart shows you some of the common **vowel digraphs**, which are combinations like *ea* and *oa*. Two vowels together are called vowel digraphs. Usually, vowel digraphs represent the long sound of the first vowel.

Vowel Digraphs	Examples of Usual Sounds	Exceptions
ee and *ea*	steep, each, treat, sea	head, sweat, dread
ai and *ay*	plain, paid, may, betray	aisle
oa, ow, and *oe*	soak, slow, doe	
ie, igh, and *y*	lie, night, delight, my	myth

As you read, sometimes the only way to know how to pronounce a word with an *ea* spelling is to see if the word makes sense in the sentence. Look at this example:

The water pipes were made of *lead*.

First, try out the long sound "ee." Ask yourself if it sounds right. It does not. Then try the short sound "e." You will find that the short sound is correct in that sentence. Now try this example.

Where you *lead*, I will follow.

WORD PATTERNS

Recognizing different vowel-consonant patterns will help you read longer words. In the following section, the **V** stands for "vowel" and the **C** stands for "consonant."

Single-syllable Words

CV–go: In two letter words with a consonant followed by a vowel, the vowel is usually long. For example, the word *go* is pronounced with a long "o" sound.

In a single syllable word, a vowel followed only by a single consonant is usually short.

CVC-got: If you add a consonant to the word *go*, such as the *t* in *got*, the vowel sound is a short *o*. Say the words *go* and *got* aloud and notice the difference in pronunciation.

Multi-syllable Words

In words of more than one syllable, notice the letters that follow a vowel.

VCC–robber: A single vowel followed by two consonants is usually short.

VCV–begin: A single vowel followed by a single consonant is usually long.

VCe–beside: An extension of the VCV pattern is vowel-consonant-silent *e*. In these words, the vowel is long and the *e* is not pronounced.

When you see a word with the VCV pattern, try the long vowel sound first. If the word does not make sense, try the short sound. Pronounce the words *model*, *camel*, and *closet*. First, try the long vowel sound. That does not sound correct, so try the short vowel sound. The short vowel sound is correct in those words.

Remember that patterns help you get started on figuring out a word. You will sometimes need to try a different sound or find the word in a dictionary.

As you read and find unfamiliar words, look the pronunciations up in a dictionary. Write the words in this chart in the correct column, to help you notice patterns and remember pronunciations.

Syllables	Example	New Words	Vowel Sound
CV	go		long
CVC	got		short
VCC	robber		short
VCV	begin open		long long
VCe	beside		long

FAQS ABOUT THE SAT®

What is the SAT®?

- The SAT® is a national test intended to predict how well you will do with college-level material.

What does the SAT® test?

- The SAT® tests vocabulary, math, and reasoning skills in three sections:
  - Critical Reading: two 25-minute sections and one 20-minute section
  - Math: two 25-minute sections and one 20-minute section
  - Writing: one 35-minute multiple-choice section and one 25-minute essay

Why should you take the SAT®?

- Many colleges and universities require you to submit your SAT® scores when you apply. They use your scores, along with other information about your ability and your achievements, to evaluate you for admission.

How can studying vocabulary help improve your SAT® scores?

- The Critical Reading section of the SAT® asks two types of questions that evaluate your vocabulary.
  - Sentence Completions ask you to fill in one or more blanks in a sentence with the correct word or words. To fill in the blanks correctly, you need to know the meaning of the words offered as answers.
  - Vocabulary in Context questions in Passage-based Reading ask you to determine what a word means based on its context in a reading passage.
- With a strong vocabulary and good strategies for using context clues, you will improve the likelihood that you will score well on the SAT®.

Using Context Clues on the SAT®

When you do not know the meaning of a word, nearby words or phrases can help you. These words or phrases are called *context clues*.

Guidelines for Using Context Clues

1. Read the sentence or paragraph, concentrating on the unfamiliar word.
2. Look for clues in the surrounding words.
3. Guess the possible meaning of the unfamiliar word.
4. Substitute your guess for the word.
5. When you are reviewing for a test, you can check the word's meaning in a dictionary.

Types of Context Clues

Here are the most common types of context clues:

- formal definitions that give the meaning of the unfamiliar word

- familiar words that you may know that give hints to the unfamiliar word's meaning

- comparisons or contrasts that present ideas or concepts either clearly similar or clearly opposite to the unfamiliar word

- synonyms, or words with the same meaning as the unfamiliar word

- antonyms, or words with a meaning opposite to that of the unfamiliar word

- key words used to clarify a word's meaning

Note-taking List several new words that you have learned recently by figuring out their meanings in context. Then, explain how you used context to decide what the word meant.

New Word	How You Used Context to Understand the Word

Sample SAT® Questions

Here are examples of the kinds of questions you will find on the SAT®. Read the samples carefully. Then, do the Practice exercises that follow.

Sample Sentence Completion Question:

Directions: The sentence that follows has one blank indicating that something has been omitted. Beneath the sentence are five words or sets of words labeled A through E. Choose the word or set of words that, when inserted in the sentence, best fits the meaning of the sentence as a whole.

1. Though he is _____, his nephew still invites him to Thanksgiving dinner every year.

   A cheerful

   B entertaining

   C misanthropic

   D agile

   E healthy

The correct answer is *C*. The uncle is *misanthropic*. You can use the context clues "though" and "invites him" to infer that the uncle has some negative quality. Next, you can apply your knowledge of the prefix *mis-* to determine that *misanthropic*, like *mistake* and *misfortune*, is a word indicating something negative. Eliminate the other answer choices, which indicate positive or neutral qualities in this context.

Sample Vocabulary in Context Question:

Directions: Read the following sentence. Then, read the question that follows it. Decide which is the best answer to the question.

Martin Luther King, Jr., whose methods motivated many to demand equal rights in a peaceful manner, was an <u>inspiration</u> to all.

1. In this sentence, the word *inspiration* means—

A politician

B motivation to a high level of activity

C the process of inhaling

D figurehead

The correct answer is *B*. Both *B* and *C* are correct definitions of the word *inspiration*, but the only meaning that applies in the context of the sentence is "motivation to a high level of activity."

Practice for SAT® Questions

Practice Read the following passage. Then, read each question that follows the passage. Decide which is the best answer to each question.

Many people are becoming Internet <u>savvy</u>, exhibiting their skills at mastering the Web. The Internet is also becoming a more *reliable* source of factual information. A <u>Web-surfer</u> can find information provided by <u>reputable</u> sources, such as government organizations and universities.

1. In this passage, the word *savvy* means—

A incompetent

B competent

C users

D nonusers

2. The word *reliable* in this passage means—

A existing

B available

C dependable

D relevant

3. In this passage, the term *Web-surfer* means—

   A someone who uses the Internet

   B a person who uses a surfboard

   C a person who know a great deal about technology

   D a student

4. The word *reputable* in this passage means—

   A an approved Internet provider

   B well-known and of good reputation

   C purely academic

   D costly

Practice Each sentence that follows has one or two blanks indicating that something has been omitted. Beneath the sentence are five words or sets of words labeled A through E. Choose the word or set of words that, when inserted in the sentence, best fits the meaning of the sentence as a whole.

1. "I wish I had a longer _____ between performances," complained the pianist. "My fingers need a rest."

   A post-mortem   C prelude   E solo

   B circumlocution   D interval

2. Instead of revolving around the sun in a circle, this asteroid has a(n) _____ orbit.

   A rapid   C interplanetary   E regular

   B eccentric   D circular

3. He was the first historian to translate the _____ on the stone.

   A impulsion   C excavation   E inscription

   B aversion   D circumspection

4. To correct your spelling error, simply _____ the *i* and the *e.*

   A translate   C transcent   E integrate

   B transpose   D interpolate

5. Spilling soda all over myself just when the movie got to the good part was a(n) _____ event.

   A fortunate   C tenacious   E constructive

   B premature   D infelicitous

COMMUNICATION GUIDE: DICTION AND ETIQUETTE

Diction

Diction is a writer's or a speaker's word choice. The vocabulary, the vividness of the language, and the appropriateness of the words all contribute to diction, which is part of a writing or speaking style.

- Hey, buddy! What's up?
- Hi, how're you doing?
- Hello, how are you?
- Good morning. How are you?

These four phrases all function as greetings. You would use each one, however, in very different situations. This word choice is called *diction*, and for different situations, you use different *levels of diction*.

Note-taking Here are some examples of levels of diction. Fill in the blanks with the opposite level of diction.

Level of Diction	Formal	Informal
Example	Good afternoon. Welcome to the meeting.	
Level of Diction	Ornate	Plain
Example		I need more coffee.
Level of Diction	Abstract	Concrete
Example		The mayor has asked for volunteers to pick up litter along the river next Saturday.
Level of Diction	Technical	Ordinary
Example	My brother is employed as a computer system design manager.	
Level of Diction	Sophisticated	Down-to-Earth
Example	Thank you very much. I appreciate your help.	
Level of Diction	Old-fashioned	Modern/Slangy
Example	Yes, it is I. Shall we sample the bill of fare?	

With close friends and family, most of your conversations will probably be informal, down-to-earth, even slangy. In school or in elegant surroundings, or among people you do not know well or people who are much older than you, you will probably choose language that is more formal. Sometimes the distinctions can be subtle, so try to take your cues from others and adjust your diction accordingly.

Note-taking Complete the following activities.

1. Make a list of words and phrases that would be appropriate for you to use as you escort a visiting school board member on a tour of your school.

_____

_____

_____

2. Make a second list of words and phrases that you might use as you escort your teenage cousin on a tour of your school.

_____

_____

_____

3. Study the following pairs of phrases. Then, identify one phrase in each pair as formal and the other as informal.

	Phrase	Formal / Informal	Phrase	Formal / Informal
1.	Hello, it's nice to meet you		How do you do?	
2.	What is your opinion, Professor Hughes?		What do you think, Pat?	
3.	Please accept my deepest sympathy.		That's too bad.	
4.	Sorry. I didn't hear you.		I beg your pardon. Please repeat the question	
5.	I don't get it.		I do not quite understand.	

4. List several common phrases. Then, identify whether each phrase is formal or informal, and give its formal or informal opposite.

	Phrase	Formal / Informal	Phrase	Formal / Informal
1.				
2.				
3.				
4.				
5.				

Etiquette: Using the Vocabulary of Politeness

No matter how many words you know, the way you use those words will impact how your friends, your family, your teachers, and all the people in your life react to you. For almost every interaction you have, choosing a vocabulary of politeness will help you avoid conflicts and communicate your ideas, thoughts, and feelings effectively to others.

When in doubt, always choose the polite word or phrase.

Formal or Informal?

Polite vocabulary does not have to be formal. In fact, the definition of the word *polite* is "behaving or speaking in a way that is correct for the social situation." People often think that *etiquette*, which consists of rules for polite behavior, applies only in formal situations. All interactions with other people, though, should follow the etiquette that is appropriate for the situation.

Etiquette for Classroom Discussions

Use the following sentences starters to help you express yourself clearly and politely in classroom discussions.

To Express an Opinion

- I think that _____.
- I believe that _____.
- It seems to me that _____.
- In my opinion, _____.

To Agree

- I agree with _____ that _____.
- I see what you mean.
- That's an interesting idea.
- My idea is similar to _____'s idea.
- I hadn't thought of that.

To Disagree

- I don't completely agree with _____ because _____.
- My opinion is different from yours.
- My idea is slightly different from yours.
- I see it a different way.

To Report the Ideas of a Group

- We agreed that _____.
- We concluded that _____.
- We had a similar idea.
- We had a different approach.

To Predict or Infer

- I predict that _____.
- Based on _____, I infer that _____.
- I hypothesize that _____.

To Paraphrase

- So you are saying that _____.
- In other words, you think _____.
- What I hear you saying is _____.

To Offer a Suggestion

- Maybe we could _____.
- What if we _____.
- Here's something we might try.

To Ask for Clarification

- Could you explain that another way?
- I have a question about that.
- Can you give me another example of that?

To Ask for a Response

- What do you think?
- Do you agree?
- What answer did you get?

Practice With a partner, discuss an issue about which you disagree. At the end of five minutes, list five or more polite words or phrases that you used to communicate your conflicting opinions.

_____

_____

WORDS IN OTHER SUBJECTS

Use this page to write down academic words you come across in other subjects, such as social studies or science. When you are reading your textbooks, you may find words that you need to learn. Following the example, write down the word, the part of speech, and an explanation of the word. You may want to write an example sentence to help you remember the word.

dissolve *verb* to make something solid become part of a liquid by putting it in a liquid and mixing it

The sugar *dissolved* in the hot tea.

_____
_____
_____
_____
_____
_____
_____
_____
_____
_____
_____
_____
_____
_____
_____
_____
_____
_____
_____

Use these flash cards to study words you want to remember. The words on this page come from Unit 1. Cut along the dotted lines on pages V29 through V32 to create your own flash cards or use index cards. Write the word on the front of the card. On the back, write the word's part of speech and definition. Then, write a sentence that shows the meaning of the word.

confederate	entreated	subsisted
protruded	deliberation	mortality
ablutions	disposition	feigned

VOCABULARY FLASH CARDS

adjective united with others for a common purpose The *confederate* Iroquois nations worked well together.	*verb* jutted out A tuft of hair *protruded* from under her hat.	*noun* cleansing the body as part of a religious rite The people performed their *ablutions* before beginning the scared dance.
verb begged; pleaded The children *entreated* the parents not to be angry with them.	*noun* careful consideration After much *deliberation*, we decided to go to the Grand Canyon for our vacation.	*noun* an inclination or tendency Neither side shows a *disposition* to compromise in the conflict.
verb remained alive; were sustained The lost hunters *subsisted* on berries and tree bark.	*noun* death on a large scale The infant *mortality* rate has been on the increase in certain areas.	*verb* pretended; faked Joe *feigned* sleep so that his brother would not talk to him.

VOCABULARY FLASH CARDS

Use these flash cards to study words you want to remember. Cut along the dotted lines on pages V29 through V32 to create your own flash cards or use index cards. Write the word on the front of the card. On the back, write the word's part of speech and definition. Then, write a sentence that shows the meaning of the word.

VOCABULARY FLASH CARDS

Use these flash cards to study words you want to remember. Cut along the dotted lines on pages V27 through V32 to create your own flash cards or use index cards. Write the word on the front of the card. On the back, write the word's part of speech and definition. Then, write a sentence that shows the meaning of the word.

Use vocabulary flash cards to help you remember the words you want to remember. Cut along the dotted lines in pages V32 through V38 to make your own flash cards. For the Index, V18, write the word in front of the card. On the back, write the word, the part of speech and definition. Then, write a sentence that shows the meaning of the word.

VOCABULARY FOLD-A-LIST

Use a fold-a-list to study the definitions of words. The words on this page come from Unit 1. Write the definition for each word on the lines. Fold the paper along the dotted line to check your definition. Create your own fold-a-lists on pages V35 through V38.

exquisite _____

_____

affliction _____

_____

indications _____

_____

abundance _____

_____

pilfer _____

_____

palisades _____

_____

conceits _____

_____

mollified _____

_____

peril _____

_____

loath _____

_____

Fold

VOCABULARY FOLD-A-LIST

Write the word that matches the definition on each line.
Fold the paper along the dotted line to check your work.

very beautiful; delicate;
carefully wrought   _____

something causing
pain or suffering   _____

signs; things that point
out or signify   _____

a great supply;
more than enough   _____

steal   _____

large, pointed stakes set
in the ground to form a
fence used for defense   _____

strange or fanciful ideas   _____

soothed; calmed   _____

danger   _____

reluctant; unwilling   _____

Fold

VOCABULARY FOLD-A-LIST

Write the words you want to study on this side of the page. Write the definitions on the back. Then, test yourself. Fold the paper along the dotted line to check your answers.

Word: _____

_____

Word: _____

_____

Word: _____

_____

Word: _____

_____

Word: _____

_____

Word: _____

_____

Word: _____

_____

Word: _____

_____

Word: _____

_____

Word: _____

_____

Fold →

VOCABULARY FOLD-A-LIST

Write the word that matches the definition on each line.
Fold the paper along the dotted line to check your work.

Definition: _____

_____

Definition: _____

_____

Definition: _____

_____

Definition: _____

_____

Definition: _____

_____

Definition: _____

_____

Definition: _____

_____

Definition: _____

_____

Definition: _____

_____

Definition: _____

Fold

VOCABULARY FOLD-A-LIST

Write the words you want to study on this side of the page. Write the definitions on the back. Then, test yourself. Fold the paper along the dotted line to check your answers.

Word: _____

_____

Word: _____

_____

Word: _____

_____

Word: _____

_____

Word: _____

_____

Word: _____

_____

Word: _____

_____

Word: _____

_____

Word: _____

_____

Word: _____

_____

Fold →

VOCABULARY FOLD-A-LIST

Write the word that matches the definition on each line.
Fold the paper along the dotted line to check your work.

Definition: _____

_____

Definition: _____

_____

Definition: _____

_____

Definition: _____

_____

Definition: _____

_____

Definition: _____

_____

Definition: _____

_____

Definition: _____

_____

Definition: _____

_____

Definition: _____

Fold

COMMONLY MISSPELLED WORDS

The list on these pages presents words that cause problems for many people. Some of these words are spelled according to set rules, but others follow no specific rules. As you review this list, check to see how many of the words give you trouble in your own writing. Then, add your own commonly misspelled words on the lines that follow.

abbreviate	auxiliary	census	deficient
absence	awkward	certain	definitely
absolutely	bandage	changeable	delinquent
abundance	banquet	characteristic	dependent
accelerate	bargain	chauffeur	descendant
accidentally	barrel	chief	description
accumulate	battery	clothes	desert
accurate	beautiful	coincidence	desirable
ache	beggar	colonel	dessert
achievement	beginning	column	deteriorate
acquaintance	behavior	commercial	dining
adequate	believe	commission	disappointed
admittance	benefit	commitment	disastrous
advertisement	bicycle	committee	discipline
aerial	biscuit	competitor	dissatisfied
affect	bookkeeper	concede	distinguish
aggravate	bought	condemn	effect
aggressive	boulevard	congratulate	eighth
agreeable	brief	connoisseur	eligible
aisle	brilliant	conscience	embarrass
all right	bruise	conscientious	enthusiastic
allowance	bulletin	conscious	entrepreneur
aluminum	buoyant	contemporary	envelope
amateur	bureau	continuous	environment
analysis	bury	controversy	equipped
analyze	buses	convenience	equivalent
ancient	business	coolly	especially
anecdote	cafeteria	cooperate	exaggerate
anniversary	calendar	cordially	exceed
anonymous	campaign	correspondence	excellent
answer	canceled	counterfeit	exercise
anticipate	candidate	courageous	exhibition
anxiety	capacity	courteous	existence
apologize	capital	courtesy	experience
appall	capitol	criticism	explanation
appearance	captain	criticize	extension
appreciate	career	curiosity	extraordinary
appropriate	carriage	curious	familiar
architecture	cashier	cylinder	fascinating
argument	catastrophe	deceive	February
associate	category	decision	fiery
athletic	ceiling	deductible	financial
attendance	cemetery	defendant	fluorescent

foreign
fourth
fragile
gauge
generally
genius
genuine
government
grammar
grievance
guarantee
guard
guidance
handkerchief
harass
height
humorous
hygiene
ignorant
immediately
immigrant
independence
independent
indispensable
individual
inflammable
intelligence
interfere
irrelevant
irritable
jewelry
judgment
knowledge
lawyer
legible
legislature
leisure
liable
library
license
lieutenant
lightning
likable
liquefy
literature
loneliness
magnificent
maintenance
marriage
mathematics
maximum
meanness
mediocre
mileage
millionaire
minimum

minuscule
miscellaneous
mischievous
misspell
mortgage
naturally
necessary
neighbor
neutral
nickel
niece
ninety
noticeable
nuisance
obstacle
occasion
occasionally
occur
occurred
occurrence
omitted
opinion
opportunity
optimistic
outrageous
pamphlet
parallel
paralyze
parentheses
particularly
patience
permanent
permissible
perseverance
persistent
personally
perspiration
persuade
phenomenal
phenomenon
physician
pleasant
pneumonia
possess
possession
possibility
prairie
precede
preferable
prejudice
preparation
previous
primitive
privilege
probably
procedure

proceed
prominent
pronunciation
psychology
publicly
pursue
questionnaire
realize
really
recede
receipt
receive
recognize
recommend
reference
referred
rehearse
relevant
reminiscence
renowned
repetition
restaurant
rhythm
ridiculous
sandwich
satellite
schedule
scissors
secretary
siege
solely
sponsor
subtle
subtlety
superintendent
supersede
surveillance
susceptible
tariff
temperamental
theater
threshold
truly
unmanageable
unwieldy
usage
usually
valuable
various
vegetable
voluntary
weight
weird
whale
wield
yield

PHOTO AND ART CREDITS

Cover: *Flag on Orange Field*, 1957, oil on canvas, Johns, Jasper (b.1930)/Ludwig Museum, Cologne, Germany, Lauros/Giraudon;/www.bridgeman.co.uk/ Cover art © Jasper Johns/Licensed by VAGA, New York, NY; **3:** Nicole Galeazzi/ Omni-Photo Communications, Inc.; **4:** Corel Professional Photos CD-ROM™; **5:** Silver Burdett Ginn; **6:** *Red Jacket*, George Catlin, From the Collection of Gilcrease Museum, Tulsa; **13:** Jeff Greenberg/Photo Researchers, Inc.; **16:** Erich Lessing/Art Resource, NY 19 *The First Day at Jamestown, 14th May 1607*, from "The Romance and Tragedy of Pioneer Life" by Augustus L. Mason, 1883, William Ludlow Sheppard/Bridgeman Art Library, London/New York; **24:** *The Coming of the Mayflower*, N.C. Wyeth, from the Collection of Metropolitan Life Insurance Company, New York City, photograph by Malcolm Varon; **31:** *Anne Bradstreet, The Tenth Muse Lately Sprung Up in America*, Ladonna Gulley Warrick, Courtesy of the artist; **34:** Bettmann/CORBIS; **42:** The Granger Collection, New York; **48:** The Granger Collection, New York; **51:** National Maritime Museum, London; **57:** Courtesy National Archives; **58:** ©Archive Photos; 64: Liberty and Washington, New York State Historical Association, Cooperstown; **73:** *Patrick Henry Before the Virginia House of Burgesses 1851*, Peter F. Rothermel, Red Hill, The Patrick Henry National Memorial, Brookneal, Virginia; **77:** Bettmann/CORBIS; **80:** *Building the First White House*, 1930, N.C. Wyeth, Copyrighted © by the White House Historical Association, photo by the National Geographical Society; **84:** *Independence (Squire Jack Porter)*, 1858, Frank Blackwell Mayer, National Museum of American Art, Smithsonian Institution, Bequest of Harriet Lane Johnson, Art Resource, New York; **90:** Leonard Lee Rue III/Stock, Boston; **99:** *Seashore in Normandy*, 1893, Maximilien Luce, Erich Lessing/Art Resource, NY; **108:** *Lewis and Clark with Sacajawea at the Great Falls of the Missouri*, Olaf Seltzer, #0137.871. The Thomas Gilcrease Institute of Art, Tulsa, Oklahoma; **109:** Corel Professional Photos CD-ROM™;

112: "I at length...," Edgar Allan Poe's Tales of Mystery and Imagination (London: George G. Harrap, 1935), Arthur Rackham, Print Collection, Miriam and Ira D. Wallach Division of Art, Prints and Photographs, The New York Public Library; Astor, Lenox and Tilden Foundations; **121:** New York State Historical Association, Cooperstown, New York; **124:** *Moby-Dick*, 1930, pen and ink drawing, The Granger Collection, New York; **127:** Ralph Waldo Emerson (detail), Frederick Gutekunst/National Portrait Gallery, Smithsonian Institution, Washington D.C./Art Resource, NY; **128:** Tom Bean/CORBIS; **129:** Frank Whitney/Getty Images; **132:** ©Lee Snider/CORBIS; **139:** Getty Images; **142:** eStock Photography, LLC; **145:** Courtesy of the Library of Congress; **148:** Courtesy National Archives; **153:** *Young Soldier: Separate Study of a Soldier Giving Water to a Wounded Companion*, (detail) 1861, Winslow Homer, Oil, gouache, black crayon on canvas, 36x17.5 cm., United States, 1836-1910, Cooper-Hewitt, National Museum of Design, Smithsonian Institution, Gift of Charles Savage Homer, Jr., 1912-12-110, Photo by Ken Pelka, Courtesy of Art Resource, New York; **156:** Courtesy of the Library of Congress; **159:** *Frederick Douglass* (detail), c.1844, Attributed to Elisha Hammond, The National Portrait Gallery, Smithsonian Institution, Washington, D.C./Art Resource, New York; **170:** CORBIS; **175:** Courtesy of the Library of Congress; **175:** Courtesy of the Library of Congress; **178:** Courtesy of the Library of Congress; **181:** Pearson Education/PH School Division; **188:** *Edge of Town*, Charles Ephraim Burchfield, The Nelson-Atkins Museum of Art, Kansas City, Missouri; **191:** Kansas State Historical Society; **192:** National Museum of American History, Smithsonian Institution; **195:** Annie Griffiths/DRK Photo; **198:** Corel Professional Photos CD-ROM™; **204:** Stock Montage, Inc.; **207:** Joel Greenstein/Omni-Photo Communications, Inc.; **210:** George Schreiber (1904-1977), *From Arkansas*, 1939, oil on canvas, Sheldon Swope Art Museum, Terre Haute, Indiana; **214:** Corel Professional Photos CD-ROM™;